Changing Narratives of Youth Crime

CW00517861

In recent years, western societies have experienced a fundamental transformation in the way crime is understood and dealt with. Against the backdrop of a current great interest in narratives in criminology, this book draws on a narrative perspective to explore this transformation.

Drawing on data from Germany, the book focuses on changing narratives of youth crime in recent decades and the exact narratives that have been used, abandoned, invented or criticized in order to instil particular understandings of crime and measures to act against it. The author draws upon a wide range of sources, including debates on youth crime in six parliaments from 1970 to 2012; articles on youth crime in four police and six social work journals from 1970 to 2009; and case studies with 15 young defendants who were interviewed before and after their trial and whose trial was observed. In doing so, the author reconstructs narratives over several decades and, overall, reveals a fascinating and multifaceted scope of narratives of youth crime.

This book will be of great interest to students and scholars of youth crime and justice, as well as criminology, sociology, politics and social work more broadly.

Bernd Dollinger is a professor of pedagogy and social work at the University of Siegen, Germany. Youth crime is his long-standing focus of research. Bernd's special research interests relate to drug use, criminal policy, professionalism in dealing with juvenile delinquency and processes of identity negotiation of youths. He has published extensively on juvenile delinquency. His publications include handbooks, textbooks and numerous research papers. Most recently, he has been particularly interested in reconstructing measures against crime 'from below', as it were, from the often neglected perspective of the defendants and convicts. They in particular have a lot to tell, and their stories are individually linked to cultural crime discourses.

Routledge Studies in Crime and Society

For more information about this series, please visit: www.routledge.com/
Routledge-Studies-in-Crime-and-Society/book-series/RSCS

Changing Narratives of Youth Crime

From Social Causes to Threats to the Social

Bernd Dollinger

Routledge
Taylor & Francis Group

LONDON AND NEW YORK

First published 2020
by Routledge
2 Park Square, Milton Park, Abingdon, Oxon OX14 4RN

and by Routledge
605 Third Avenue, New York, NY 10017

First issued in paperback 2020

Routledge is an imprint of the Taylor & Francis Group, an informa business

British Library Cataloguing-in-Publication Data
A catalogue record for this book is available from the British Library

Library of Congress Cataloging-in-Publication Data
A catalog record for this book has been requested

ISBN 13: 978-0-367-72698-0 (pbk)
ISBN 13: 978-0-367-07469-2 (hbk)

Typeset in Bembo
by Apex CoVantage, LLC

MIX
Paper from
responsible sources
FSC   FSC™ C013985
www.fsc.org

Printed in the United Kingdom
by Henry Ling Limited

Contents

Preface

Prefaces can serve to prepare the reader. They do so successfully if they briefly outline what perspective the reader can expect. I try to do this here by starting with a quote from the Polish doctor and researcher Ludwik Fleck, who aptly describes my starting point. In his analyses, Fleck found that epistemologists each tended to observe something specific as a clear given on which they then based their theories. For some, thought, and for others, an empirical fact was "fixed", in other words unchangeable. Fleck then asked:

> Would it not be possible to manage entirely without something fixed? Both thinking and facts are changeable.
>
> (Fleck 1935/1981, 50)[1,2]

Even after decades of poststructuralist and postmodern debate (e.g. Arrigo 2003; Arrigo et al. 2005; Cunneen 2011), this critical comment is in my view still important today, particularly for criminology. One could write the history of criminology as a search for "something fixed", for a fixed constant; as the desperate pursuit of something solid and unshakable that ultimately, however, can be found neither in "thinking" nor in "facts". This was my starting point for this monograph.

Let us start with "thinking": criminological analysis is heterogeneous. Criminology has boomed in the recent past, particularly in the English-speaking world (Liebling et al. 2017). That boom has revealed its diversity all the more clearly; it is a growing interdisciplinary research field in which there is little unity or consensus. Bosworth and Hoyle (2011, 3) see a risk of criminology increasingly splitting into disparate "cliques", "where criminologists read the work of others who think like them, write for those very same people and publish only in the journals that they and their colleagues are already reading". If we look at the individual trends in criminology – evidence-based criminology, cultural criminology, developmental criminology, narrative criminology, comparative criminology, etc. – it is immediately apparent that criminology already only exists in the plural. Criminology is, according to Agnew (2011, 2), "a divided discipline". Individual criminological trends ask their own, characteristic questions and use different methods to answer those questions. The fact that contemporary criminology is varied and comprises different, distinct elements represents its interdisciplinary normality. Although criminology has enduring "core ideas, arguments and assumptions" (Watts et al. 2008, 227), these differ considerably between individual branches and trends. There is no discernible common "fixed" constant.

In criminology, even "facts" are no guarantee of such a constant. The central subject, crime, itself varies widely. What is considered crime at different times and in different countries is variable. Reiner (2016, 15) talks of a "huge cultural variation across space and time in what has been counted by the law as criminal". There are elements of continuity: for example, homicide, theft and incest were and are often perceived and treated as deviant (Peters 2017). However, this is no guarantee that such elements have had the same significance across different times and countries. According to Émile Durkheim (1893/1964, 81), the definition of crime depends on the moral sensitivity of a society. From a perspective not dissimilar to labelling theory, he argued that

> we must not say that an action shocks the common conscience because it is criminal, but rather that it is criminal because it shocks the common conscience. We do not reprove it because it is a crime, but it is a crime because we reprove it.

Crime would occur even in a community of saints, but the types of crime committed would be ones to which a 'rougher' society would hardly take exception (Durkheim 1895/1964).[3] What persists throughout time is above all *that* certain behaviour is prohibited, but not *what* is prohibited at a material level and *what significance* this has. We should therefore assume change and difference rather than continuity (Cohen 1988, 47). Attempts to define something like a constant core set of crimes, whether as "natural crime" (Garofalo 1885/1968) or in other terms, have yet to convince.[4]

Crime is only crime if it is declared to be. Its definition is not based on the nature of the matter in hand, however that might be determined or measured, as the nature of the matter is open to different interpretations. What undoubtedly exists is *the attribution* of crime. I draw here on the central finding of the labelling approach as expressed by Howard Becker, namely that "deviance is *not* a quality of the act the person commits, but rather a consequence of the application by others of rules and sanctions to an 'offender'" (Becker 1963, 9). I believe that this perspective is still sustainable today.[5] It expresses "an enduring paradigm" (Liebling et al. 2017, 7) in which crime of any form is an ascription. Deviance, and in particular crime, "consists entirely and exclusively of the activities through which it is realized as such" (Pollner 1978, 279). Whenever it is claimed that a crime has been committed, "something fixed" is *attributed*. Such labelling requires plausible interpretations. Drawing on a consistent labelling approach and seeking to develop that approach in the light of new "narrative criminology" positions (Presser/Sandberg 2015b), I assume that ascriptions are created through some kind of 'interpretation packages'. Such packages contain definitions of who is an offender, who is a victim, how the two have acted, who bears responsibility for an act, how the act unfolded, etc. I call these interpretation packages *narratives* (see Chapter 1).

Narratives ensure that a certain unity can be achieved despite all the diversity and the absence of a fixed constant (Loseke 2018). There can be no doubt about the existence of crime; it is spoken of often and is a cultural reality. Crime is an important issue not only in the field of justice, research, media or politics, but also in everyday life (e.g. Sasson 1995; Simon 2007). Crime is a frequent topic of discussion and debate despite the absence of a fixed constant. Different players give crime a special status, and this is to be analysed here: the book explores how youth crime is produced and changed over time by specific narratives. In the light of the lack of a fixed constant, I try, as far as possible, to refrain from assuming supposedly immutable facts in the analysis of the narratives. I deliberately do not seek *to explain* how narratives come about or why they change. I will not argue that neoliberalism, the late modern period, capitalism, social inequalities, a societal crisis, populist politics or anything else produces certain narratives or causes them to change, for that would suggest the existence of a fixed constant. That constant would then lie not in crime, but in social, economic or political structural conditions.

This does not mean that theoretical analyses of changes in crime narratives are not revealing or important. Many excellent studies have demonstrated the importance of theoretical analyses in reconstructing changes in perceptions of crime. However, I deliberately choose a different, more small-scale and detailed approach *by analysing specific individual narratives on youth crime using Germany as an example*. The aim is to understand the narrative creation of youth crime by different players and how those narratives change over an extended period of time. This is the objective rather than a theoretical analysis, as the changes are empirically identifiable. Theoretical analysis could follow on this basis, but is not the purpose of this book. My research questions are as follows:

> How have narratives on youth crime changed in recent decades? What exact narratives have been used, abandoned, invented or criticized from different perspectives in order to install particular understandings of crime?

The data used here have been derived from three research projects that I completed in collaboration with colleagues over the past couple of years. A special thanks, therefore, goes to these colleagues, who have contributed so much work to the following reports. During countless joint interpretations and discussions, we were able to develop perspectives that I brought together here. I would especially like to thank Henning Schmidt-Semisch, Tobias Fröschle, Thomas Klatetzki, Monika Urban, Matthias Rudolph, Dirk Lampe, Selina Heppchen, Luzie Gilde, Jenna Vietig and Sophia Eschlbeck. Particularly helpful was advice by Sveinung Sandberg. I would also like to extend my thanks to the teenagers and young people who declared their willingness to contribute to the interviews introduced in Chapter 4, which meant that despite criminal investigations being ongoing against and the threat of imprisonment hanging over them, they still allowed this research to be conducted. Furthermore, I would like to thank all other cooperation partners and sponsors of the projects. The latter especially refers to the German Research Foundation (Deutsche Forschungsgemeinschaft, DFG) for its support with the findings put forth in Chapters 2 and 3, as well as to the deanship at the University of Siegen for making the project with the young offenders (Chapter 4) possible.

Notes

1 The German original emphasises more strongly the substantival nature of "something fixed", and the author uses inverted commas to distance himself from an assumption of fixed-ness: "*Können wir nicht ohne ein 'Fixum' auskommen? Beide sind veränderlich: Denken und Tatsachen*" (Fleck 1935/1980, 69).

2 I only mention the date of first publication when citing classic works in this book. I indicate wherever highlighting is mine; otherwise, it is from the original text.

3 Think, by way of example, of the term 'insult' in a society of the early modern period and in a society of today. The name and the basic principle would be the same: a person's honourable name has been blackened, and the author of this act is to be punished. The significance, however, would be different. In early modern times, a person's honour was central to his or her entire life. Children of 'dishonourable' parents could only engage in 'dishonourable' professions (Harrington 2013; Stuart 2006). Nowadays, honour and insult are still relevant, but people's honour no longer determines how they or their children live. In public debates on crime, on the other hand, violent and sexual offences are of central importance, including in relation to youth crime (Clear/Frost 2015, 75–76; Pratt 1997). The assumption that acts of insult would have had the same significance for people in the early modern period, for example, as insults today, is surely hardly sustainable. There is no reason to assume anything other for homicide, theft, etc. than the possibility that they may take on modified meanings over time.

4 The same applies to attempts to take crime seriously by placing the criminological focus on the harm crime causes. Crime is indeed associated with harm, which must of course be taken seriously. Nonetheless, this association is not sufficient grounds for regarding harm as a fixed material constant of crime, for the connection between harm and crime tends to be arbitrary or unclear (Lacey/Zedner 2017, 64). For example, there are offences (such as drug offences) in which it is not evident whether others have been harmed. Harm must, moreover, be selected and assessed before it can be relevant in criminal proceedings; many forms of harm are not primarily categorised under criminal law (warfare, legal abortions, pollution from cars, etc.). Harm alone cannot explain why one specific type of behaviour is punished and another not. Looking at the question from the opposite angle, we could say that crime does not exist because it causes harm, but that when something is defined as criminal, this officially legitimises the deliberate infliction of harm (Christie 1982). When people have to pay fines, are forced to work as a criminal sanction or are imprisoned, this constitutes inflicting harm. Is criminal law therefore criminal? Is the judge an offender because he or she is responsible for harming others? If intentionally inflicting harm is criminal, why is the criminal justice system not abolished, as it serves precisely this purpose: the intentional infliction of harm?

5 Becker himself did not argue on the basis of a consistent labelling approach (Pollner 1978). Crime was to him a label, but also included a violation of the rules that was *irrespective* of labels. To demonstrate how far-reaching a consistent approach would be, I would like to point out that labelling could not be argued to cause recidivism on such a basis, for recidivism would then be an objective quality of the act. Anyone who holds that labelling causes crime is implicitly claiming that subsequent crime ("secondary deviation" as defined by Lemert (1951/1981) or a "deviant career" according to Becker (1963)) is identifiable

without ascriptions. This assumption contradicts a consistent labelling perspective, which states that labelling is "contingent" (Rock 2017, 46), even in the case of recidivism. For a detailed discussion of the labelling approach, see e.g. Brown et al. (2010, 321–335); Lilly et al. (2011, 139–165); Pfohl (1994, 345–398). I do not interpret the labelling approach as a comprehensive theory, but rather as an approach that can be integrated into various other perspectives, including ethnomethodology (Garfinkel 1967) and the discourse theories of Foucault (1972) and Laclau and Mouffe (1985).

1 Narrating crime

This book is about narratives of youth crime. Its aim is not to reveal the latest state of criminal policies, but to provide fundamental insights into changes of youth crime narratives. This raises two fundamental questions that need to be addressed. Why is youth crime an interesting subject for narrative analyses (1.1)? What is the meaning of narratives in the context of youth crime (1.2)?

1.1 Disputes on youth crime

Isn't that scary?

I will begin with an example from the USA. The phrase above comes from a key ruling by the United States Supreme Court that I would like to use to demonstrate the importance of conflicting discourses surrounding the interpretation of youth crime. In 2005, the narrowest possible majority of five to four judges ruled that the death penalty for persons over the age of 15 but under the age of 18 at the time of an offence constituted "cruel and unusual punishment", i.e. breached the Eighth Amendment and thus the United States Constitution (*Roper v. Simmons* 543 U.S. 551 (2005)). Since then, it has not been possible to sentence persons in that age group to death. According to Drinan (2018, 84), the ruling is connected to other decisions by the Supreme Court that open up certain possibilities for revising the US trend towards increasing punitiveness. That "punitive turn" in the approach to crime began in the USA back in the 1960s (Beckett/Sasson 2000, 47–74; Clear/Frost 2015, 71–112) and gradually became a project of imposing harsher sentencing that is unique in history. Prison sentences experienced a lasting renaissance. Although they are hardly an effective means of preventing reoffending (Cullen et al. 2011; Nagin et al. 2009; Travis et al. 2014), they were widely used as a way of responding to crime and in particular to recidivism. Political decisions (Beckett 1997; Tonry 2016) were primarily responsible for the trend described as "mass imprisonment" (Garland 2001b). Rising or falling rates of imprisonment are not a systematic function of rising or falling crime rates (Lappi-Seppälä 2010, 978; Muncie 2008, 117; Tonry 2007, 2–3). Changes are instead largely a result of political decisions to imprison more or fewer people for specific offences. It is not rising rates of crime or violence but political decisions that are at the heart of why approaches to crime and offenders have changed. In countries such as England/Wales and the USA, for example, there has been a remarkable trend towards more punitive penal policies (e.g. Garland 2001b; Pratt et al. 2005; Wacquant 2010; for European trends in imprisonment: Lappi-Seppälä 2014; for Germany: Sack 2013). Statistically speaking, the primary subject or victims of such policies were the socially disadvantaged and dark-skinned people (e.g. Alexander 2010; Western 2006; Wacquant 2009).

I do not want to go into any further detail here. Criminal policy will be the focus of the second chapter. What is more important at this point is that young people were also affected by the trend towards more punitive measures.[1] While future trends in the USA towards less or even greater punitiveness will be foreseeable, the above ruling decision illustrates a central aspect for this book: *youth is a highly contentious area*. When young people commit an offence, it can be interpreted in very different ways. In principle, the same applies to adults. Here too, there are different principles for dealing with crime, which vary between a sympathetic focus on help and support on the one hand and a rather hostile focus on mere punishment and retribution on the other (Melossi 2000). However, youthfulness often is a blank canvas onto which both hopes and fears are projected. It is a particularly contentious area. The mere age of a person is not particularly important; the decisive factor is how age is *interpreted* and *what significance* is attached to the perception that relatively young people commit offences.

One illustration of this is the passage below, which is taken from the opinion announcement in which Justice Anthony M. Kennedy set out the majority ruling of the court in *Roper v. Simmons* as to why the death penalty for juveniles is unconstitutional. The passage relates to the case of the defendant Christopher Simmons. He had admitted to being involved in a burglary and a planned murder at the age of 17. He was charged with the offences in Missouri, found guilty and sentenced to death. Following a number of unsuccessful appeals by the defendant, the United States Supreme Court finally issued the above ruling that the death penalty for juveniles was unconstitutional. During the trial in Missouri that had led to the death sentence subsequently revoked, the following interaction occurred:

> During closing arguments, both the prosecutor and defense counsel addressed Simmons' age, which the trial judge had instructed the jurors they could consider as a mitigating factor. Defense counsel reminded the jurors that juveniles of Simmons' age cannot drink, serve on juries, or even see certain movies, because "the legislatures have wisely decided that individuals of a certain age aren't responsible enough". Defense counsel argued that Simmons' age should make "a huge difference to [the jurors] in deciding just exactly what sort of punishment to make". In rebuttal, the prosecutor gave the following response: "Age, he says. Think about age.

Seventeen years old. Isn't that scary? Doesn't that scare you? Mitigating? Quite the contrary I submit. Quite the contrary".

(*Roper v. Simmons* 543 U.S. 551 (2005))

The defendant was 17 years old at the time of the crime, but age is in itself irrelevant, as it is open to different interpretations. In particular, age can be associated with particular moral characteristics and with a smaller or larger ability to know what one is doing. "Thus, through the official administration of 'age' categories are such characterizations as 'guilt' and 'innocence' rendered available or unavailable for deciding particular outcomes" (Atkinson 1980, 44). The public prosecutor and the defence counsel demonstrate two different possible assessments. According to the *defence counsel*, youth is a "mitigating factor". Anyone who cannot yet drink alcohol, serve on a jury or watch certain films cannot be considered to bear full responsibility for an act – and should therefore not be sentenced to death. From this perspective, age is a protection against harsh sentences. The *prosecutor* argues the exact opposite: if young people commit serious crimes, their age should not be interpreted in their favour; rather, it should be counted against them. A criminal who is already committing the most serious crimes at an early age must surely be a particularly dangerous criminal. From this perspective, age is a reason for harsh sentences. Obviously, these two assessments of age are diametrically opposed. They are, however, part of a long tradition of conflicting interpretations.

The *defence counsel's* line of argument follows the tradition that perceives young people as in need of particular protection and as less responsible than adults. This approach shields young people from claims that they require particularly harsh punishments. Despite fairly significant differences in the detail, criminal law systems internationally have one aspect in common: regulations that respond to young offenders with supportive, welfarist and less punitive measures than to adults (Cavadino/Dignan 2006; Dünkel et al. 2010a). This line of argument has existed historically for a relatively long time. Bernard and Kurlychek (2010, 16) refer to "the code of Moses in the Bible" when talking about special youth laws. They also note that the "Code of Hammurabi", written 4000 years ago, already stipulated that young people should be treated more leniently than adults. A modern concept of youth crime was then established around 1800 (Bernard/Kurlychek 2010, 34), and the first youth court in the USA started operating in 1899.[2] The fundamental principle of this special treatment of young people is a welfarist approach: crime committed by young people is seen as a sign that they need help, and that help is supposed to prevent future crime. At the centre of such reforms is the welfare of the individual child, even above and beyond a response to individual offences (Garland 1985/2018, 21). In reality, it was difficult to respect this principle in practice. It often subjected young people to state control, coercive power and discipline (Oberwittler 2000; Muncie 2015, 266–276). For the young people concerned, it was not always possible to distinguish between help and punishment (Steinacker 2007). However, the core principle is that of help: support is supposed to respond to a young person's problems and to challenges in his or her environment and thus to address the underlying causes of criminal acts. As those causes exist, a young offender is not fully responsible for offences. Recent neuroscientific findings seem to confirm this, and were cited by the United States Supreme Court in its abovementioned decision that young offenders should be treated with a degree of leniency. The findings suggest that young offenders "are less culpable by definition; that their moral character is fluid; and that they are more amenable to rehabilitation than adult offenders" (Drinan 2018, 132). This assessment is the basis on which the defence counsel is demanding leniency.

The *prosecutor's* line of reasoning follows a different tradition, which argues that young people are particularly dangerous to current society. Moral immaturity and suggestibility are presented as arguments to support restrictive treatment rather than leniency. In criminology, Stanley Cohen's (1972/2002) analysis of "moral panics" strikingly described the ways in which the conduct of young people can be dramatised, and the punitiveness that can result.[3] In this process, in which individual violations of norms are presented in exaggerated terms, social control is extended and problems can be intensified. As Cohen demonstrates, norm violations by young people are a typical subject of "moral panics". Moral panics also have a long history (Bernard/Kurlychek 2010, 20–21). Historically, young people have repeatedly been criticised for their supposed amorality and violations of the norms (Pearson 1983). Such accusations already featured on clay tablets in 2000 B.C. (Kreuzer 2008, 128), and younger generations are still regularly denounced for the alleged risk they pose to the social and moral order today. Drawing on Pearson, McRobbie and Thornton (1995, 561–562) describe a permanent moral panic:

> The same anxieties appear with startling regularity; these involve the immorality of young people, the absence of parental control, the problem of too much free time leading to crime, and the threat which deviant behaviour poses to national identity and labour discipline.

An extreme form of moral indictment has also been significant in the context of the punitive turn of criminal policy in the USA. On the basis of statistical projections in the 1990s, there were predictions that a relatively large number of brutal, unscrupulous young people ("super-predators") would commit serious violent crimes in the near future. John DiIulio (1995) warned of "elementary school youngsters who pack guns instead of lunches. We're talking about kids who have absolutely no respect for human life and no sense of the future". Young people were supposedly to become increasingly brutal and ruthless. Yet this predicted wave of cold-blooded young violent offenders did not occur. Serious violent crimes committed by young people in the USA did not increase; in fact, they decreased in the mid- and late 1990s (Zimring 2014). The youthful "super-predators" remained a figment of the imaginations of a few individual criminologists, journalists and politicians. Nevertheless, the warning against them was in line with trends towards a punitive turn in US criminal policy, in which offences committed by young people were considered particularly threatening and treated restrictively (Drinan 2018, 5–6; Stevenson 2014, 159–160). In this line of argument, youthfulness does not lead to calls for leniency and rehabilitation, but instead symbolises a dramatic danger that must be neutralised using repressive means. The fact that young offenders are morally immature and can be influenced is acknowledged here just as much as in the welfarist image of youth. However, these assumptions lead in this case to completely different conclusions.[4]

These two interpretations demonstrate something important: youthfulness as an objectively definable age is largely irrelevant to the way youth crime is perceived.[5] Key to understanding youth crime is not the age of an offender, what specific offences have been committed or the frequency of offending over time, but the *interpretations* of offences and offenders. Narratives on youth crime are not a reflection of a 'genuine' reality of crime; they are a form of production of that crime reality in their own right. Different, competing narratives exist from which different conclusions can be drawn.

One could argue that scientific findings make it possible to decide which interpretation of youth or youth crime is 'correct'. Indeed, there are relevant findings in the field on options for effectively responding to youth crime in the sense of reducing recidivism (e.g. Cullen/Jonson 2011; Howell et al. 2014; Lipsey 2009; Lösel 2012; Welsh/Farrington 2012). Yet, although these findings exist, their relevance to the question of how youth crime is narrated politically and culturally should not be overestimated. Take the case of the "super-predators", for example: statistical findings clearly showed that they were an unsustainable myth, but myths can also shape cultures (Barthes 1972). Even when fear of crime may be unreasonable, it is still "a potent cultural and political force" (Pearson 1983, 211). What is key to the political and cultural understanding of youth crime, as I will argue below, is which narratives can be successfully established in face of others. Scientific findings are only one possible point of reference in conflicting narratives. Using the example of US criminal policy, Tonry notes that while many high-quality scientific studies are available to guide criminal policy, those studies have often not been used. "Policy making on some subjects has occurred mostly in an evidence-free zone" (Tonry 2013, 1). Neuroscientific findings are also only relevant to criminal policy if the policy-makers are interested in them and take them seriously. Whether or not this happens follows political, not scientific, principles.

For one illustration, let us go back to the case of *Roper v. Simmons*. Justice Antonin Scalia disagreed with the decision that young people should be spared the death penalty. In his opinion announcement, he expressed his dissenting opinion as follows, criticising the majority of his fellow judges in the Supreme Court who, in his view, wrongly trusted science:

> The court relies selectively on social scientific studies, failing to acknowl-
> edge that for every study telling the court what it wants to hear there is

another that says the opposite. Indeed there are sometimes contradictory assurances from the same supposedly scientific source.[6]

This opinion explicitly discredits scientific findings as the basis for criminal policy. In view of the narrow decision – a majority of only five to four judges – in favour of abolishing the death sentence for juveniles in *Roper v. Simmons*, and in view of the fluctuating and politically influenced make-up of the body of judges in the United States Supreme Court, this is to be taken seriously. Although only an example, it is an unusually transparent illustration that scientific knowledge is not directly applied to non-scientific areas. If we are to understand the political and cultural talk of youth crime, we therefore need to take seriously and to analyse conflictual and historically changing interpretations of youth crime in their own right. This can be done using narrative analysis.

1.1.1 *Whose narratives?*

Two points need to be clarified before I outline my understanding of narratives and their analysis in more detail in 1.2. If narratives of youth crime are to be analysed, we first need to define *whose* narratives and *over what period*.

First, the question of *whose* narratives is important. We have already seen that *politics* is crucial to a reconstruction of the interpretations of youth crime. Politics is the most important party in disputes on youth crime, as the legal definition of crime and the determination of how it should be treated are, above all, a matter of politics. The first empirical chapter, Chapter 2, will therefore look at politics.

However, youth crime is not solely a political issue. If youth crime is to be understood as a cultural phenomenon, we need to examine the people who work with the label "youth crime" on a daily basis and manage and apply it in their professional practice: *the professionals*. They are indispensable to dealing with crime in the long term. Howard Becker (1963, 153) appositely calls them an "enforcement machinery" that enables the long-term processing of a social problem. Political debates and decisions represent moral attitudes and ideas for dealing with crime, whereas this "machinery" perpetuates and modifies them in its daily institutional "social problems work" (Holstein/Miller 2003; Miller/Holstein 1997; see also Lipsky 2010; Maynard-Moody/Musheno 2003). The machinery ensures that *certain* conceptualisations of crime last and appear persistently legitimate. I select two occupations from the relevant professionals. Firstly, the police as a central criminal justice institution. Its relevance in the area of crime and youth crime is undisputed. Secondly, social work, as an institution that is of key importance in the field of *youth* crime in particular (Gensing 2010, 1605–1609). Internationally, one characteristic feature of approaches to offences by young people is that special attention is to be paid to the personality of offenders (Dünkel et al. 2010a). Trials of young people focus not just on individual acts but also on young people as persons (Emerson 1969; Rap/Weijers 2014). Welfarist institutions such as social work are supposed to support this approach. It is precisely this support function of welfare professionals that comes under pressure from calls for increasingly punitive responses to crime (Garland 2001b, 150). For this reason, an analysis of social work narratives of youth crime is highly relevant, as they offer a particularly sensitive record of potential transformations. Together with the police, social work is therefore the focus of Chapter 3.

In addition to political and professional stakeholders, the narratives of *young persons charged with crime, i.e. defendants,* are also analysed (in Chapter 4). Although often disregarded in criminology, offenders and their stories are the subject matter of criminal proceedings. In their course, stories of (alleged) offenders are considered with a narrow focus on – narratively structured (Brooks/Gewirtz 1996; Olson 2014; Scheppele 1994) – fact-finding and decision-making. Beginning particularly with the Chicago School of Sociology (Hardyns/Pauwels 2018), a broader criminological interest in offender narratives grew. It recently gained momentum in the context of "narrative criminology" (Presser/Sandberg 2015b). In this tradition, it is essential to consider narratives of (alleged) offenders if different angles on crime are to be taken seriously. But this results in a serious challenge. Political narratives and narratives of professionals are empirically accessible as historically altering conceptions of crime. In Chapter 2 parliamentary debates and in Chapter 3 journals of professionals will be analysed in this regard. Yet there is no corresponding option to reconstruct offenders' narratives in a historical process. The best way to gather their narratives is by interviewing them – which results in synchronic, not in diachronic data. Although this represents a particularity, I decided to include the respective narratives in this volume in order to consider them as an important angle in the narration of crime. After all, offenders' narratives are cultural products (Maruna 2001). They are predicated on culturally pervasive options to devise stories on crime and, particularly important for offenders, on individual responsibility and guilt. Historically established narratives on crime are likely to be mirrored in offenders' stories (Dollinger 2017). Narratives that emerge in the political and professional sphere are in all probability also to be found among young defendants. If, in the case of an accusation or charge, people are forced to present or deny offences and justify themselves, they have to use culturally available and 'understandable' means for their self-portrayal (Scott/Lyman 1968; Komter 1998). Considering the narratives of young defendants can therefore show how those individual narratives relate to political and professional narratives. The narratives of defendants are not abstract, purely individual stories; defendants do not simply make up arbitrary tales. Instead, their narratives are embedded in cultural narratives, and this can be explored empirically. Narrative analyses in criminology often focus on individual offenders (e.g. Dickinson/Wright 2017; Maruna 2001; O'Connor 2000; Presser/Sandberg 2015b; Rajah et al. 2014). Working on this basis, links between the individual accounts of defendants and the accounts of politicians and professional practitioners can be explored. Narratives of the young defendants are also interesting and revealing if analysed without such connections. However, it is particularly interesting to examine if and how the other narratives resonate in the narratives of the defendants. The basis of individual narratives is not facts or social structures, but other narratives: if one is looking for what's behind narratives, then it is "narratives all the way down" (Scheppele 1994, 93). This narrative interconnection makes it possible to relate the narratives of politicians, professionals and defendants to each other. On that basis, we can ask which narratives have become particularly important over time and look for *dominant or hegemonic* narratives.[7] This is the focus of Chapter 5.

The narratives are analysed *using the example of Germany*. I do not assume that the findings can be applied in detail to other countries, as criminal policy and criminal law systems are shaped by national systems and circumstances (see Chapter 5.3). Nevertheless, the findings should still be relevant internationally. As there is a strong Anglo-American influence on international criminology, it should be interesting to obtain findings from a non-English-speaking country. Certain basic principles of how youth crime is narrated are also reconstructed below. Even if there has been a lack of narrative-based international comparative studies to date, it can be assumed that these principles most likely do not only apply to Germany. They should also be relevant for other industrialised modern societies, even if further research is required to find precise evidence of this.

1.1.2 Periods covered

We need to define specific periods before we can analyse narratives. This applies below to political and professional narratives, as – unlike the narratives of the defendants – these narratives can be analysed historically. I choose the 1970s as a starting point as this period is internationally deemed dominated by "penal welfarism", i.e. a hybrid construct that combines "the liberal legalism of due process and proportionate punishment with a correctionalist commitment to rehabilitation, welfare and criminological expertise" (Garland 2001b, 27). In other words, penal welfarism implies a strong political will to address crime with rehabilitation, social welfare and social work programs. Custodial sentences and other 'tough' measures were relevant in this period; in the words of Bottoms (1977, 89), they were reserved in particular for "the 'mad' and the 'bad'", i.e. for offenders considered dangerous, e.g. because of psychological problems or a particular inclination towards harmful crime. The rehabilitation of offenders was nonetheless the programmatic key focus of intervention. Social policies and programs were thriving, and so were professions like social work. For the decades that follow – internationally since around the mid-1970s (Melossi 2008); in Germany somewhat later (Doering-Manteuffel/Raphael 2012) – a transformation is then diagnosed. As described above, that transformation apparently involved increasing punitiveness. In order to be able to analyse such (possible) changes, I continue the reconstruction of relevant narratives into the 2000s. More detailed information can be found at the beginning of the second and third chapters.

1.2 Crime as a narrative

What is a narrative and how can it be analysed? To avoid any misunderstanding, it should be noted that I am deliberately conducting a narrative analysis and not a discourse analysis. I have chosen Michel Foucault's (1972) definition of discourse from among the many terms currently used in order to illustrate the difference. Foucault characterised his understanding of discourse in part in the context of the "archaeology of knowledge". In his words, a discourse is a historically established regularity of statements about an object. That object does not exist as an objective fact that is then discussed; discourses are instead practices that make it possible to perceive an object as such. In his words, discourses are "practices that systematically form the objects of which they speak" (Foucault 1972, 49). Discourses are formations that vary historically and make certain statements possible or impossible at certain points in history. Discourses determine what and how something can be said and the status of those statements, for example by defining whether they can be regarded as true or untrue. Discourses are a "principle of dispersion and redistribution" (Foucault 1972, 107), as they regulate options for speaking. Discourses make it possible to know something and assign it a certain meaning; subjects are themselves shaped discursively in terms of their ability and opportunity to talk about themselves and experience themselves as subjects (Dreyfus/Rabinow 1983; see also Butler 1997).

Foucault became highly influential across various disciplines through his discourse theory and related theory of power, and studies on questions such as punishment and the history of prison (Foucault 1975/1979). In criminology, he is a key point of reference (Voruz 2010; see e.g. Garland 1993, 2001a). My narrative approach gained important insights from Foucault, in particular regarding the impossibility of perceiving objects or facts without presuppositions. The perception and identification of any matter is based on historically established conditions that can be empirically reconstructed. The presuppositions behind and options for speaking about a given matter are powerful, for they establish relationships and communicate evaluations. This is exactly what discourses and narratives do. As I describe in more detail in this chapter, narratives make it possible for youth crime to be identified and discussed as such in the first place. Youth crime is *in itself* a narrative. Narratives have the power to determine the existence and the specific nature of youth crime. I also share Foucault's criticism of attempts to define clear and unambiguous causes underlying discourses. For Foucault, discourses are genuinely historical. They are interrelated, emerge unexpectedly and disappear again. Foucault (1972, 170) argues that one should not, therefore, ask of a discourse "how and why it was able to emerge and become embodied at this point in time". I agree with this judgement with regard to narratives. That is why I deliberately do not search for supposedly 'objective' social, political or other reasons why narratives surface or change.[8] Nevertheless, I depart from Foucault's concept of discourse on a crucial point, as narratives are more specific than discourses. A discourse is a relatively abstract regularity of statements. Narratives, on the other hand, as I detail below, provide specific communicative and formal ascriptions regarding what crime is, who is involved in it and how it unfolds over time. In the following chapters, I do talk about discourses when it comes to crime in general. However, key to a narrative analysis of crime are *specific* statements on crime as a phenomenon with particular characteristics, participants and meanings. Although it has links to discourse theory, my narrative analysis focuses more closely on individual statements in special contexts than discourse analysis according to Foucault. Discourses form a backdrop against which specific narratives can be analysed, and that analysis will be the focus of the following pages.

A second distinction is important. I already referred to the concept of "moral panics" popularised by Cohen's study of "Mods and Rockers" (1972/2002). This concept also enables relatively specific analyses of the way in which youth crime is discussed. Cohen's study is rightly regarded as a classic work of criminology (Findlay 2010). Despite the major importance of this study and other analyses of "moral panics", I choose a different approach. In my view, "moral panics" do open up an important opportunity to analyse how dramatisations of young people's conduct can emerge and escalate. However, the opposite process is also relevant: routines and everyday narrative practices. For some players, social problems are "just another day at the office" (Hilgartner/Bosk 1988, 57). Stereotyping and ascriptions from specific perspectives, as defined by Cohen (1972/2002, 1) as core elements of a "moral panic", are indeed of central importance in times of moralising campaigns. Yet they are always important; without them, we could not talk of youth crime. Even if "moral panics" may currently be articulated "on a daily basis" (McRobbie/Thornton 1995, 560) or if there is a "permanent moral panic" (Cohen 1972/2002, xxix), the assumption of a "moral panic" is different from a narrative perspective on youth crime. Narratives as understood here are of constitutive importance to the perception of delinquency, regardless of any possible particularly moralising or exaggerated response in a "moral panic". Typified categories such as offender, victim, witness, etc. are in constant use to attribute meaning to certain events, both in everyday and in institutional contexts (Mäkitalo 2014; Miller/Holstein 1997). There is no doubt that analyses of "moral panics" make it possible to reconstruct dramatisations of drug use, violence, youth cultures, etc. However, my research focus is different: it is to allow for the possibility that youth crime is constituted narratively without specific dramatisation. Even where it is not the target of particular attention or special social control, youth crime is generated by narratives. To say that youth crime is dramatised through "moral panics" is itself a narrative of youth crime, for narratives are always at play when we talk about youth crime.

1.2.1 What is a narrative?

It is now about time to clarify what a narrative is and why it does make sense to analyse crime as a narrative. To conceive crime as a narrative does not mean that crime is being spoken about – even though it is more than obvious that crime is a widely handled topic among the public arena, politics, media, science and in everyday life. It can even be the case that crime is being discussed far more than it needs to be. In many ways, crime is exploited for various purposes – whether that be in the economic or political arenas or in some other way (Cohen 1972/2002; Pratt 2007; Roberts et al. 2003; Simon 2007). According to this understanding, crime is over-represented in narratives because it is concentrated on too often as a topic and with special interest. But this is not the focus of this study. Crime as a narrative, as I understand it, assumes that crime *in itself* is a narrative. This follows what Baldwin (2013, 7) calls a "strong programme" of narrativity. A weaker version would mean talking about crime. Crime would be a fact, which exists in itself, before it is embedded in narratives. The strong programme, on the other hand, includes "narrative as performing the task of constructing" (Baldwin 2013, 7) the involved persons, phenomena and the world around them. For the criminology perspective, Presser (2009, 184) speaks about a "constitutive view", meaning that a reality of crime is actually created by narrations. According to this view, there are no experiences that are directly related to a reality, which would subsequently be packed into stories and interactively represented. Experiences of and approaches to reality are instead narratively structured.[9]

Very different academic positions compete in relation to the question of which ratio narrations, reality and experiences stand with respect to each other (e.g. Freeman 2015; Kreiswirth 2000; Meuter 2014; Presser/Sandberg 2015a). The corresponding fundamental questions cannot be ultimately clarified by determining 'correct' and 'incorrect' statements and drawing 'logical' conclusions. It is obvious that different positions are in competition, each of which assumes distinctive images of people, of social life and, in this particular case, of crime (Lilly et al. 2011, 1–14; Melossi 2000; Pfohl 1994). With respect to crime, it can at least be said with certainty that it is very differently devised, and I assume this diversity in the following. If a situation is disputed, it makes sense to harness exactly this disagreement as a focal point, and to analyse different ways of narrating. Observing a stance of "ethnomethodological indifference" (Garfinkel/Sacks 1970, 345),[10] presuppositions and evaluations concerning a 'real', putatively non-discursive nature or experience of crime have to be abandoned in order to fathom the contentious, narrative constitution of crime. The following analyses are therefore not bound to presuppositions in such a way as to think that offenders are 'bad people', victims are 'innocent', judges hand down 'just/unjust judgements' etc. Instead, respective reasonings are to be found in the empirical material that I will present in Chapters 2 to 4 of this volume.

The analytical starting point to approaching the empirical data is a "constitutive" view which states that crime is *a discursively constituted phenomenon* and, more specifically, that *narratives as a special type of discursive communication* imply a key option to understanding crime and the way people are dealing with it. This assumption is a recourse to traditions of symbolic interactionism, ethnomethodology and (in the way stated above) the Foucault discourse theory. If we look at symbolic interactionism as an example, it assumes the premises, among other things, that people act in a meaning-based manner, that these meanings are interactively negotiated and can be altered (Blumer 1969; Denzin 2003). In lieu of 'larger' theories with extensive presuppositions on specific subject matters, this position suggests "to describe the recurring meanings and practices which persons produce when they do things together" (Denzin 1992, 23). Instead of applying the premise that crime is something bad that has to be prevented and is to be theoretically explained, talk on crime should be contextually located. Situationally attributed meanings and evaluations should be explored. The fruitfulness to do so is nicely illustrated by the following ironic quote from the statistician Walter Krämer (2006, 147):

> Whoever after drinking eleven beers is still able to drink a twelfth is regarded a real manly man in Munich and in Tehran as a criminal; con- scientious objectors to military service, adulterers, environmental polluters, blasphemers, animal abusers, rapists are sometimes criminals and sometimes they are not, and for certain crimes such as torture you can end up in prison here, but there you end up on a list for a medal.

Crime is thus flexible. It is "behavior that people so label" (Becker 1963, 9). The process of labelling relates back to stories, which allocate roles, attributes and responsibilities. A simple example can clarify this: the word *theft*. Such a term invokes culturally pervasive designations (Watson 1976). When there is a theft, there must be a thief ("offender"); furthermore, someone who has been stolen from ("victim"); as well as an action of stealing with a certain temporal sequence of events (according to which the person stolen from previously owned some- thing that the thief then appropriated). There were perhaps also witnesses, and a legitimate reason to undertake a criminal prosecution has occurred, including criminal investigations, interviews and interrogations of people ("suspects"). As a result, punishments can be handed down and the media can report about the event in question (especially when something expensive was stolen) etc. In this regard, a simple word like "theft" implies a whole range of assump- tions and ascriptions, virtually a *package of interpretations*. Watson (1997, 79) uses the example of police interrogations to refer to a corresponding "background scheme of interpretation", because for police officers – but also in everyday situations and in other institutional contexts – it is clear that in the case of a theft, it was perpetrated by a thief, there is a victim etc. Categories of crime are never free of these types of references; "what we have is a mass of knowledge known about every category" (Sacks 1979, 13).

Against this background, it becomes clear that everything that has to do with crime is based on categorisation (Dollinger/Fröschle 2017). Crime 'needs' offenders, victims, witnesses etc. to be crime. What also becomes evident is the *narrative* 'nature' of crime. An important aspect hereof is that crime centres upon the assignment (or rejection) of *responsibility* for the infringement of norms (e.g. Andersson 2008; Atkinson/Drew 1979; Ewick/Silbey 2003; Lagasnerie

2016; Watson 1976). Narratives are based on exactly this: on the negotiation of guilt and responsibility (Bruner 2003, 111; Hall 1997, 27; Labov 2011). It is therefore not a coincidence that talking about crime has a narrative quality to it. It is in this way that the example of theft illustrates a narrative structure: the talk of crime organises narratively the categories, actions and background expectations revolving around an imputed act of e.g. 'stealing'.

So, what is a narrative? Particularly known are statements by Labov (1997, 2011) or Labov and Waletzky (1967), who argue that narratives comprise several structure elements (abstract, orientation, complicating action, evaluation, resolution and coda). Not all of these structural elements need be present to identify a narrative. Nevertheless, Labov's model involves the specification of defined elements that supposedly characterise a narrative. The model indicates that a narrative can be divided into typical, clearly definable sections or stages that communicate a temporal sequence. A narrative starts with an *abstract* that gives a summary of an event. This is often followed by an *orientation* providing a basic guide to the story and those involved. The *complicating action* then conveys the essence of the event, which is evaluated and commented upon in the *evaluation*. The *resolution* follows and relates to the complicating action. The *coda* completes the narrative. The wide reception received by this model shows how fruitful it is when it comes to analysing narratives. However, it is often difficult to identify specific structural elements of a (possible) narrative – and perhaps this identification is even unnecessary, as the model is criticised as being "too static" (De Fina/Georgakopoulou 2012, 36). It provides the impression of a context-independent, universally applicable structure of stories. This understanding of stories contrasts in particular with the variety of narratives that arise during actual interactions (Benwell/Stokoe 2006, 134–135). According to Hall (1997, 26–27), it is misleading to assume specific structure elements of narratives, while it is more useful to assume interactively created structuring, which particularly, as stated by Benwell and Stokoe (2006), leads to interactionist or ethnomethodological positions (see also Goodwin 2015). These positions focus predominantly on the production of narratives as a situationally contextualised achievement. Stories are therefore "*interactive* productions, co-constructed by teller and recipient and tailored to the occasions of their production" (Mandelbaum 2014, 492). Accordingly, De Fina and Georgakopoulou (2012, 117) refer to narratives as "discourse engagements that engender specific social moments and integrally connect with what gets done on particular occasions and in particular settings".

This understanding of narratives highlights discursive performances that narrators undertake in an interactive process with a specific (actual or fictive) audience. A minimum requirement can apply here: "A narrative is an account of events occurring over time" (Bruner 1991, 6). Labov and Waletzky (1967, 28) provide the definition: "Any sequence of clauses which contains at least one temporal juncture is a narrative". However, instead of focusing on 'large', fully developed and specifically structured narratives, it makes more sense for analyses of relating crime to engage a wide interpretation of narrativity. Whether a narrative exists is not a dichotomous issue of narrativity or non-narrativity, but instead a question of "more or less" (De Fina/Georgakopoulou 2012, 117), i.e. statements can have greater or lesser narrative characteristics.

The following five dimensions clarify more specifically what narrativity means in this regard. They do not represent structural elements of narratives but rather basic aspects that play a significant role in stories. Take for example the following headline in the "Financial Times" from 19 April 2017:

Man wanted in Facebook murder video kills himself, police say.

a) **Categorisation:** According to Mäkitalo and Säljö (2002, 160), categorisation is "basic to human life" and a "necessity in the coordination of human activities". As an allocation of objects and persons to groups based on ascriptions of differences and similarities, categorisation is a normal part of how humans live their everyday life.[11] It plays a distinctive role in crime. Even a unique case of crime requires references to 'typical' actions and persons. In the example, a particular name is mentioned ("Facebook murder video"), which underlines the particularity of the event in question. Still, the depiction rests on a typification. Where a murder is committed, there is a murderer, a victim and possibly witnesses, as well as police officers who investigate the case and, later down the line, a judge or a jury that will hand down a verdict. According to this, people associated with criminal actions are never – not even in a "Facebook murder video" – just individuals, but members of categories such as offenders, victims, witnesses etc. With a particular (possibly) criminal offence, the respective persons are typified (Watson 1976, 62). In the corresponding narratives, neither tellers nor listeners need to have legal expert knowledge because crime is talked about at many times and outside the bounds of criminal law. The central categories for the narrative creation of crime "victim and offender (and transformations of these terms, e.g. perpetrator, aggressor, etc.) are common sense designations in ordinary language" (Watson 1976, 61; see also Sasson 1995). These commonsensical designations relate to talk about offenders and victims in the media and in politics (Ferrell et al. 2015). In the respective discourses, narratives revolve around culturally available categories of crime, which they use and adjust in a context-specific manner.

b) **Relations:** Individual categories do not exist alone. They are part of collections and point to other categories. Narratives fulfil the function to determine these relations and to reproduce them. As "cultural artifacts" (Maruna 2001, 39), narratives adhere to culturally available interpretations, which bring together the categories in an understandable and plausible manner and combine both events and people. Referring to crime, there exists a basic scheme because an offender is a person with (imputed) responsibility for something unwanted, while a victim is the aggrieved party negatively affected by criminal action. We can also view the example here: the title of an event is "Facebook murder video". It is obvious that Facebook did not kill somebody nor was it murdered itself; instead, a specific type of relationship is strongly suggested. Because the case is categorised as "murder", then there must be a "murderer". The only person that is specifically addressed in the title is a "man", who we can assume is (possibly) the murderer. The institution of the police also emerges, which refers to the man's former status of being wanted. The police are the entity that defines the situation and it does this so prominently that a well-known newspaper reported this. Also present, but not explicitly addressed, is the person of the victim: in a murder case, in addition to a murderer, there is a person who has lost their life. The title therefore describes a relationship pattern: a person (a murderer) robbed another person (victim) of their life by committing a serious offence, and an institution (police) prosecutes the offence and can clarify the status of those involved, which is an important event worthy of reporting by a newspaper (*Financial Times*). In this sense, categories relate to one another. This can include persons, objects and institutions that are not explicitly referred to.

c) **Evaluations:** Evaluations are a core element of narratives (Labov/ Waletzky 1967). This is evident in the case of crime as a violation of legal and moral norms (Hester/Eglin 2017, 7). Nobody has to state explicitly that a "murder" is terrible, because such an evaluation is part and parcel of a respective narrative. In individual cases, the public negative evaluation is reversed if crime is regarded and described as fun and exciting for offenders (Katz 1988). There is a possible appeal in violating norms, to flout the rules and have exciting experiences by consuming drugs or taking 'irrational' risks when speeding in traffic (Lyng 2004; O'Malley 2010). Yet this still implies an evaluation, which distances itself from the publicly assigned disapproval by contrasting it with emotional stimulation from the transgression against legal norms. Regardless of such an exception, there is a predominant negative evaluation of crime, which defines it as such. In the case of particularly drastic crimes such as murder, a positive evaluation is pretty much excluded (a newspaper would categorise the positive evaluation of the killing of a human being in a different fashion, not as a 'murder' case; see Benwell/Stokoe 2006, 106). If a murderer should regard what they have done as something positive and not show any remorse, they would be all the more a sustained case for the criminal courts or even the psychiatric ward. By contrast, a milder evaluation would probably occur in the case of 'lighter' offences, such as consuming cannabis. Offenders are confronted with different normative evaluations; narratives lay down which evaluation is 'justified'. In the case of the "Facebook murder video", the evaluation is extremely negative because, as the title would suggest, the murder was even 'posted' on Facebook. A comparable, yet inverted, ranking order of evaluations refers to victims. Victims of crime "may be characterized as bearing no responsibility for their plight, and therefore mereting society's support and sympathy" (Best 2008, 35). As Loseke (2003, 78–79) explains, sympathy is particularly forthcoming when a victim is not responsible in any way for the negative event that they had to endure. The same applies if they are seen to be people with moral integrity and their suffering – possibly including the suffering of the victim's family and friends (Tabbert 2015, 154) – is to be regarded as serious. Our example is also meaningful in this case: the title "*Man wanted in Facebook murder video kills himself, police say*" indicates that two people have died. Yet only one of them emerges as a victim, namely the person that was (probably) murdered by "man". The status of the "man" who is also dead is far different. As a (potential) murderer, he is obviously not a morally integral person, and he himself seems to be responsible for his (possible) suicide. The category victim and the associated evaluation do therefore not apply to him. Irrespective of the presumption of innocence, he is a "murderer", i.e. the active and evil protagonist in the crime story.

d) **Temporal Processes:** Narratives imply that time passes and changes happen. Temporal sequences can be varyingly extensive and affect different story lines. Our exemplary title story indicates a temporal sequence consisting of four sequences. A man has (possibly) killed someone; a video of the murder was uploaded to Facebook; the police sought the murderer; probably during the search, the murderer took his own life. Events like murder (or other offences) are 'understandable' when they are part of a story with a respective course. It would not make sense, for example, to assume that the man could have killed himself in the time before the murder was committed. A crime in this sense has a temporal sequence integrated into it. During the institutional handling of a case, relevant sequences have to be ascertained and (re-)constructed (Arnauld/Martini 2015; Komter 2014; Olson 2014). An important reference point is the biography of an offender. As Foucault (1975/1979), among others, pointed out, the criminological and criminalistic interest in individual biographies presumes a special, historically established understanding of crime. This understanding is currently of particular relevance in the area of youth crime, where the commission of crimes is deemed strongly connected with negative events in the biography of an offender (Dünkel et al. 2010a). In their handling of a case, youth courts expect corresponding life stories.[12] Young people seem to be well advised to narrate a difficult life history when faced with a potentially harsh penal sanction, and this illustrates that, in narratives, temporal sequences are not just aligned retrospectively (Chase 2011, 430; see also Boje 2008, 13–15). Narrating biographies brings about effects in the present for the future. When a (potential) offender remorsefully tells his or her problem-laden life story before a court, s/he may do this because s/he hopes to influence the judge and public prosecutor positively. A narrator relates the past within a particular present-situational framework of the narration. The expected future consequences of the narration are an integral part of this framework.

e) **Performance:** Drawing on ethnomethodological tenets, the telling of stories, just like communication on the whole, is "recipient designed", meaning that "speakers should design their talk for recipients" (Sacks 1995, II,

445). An audience is even relevant in a narrative when not physically present, so the telling of stories is an interactive achievement. As social action, a narration is involved in mutual negotiations of meaning and the constitution of interactional relations. Mandelbaum (2014, 504) states that "all stories in conversation appear to be both designed by tellers and understood by recipients to be *doing* something". Accordingly, a performance lies not just within a story as the (re-)production of a "connected series of events" (Hall/Matarese 2014, 80). As a further level of performance, the telling of a story has to be heeded, i.e. "the act of narration itself" or "the actions of the narrator" (Berns 2014, 677). Without the practical act of narrating an offence, crime would not exist. Hereby, the situational context of telling and listening (or writing and reading) characterises the content and type of narrative in a constitutive manner. Fitting examples are provided by Toch (1993, 195), who compares public and private accounts of violence:

> Public accounts are not designed for audiences of intimates or peers, whose understanding and loyalty the aggressor expects. No self-respecting delinquent tells another delinquent, 'I really can't imagine what came over me to make me violent. Everybody knows I wouldn't hurt a fly. I guess something must have snapped'. No hockey player says to his team, 'You can imagine my chagrin when I misjudged the distance between Big Pierre and myself and knocked his teeth out with my stick'.

This shows not only the principle of "recipient design" but also the active processing of social relationships through narratives. A teller adapts to external expectations that they integrate into the story, and listeners react correspondingly and evaluate or honour to what extent this has been successful (Mandelbaum 2014). In the case of deviance or crime, this is relevant in a particular way because the moral qualities of those involved are handled here and corresponding care has to be shown when assuming or rejecting responsibility for the incorrect behaviour in question (Scott/Lyman 1968). This also has significance for the "Facebook murder video", even when the person does not report on their crime in this particular case. Within the complex of writing/reading, a certain form of interaction and moral communication is realised: the newspaper assumes an interest in the unusual murder case among readers. It can act on the assumption that the categories used are generally known. Facebook is a communication platform that many people use, and there is a general (at least rudimentary) understanding of what a murder and murderer are. Such drastic violent crimes often attract a great deal of public and media attention. Title and reader interact, whatever the exact interpretation in the end is. Stories do not just convey messages on events and persons but are interactive, performative achievements (Hall/Matarese 2014, 84–86). This notion is particularly important here, as it highlights what politicians, professionals and defendants say about themselves as well as the situation they find themselves in and their audiences when they speak about crime.

These five dimensions illustrate my understanding of narrativity. There are, of course, alternatives and possible extensions, but the dimensions reflect the central lines, which I will use in the following reasoning.[13]

1.2.2 Stories and nonstories

The example of the "Facebook murder video" shows that crime can even be narrated in short allusions. Crime is an event with strong moral connotations, so that individual words or suggestions can suffice to impart wide interpretative references (Beckett 1997, 65–66; Rapley 2012). Small suggestions and ambiguities are, as Sandberg (2016) explains, analytically insightful because they imply and reveal wide contexts related to the meaning attributed to crime. In this respect, narrative research is dealing with so-called *small stories*. This concept draws on the abovementioned scepticism directed at comprehensive structural elements of narratives as the sole subject matter of narrative analyses. Instead, proponents of "small story"-research emphasise mundane, inconspicuous narratives or allusions with more or less narrative qualities. De Fina and Georgakopoulou (2012, 116) talk about small stories as an

> umbrella term, that captures a gamut of under-represented narrative activities, such as tellings of ongoing events, future or hypothetical events, shared (known) events but also allusions to (previous) tellings, deferrals of tellings and refusals to tell. These tellings are typically small when compared to the pages and pages of transcripts of interview narratives.

Because small stories include allusions and hidden references, the reconstruction of the relationship between teller and listener, as well as the appraisal of the teller's situation, gains special weight (Chase 2011, 425). Small stories don't represent a clearly definable category of narratives. Instead, the concept calls for attention that a researcher has to pay to the function of telling for the development of an interactive situation and the identity construction of participants in the situation (Bamberg/Georgakopoulou 2008).

This important notion is taken one step further here, with *nonstories* also supposed to be analysable as stories. Narrators sometimes avoid the impression of being narrators. Or, in other words, some accounts fulfil 'storylike' functions even though (or by the very fact that) they assume to be particularly neutral and realistic. According to Loseke (2018, 2), "the most socially consequential [stories; B.D.] are told as fact", and this particularly applies to crime. Nonstories are often told within the context of crime in order to report in a serious manner about the infringement of legal standards and to render narrators as rational persons who are in possession of expert knowledge. This is what Bruner (2003, 48) says about attorneys and judges:

They work hard to make their law stories as unstorylike as possible, even anti-storylike: factual, logically self-evident, hostile to the fanciful, respectful to the ordinary, seemingly 'untailored'. Yet in pleading cases, they are creating drama, indeed, are sometimes carried away by it.

Accordingly, avoiding the impression of telling a story can imply a special story in itself. An example from the corpus of the data presented in Chapter 2 from debates that took place in German parliaments can illustrate this point. It involves an excerpt from a debate held in 1993 in the German Federal Parliament (Bundestag). At the time, the German federal government was a coalition of the conservative CDU/CSU and the liberal FDP. The debate was on "security" and "mass crime". Jürgen Meyer, a representative of the opposition Social Democratic Party (SPD), made the following statement:[14]

1   *Crime victims* are often socially weaker. In the case of snatched purses, 55.6% of the victims are older
2   people over 60 years of age. Equally worrying is the fact that in the case of other street robberies, 14.9%
3   % of the victims were teenagers, 8.9% adolescents and 8.7% were children above the age of six.
4   Increased crime, falling rates of crimes being solved and the diminishing feeling of being safe among
5   the population are sad events, especially after over ten years of conservative change politics. The
6   figures speak for themselves.
7   (Hans-Joachim Otto [Frankfurt] [F.D.P.]: This argument really opens one's eyes!)
8   There is no ideal solution to all current problems, but there are very concrete possibilities to take
9   action, that are undisputed among experts by the way, with which the worrying development could be
10 clearly counteracted. [Meyer, BT, 1993, 182. Session of parliament, 15774]

This excerpt does not represent a 'complete' or 'large' story. There is no single changing event whose depiction would be initiated with an abstract and an orientation, and which would be ended with be ended with a coda. The speaker conveys facts and numbers, particularly at the beginning of the excerpt. Still, he delivers a telling story about himself, his audience and crime. Predicated on the dimensions of narrativity depicted in Chapter 1.2.1, there is a *categorisation* of crime victims (line 1): they are the sufferers of different types of crime, and they are categorised on the basis of their social status and their age. Young and old people in particular are made the subject of the discussion. The speaker provides numbers relating specifically to the crimes, and based on the allegedly exact numbers, he outlines the burden on these groups (lines 1–3). He also reports *relations*: Victims of different types of crimes have a connection with each other and they are linked to the implicitly indicated category offender; there are also trends such as increasing rates of crime while the probability of crimes being solved continues to decrease; and there is a decrease in the "feeling of security among the population" (lines 4–5). Crimes, becoming a victim, feelings of the population and crime-related policy are apparently relationally connected with one another. *Evaluations* also occur, to the extent that the speaker does not allow any doubts to arise that, as a matter of fact, he describes a new negative situation or development ("worrying", line 2; "sad events", line 5). *Temporal sequences* also occur in relation to crime, activities of the police, perceptions of the population, decision-making practices of the government parties and with respect to the speaker: there are growing amounts of crime, which results in ever more victims of crime. It would appear that the police are not able to deal with the situation, as is reflected in the fact that ever decreasing numbers of these crimes are being solved, which in turn leads to a decreasing feeling of safety and security among the general public. Decisive for the self-categorisation and positioning of the speaker is the way he depicts the temporal development of the government's work, because he attests that it has not been effective: Despite "over ten years" (line 5) of government activity, the negative situation reported about has established itself. The logical conclusion is that the government has failed in the fight against crime. This (alleged) fact delegitimises the government parties and supports the opposition, including the speaker himself. He categorises himself *performatively* as a crime politician, who not only knows the current crime situation exactly, which the numbers referred to would certainly seem to suggest. He is furthermore worried emotionally about the population, especially with respect to particularly vulnerable older and younger persons as (potential or actual) victims of crime. Associated with this knowledge and emotional concern is a self-categorisation as a knowledgeable and prudent politician who knows exactly what needs to be done. Typical for the current crime-policy discourse in Germany, in which at least a rhetorical appeal to experts plays a major role (Dollinger et al. 2017c), the speaker refers to "experts" (line 9), meaning that he develops himself as someone who has made the effort to view the statistics and to contact professionals in order to have a comprehensive basis of information for his decisions. He does not appear to be a person who, despite being emotionally affected, makes decisions based on his gut and simply acts in a punitive and hard manner. Instead, he comes across as worried, caring and rational. He orchestrates a down-to-earth and allegedly sensible form of criminal policy that is better than what the government has done.

This form of narrative may be interpreted as a small story. But it became clear that the decisive point here is not only that something is suggested or referenced, but that the speaker tries to avoid the interactive impression that he 'only' tells stories. He strives to come across as competent and successful by communicating in a rational and sober manner, *unstorylike* from Bruner's perspective. The sentence "The figures speak for themselves" (lines 5–6) sums this up exactly: no stories are meant to be told, just the facts are to be talked about. Not even "refusals to tell" (De Fina/Georgakopoulou 2012, 116) in the abovementioned sense referring to "small stories" have been expressed. The speaker avoids creating the impression that there could actually be a story behind the facts. But of course numbers do not speak for themselves; when viewed in isolation, "numbers and research findings do not have any meaning" (Loseke 2003, 89). In the communication of social problems and crime, they only have a meaning when woven into stories, and that is exactly the case here. The numbers provide a "disguised judgement"

(Becker 2007, 140), because the orchestrated neutrality blames the sitting government for a development, which the audience of the nonstory must regard as negative. The speaker is telling a nonstory in order to portray himself as a successful crime politician and to discredit the competing parties. Interwoven with this is a special depiction of crime, and corresponding narratives will be discussed in this volume. It is most likely useful in this regard to assume the possibility of nonstories in the manner described. They emphasise the interactive function of narratives, which are narratively deprived of 'storylike' qualities.

1.2.3 On categories in crime narratives

Crime as a narrative comprises individual categories (such as offender, victim etc.), which a performative and evaluative practice brings into a temporally structured relation. How can these narratives be analysed? The answer that is given here focuses on categorisations or, more precisely, on interpretations of categories and their associated qualities. Scientific or criminalistic studies may be able to determine which act with specific consequences was 'really' carried out by a person. Yet, what constitutes crime is based on something different: it is narrative *categorisations* as "ordinary practices in which members are engaged in the characterization of themselves and of one another" (Stetson 1999, 78; referring to Harvey Sacks). The focus is not on statutory stipulations or 'objective' qualities of certain acts or persons, but on the communicative identification of crime within particular contexts. In principle, there are always numerous ways to categorise acts or persons. An offender is never only an offender. He can be 40 years old, a man, left-handed, underweight, a hockey player, a tradesman, a husband, a father and much more besides. These kinds of designations can accurately describe individual people (Sacks 1995, I, 41). But in the context of crime, they are not important per se. To make somebody an 'offender', a reason must be established through communication; s/he must be involved in a "moral discourse" (Watson 1976, 68) that provides evaluations, lays down responsibilities and establishes pertinent categories. The person has to be ascribed characteristics "which one might term blameworthiness, guilt, responsibility, while the category victim has the bound property of blamelessness or innocence (of the offense or of responsibility for its ill effects)" (Watson 1976, 65). In particular when it is found that someone intentionally caused harm, accusations of guilt appear justified, the person becomes an offender and the call for punishment appears justified (Loseke 2003, 83). This also includes motives. If a person who is suspected of having committed a crime is said to have motives 'fitting' to the (alleged) crime, the status of a delinquent is then ensured. In this respect, motives are not pre-discursive reasons to take action but instead "constituent features of the description of deeds and of accounts 'surrounding' those descriptions" (Watson 1997, 90; see also Komter 1998, 62–70; Mills 1940).

Assignments of motives and guilt are actually rather complicated; there can be many plausible reasons or pretexts put forward as to why e.g. somebody intentionally caused harm (Scott/Lyman 1968; Sykes/Matza 1957). However, imputations of motives and guilt are core conditions of the talk about crime, be it in everyday or in institutional contexts. In most cases, a person who is guilty of having wilfully and for particular reasons carried out a criminal act is an offender. To the extent that this categorisation is effectively established, this can take on a dominant status for this person, and the biography of the person affected can be re-interpreted as being the biography of a criminal (Stokoe/Attenborough 2015, 61). Categories such as offender or victim are *inference rich*, which means "a great deal of the knowledge that members of a society have about the society is stored in terms of these categories" (Sacks 1995, I, 40). Categories 'explain' characteristics and activities and, inversely, characteristics and activities establish the incumbency of a category (Eglin/Hester 1992).

Harvey Sacks (1995, I, 241), who made these connections transparent within the framework of ethnomethodological analyses of stories, emphasised, among other things, "category-bound activities", which he defined as follows:

> What I mean by that is, there are a great many activities which Members take it are done by some particular category of persons, or several categories of persons, where the categories are categories from these membership categorization devices.

With "membership categorization device" (MCD), Sacks broaches the topic that categories are connected with other categories, as well as being associated with typecast activities of the respective category-incumbents. In his words, MCDs are "collections of categories for referring to persons, with some rules of application" (Sacks 1995, I, 238). Also in the case of crime, such a collection exists. An offender isn't just an offender in their own right, but they are relationally integrated into a "MCD parties to an offense", which according to Watson (1976, 62) also includes witnesses and further categories in addition to offender and victim. These categories are respectively associated with specific activities; it is mostly the case that the offender is said to have taken action, while the victim is said to have suffered passively (Bamberg 2012, 106; Tabbert 2015). Police officers, in turn, are expected to actively solve a possible crime and use, in particular, special (interview) techniques in the process (e.g. Stokoe 2009), while public prosecutors and judges assume a special task within the framework of the roles that have been assigned to them, to clarify acts of crime and sanction these if necessary (e.g. Licoppe 2015). Categories imply corresponding activities and characteristics, and they are combined with obligations and evaluations. In this regard, the category 'offender' has a pejorative meaning; it is connected with negative attributions and threatens a category-incumbent with penal sanctions and moral degradations. A victim, on the other hand, can expect to receive sympathy, at least as long as they correspond to the expectations that are associated with the category. Categorisation work is therefore morality work, and it locates category-incumbents in a status structure that shows higher and lower positions (Jayyusi 1984; Silverman 1998, 84–85).

A wide research landscape of "membership categorization analysis" (MCA) developed from Sack's notions.[15] The term MCA is supposed to emphasise membership collections and to underline the relevance of individual categories (Eglin/Hester 1992). It intends to cover "the full range of categorization practices without giving priority to any particular concept or practice" (Eglin/ Francis 2016, 8). MCA is part of the ethnomethodological programme to analyse the interactive establishment of social order as an "ongoing accomplishment" (Garfinkel 1967, VII). Especially in the focus of MCA are "peoples' routine methods of social categorisation and local reasoning practices as a display and accomplishment of 'doing' society" (Housley/Fitzgerald 2015, 5).

MCA is not undisputed, among other things with respect to the more or less significant proximity to conversation analysis (Schegloff 2007; Silverman 1998; Stokoe 2012), the possible necessity of a corpus in contrast to studies relating to single cases (Fitzgerald 2012) or the question whether (or how) cultural background knowledge can be made relevant in the empirical analyses. Despite these contentious issues, MCA developed guidelines for an empirical analysis that I can draw on, even though the following analyses will only be inspired by – and not thoroughly bound to – MCA.[16] In the following chapters, I will analyse data that mostly does not have direct interactive quality, but which is to a large extent (Chapter 2), by trend (Chapter 4) or strictly (Chapter 3) monologically oriented. Even if a (fictive) audience is always present in the respective narratives, I could only partially reconstruct mutual negotiations of the meaning of categories.

For the reasons given above, the focus of the empirical analyses in Chapters 2 to 4 will nevertheless be on how speakers and authors use categories of crime and the qualities and activities they associate with them. The respective contexts of the narrators will play a significant role in this. Categories become relevant in their practical use by people who harness them for specific purposes, thus furnishing them with context- and audience-specific denotations and connotations (Mäkitalo 2014). Despite their extra-situational origin, the meaning of categories relates to "a situated, contextually embedded sense" (Hester/Eglin 1997b, 11); it is "irredeemably occasioned" (Fitzgerald 2012, 309). That means for this volume: (penal) politicians aim to be re-elected and correspondingly direct their speeches held in parliament to the general public or electorate (Dollinger et al. 2017c). Professionals are required to legitimise their activity and carry out corresponding categorisations (Hall et al. 2006). Defendants are faced with the challenge of representing themselves before the courts in an authentic manner so as to receive no or only a clement punishment (Dollinger/Fröschle 2017; Komter 1998). There are, therefore, different audiences implicitly addressed in the respective narratives and categorisations. A reconstruction of crime narratives must heed categorisation as "occasioned", i.e. as a process of active, context- and audience-specific meaning-making.[17] It needs to be determined empirically how speakers and writers implement crime-related categories, whereby narratives are the means through which they set categories in relation to one another and make them plausible for their respective audience.

The corresponding analyses are in Chapters 2, 3 and 4. I will explain the underlying corpus of data at the start of each chapter.[18] The narrative analyses will focus on individual passages of texts. The aim is not to make the entire width of the corresponding corpora comprehensible; instead, relevant examples should be used to analyse in detail how youth crime was (and is) narratively conceptualised in the three discourses.

Conclusion

Crime is not a 'thing' that can simply be talked about without a particular perspective. It results from a special way of devising stories about it, thus creating crime as a noteworthy event and 'real' experience. Even (more or less) everyday types of crime exhibit a narrative quality. It categorises the involved persons with a special relation to each other, conveys evaluations of the respective events and persons, and performatively constitutes distinctive notions of offences.

Associated with this narrative approach is a certain kind of ambivalence. On the one hand, there are multiple ways to tell stories; narrative constructions of crime are historically, culturally and situationally contingent. On the other hand, when crime is talked about, contingency is often obscured. For instance, when a judge imposes sanctions on an offender, s/he implies that a 'real' kind of offence was at hand, that it could not be interpreted differently but deserves, by its very 'nature', an unequivocal response. In this regard, crime seems to be what it is, beyond any 'storylike' qualities. And yet it is a dynamic and context-specific narrative. Therefore, in order to reconstruct historical changes of youth crime from 1970 onwards (including synchronic narratives of young defendants), this book has to do justice to the flexible as well as the 'solidified' nature of crime. The empirical data of political, professionals' and defendants' narratives will allow for a respective assessment. The result will be a substantial transformation; delinquency gradually lost its social causes and was re-narrated as a threat to the social (Chapter 5).

Notes

1 For a more detailed analysis and explanation of punitiveness, see for example the studies by Garland (2001a), Simon (2007) and Wacquant (2009). Beckett (1997) has undertaken a major reconstruction of developments in the USA, and Green (2008) an instructive country comparison of approaches to children who commit murder. Matthews (2005) contains an interesting critical analysis of the issue of punitiveness. Key information specifically on punitiveness in the context of youth crime can be found in Muncie (2008; 2015).
2 In Germany, the first general criminal code from 1532, the *Constitutio Criminalis Carolina*, explicitly identified "*jugent*" ("youth age") as a factor that could lead to a more lenient sentence (Stump 2003). Germany's first youth courts were set up in 1908.
3 Cohen (1972/2002, 1) describes "moral panic" as follows: "A condition, episode, person or group of persons emerges to become defined as a threat to societal values and interests; its nature is presented in a stylised and stereotypical fashion by the mass media; the

moral barricades are manned by editors, bishops, politicians and other right-thinking people; socially accredited experts pronounce their diagnoses and solutions; ways of coping are evolved or (more often) resorted to; the condition then disappears, submerges or deteriorates and becomes more visible". This concept became a highly influential, albeit not uncontentious one within the field of criminology and beyond (Coomber et al. 2014, 150–155; Findlay 2010). It is seen as one important way of understanding the process by which individual events are dramatised and discursively over-represented.

4 DiIulio (1995) suggested that "moral poverty" was a major cause of the supposed "super-predators": they were brought up not by loving parents but by criminal adults "in abusive, violence-ridden, fatherless, Godless, and jobless settings". Therefore, because of their openness to social and moral influence, young people became ruthless offenders. DiIulio argued that detention and religion were necessary for dealing with such offenders.

5 The reality of youth crime policy is more complex than these two interpretations suggest. If we look at the picture internationally, there are a number of different systems (Cavadino/Dignan 2006; Dünkel et al. 2010a; Muncie/Goldson 2009; Tonry/Doob 2004). Even at a national level, we often see complex combinations of differing assessments of youth crime (McAra 2017; Muncie 2015). Interpretations of youth crime, as I have reconstructed here as distinct, polarised views on the basis of the defence counsel's and public prosecutor's assessments, mostly occur *in combination* in national systems for dealing with youth crime. Welfarist and punitive elements are weighted differently.

6 Available at www.oyez.org/cases/2004/03-633 (accessed 01 September 2018).

7 Not all relevant actors and discourses can be implicated in this volume. Especially mass media would qualify for an inclusion into the analyses undertaken here. This would reveal basic public narratives on crime. Although the corresponding findings would be relevant, public narratives can be covered here, at least partially, in Chapter 2 with the reconstruction of political narratives based on parliamentary debates. The debates are public speeches and discussions directed at the electorate. They function as an interface of politics and the public, thus attenuating the lack of further investigations of public narratives in this volume. Other candidates for an inclusion in this volume would be e.g. talk of crime in everyday life (e.g. Sasson 1995) or granular interactions in a court hearing (e.g. Atkinson/Drew 1979; Komter 2014).

8 In this regard, I also deviate from positions of critical criminology. Although those positions are relatively diverse, they often – albeit not necessarily – presume structural societal conditions that affect crime or criminalisation (for example: Hall et al. 1978; for an overview, see for example DeKeseredy/Dragiewicz 2012; Lilly et al. 2011; Lynch 2018). Such a line of argument is difficult for a narrative position if that position is to take narratives seriously in their own right (Presser 2016, 145).

9 There is therefore no crime outside of narratives. In a similar vein, Pollner (1978) noted in his criticism of Becker's labelling approach that deviance is always an ascription. Pollner argues that we should not assume that there are any rule violations without labelling. Pollner (1978, 279), with whose criticism I agree, also termed his approach "constitutive".

10 An array of concepts is related to this call for indifference, e.g. phenomenological demands to bracket presuppositions about the world according to Husserl (see Bergmann 2003, 123) or the sociology of knowledge's "Einklammerung des Geltungscharakters" ("Bracketing of the Validity Character"; Mannheim 1980, 88) of cultural phenomena. Another example would be Foucault's analysis of discursively conveyed effects of truth (Foucault 1972). The reasons behind and focuses of these concepts are different, although there are, at least regarding Mannheim and Foucault, similarities with respect to the analytical necessity of abstaining from ascertaining an 'objective' truthfulness of a specific phenomenon. In view of the approach that I develop in this volume, however, the above quote of Garfinkel and Sacks consciously refers to ethnomethodology.

11 This perspective is based on work on typification by Alfred Schütz (e.g. Schütz/Luckmann 2003). See also Edwards (1991) and Sacks (1979, 1984).

12 Young offenders who are under suspicion of having carried out serious crimes must expect to receive particularly harsh sentences if they cannot 'explain' their offences with a dire, burdensome biography (Dollinger/Fröschle 2017; for corresponding expectations in groups sessions, see Polletta et al. 2011, 116).

13 The dimensions follow premises of ethnomethodology (Garfinkel 1967), i.e. my analysis of crime as a narrative refers to the methodical, discursive and practical production of crime narratives in particular situations, within whose framework crime assumes a specific meaning. For further information on ethnomethodology, see e.g. Francis/Hester (2004); Lynch (1993); vom Lehn (2014).

14 To characterise the corpus and the rules of citation in greater detail, reference is made to Chapter 2.

15 For an overview, see Fitzgerald/Housley (2015); Have (2014); Hester/Eglin (1997a). With respect to deviance, crime and crime control, see e.g. Dollinger (2017); Eglin/ Hester (1999); Hester (2016); Lee (1984); Stetson (1999); Watson (1976, 1978).

16 For methodological and methodical guidelines, see e.g. Lepper (2000); Silverman (1998); Stokoe (2012).

17 The process of meaning-making includes the *positioning* of a narrator in different contexts (for an overview of approaches to positioning, see Deppermann 2015). According to Bamberg and Georgakopoulou (2008, 380), narrative positioning refers to three levels: the told story, the situation in which the story is told and the "global situatedness within which selves are already positioned". Despite "the locally emergent nature of positioning processes in interaction" (Clifton/Van De Mieroop 2016, 9), positioning therefore implies references to contexts beyond the situational telling of a story. In the following empirical analyses, I will repeatedly resort to this concept of positioning. A minimum knowledge of contexts of narrative situations is indispensable to analyse stories (Deppermann 2013, 83–84), and positioning analysis allows for an empirically informed ascertainment of significant contexts.

18 In particular the data from Chapters 2 (relating to parliament debates) and 3 (journal articles of social work and the police) were already partly analysed in a different manner with a focus on the width of the statements. Respective findings were presented in the publications quoted in the chapters. In this study, I will use a different type of empirical analysis by examining narratives.

2 Devising juvenile criminal law

Political debates on youth crime

Political decisions are primarily responsible for changes of penal trends. The judiciary decides on the imposition of particular sanctions on offenders, but the options and the more or less wide discretion to do so are rooted in criminal policy. It does therefore make sense to begin with narratives in the context of politics; this chapter analyses *political debates on youth crime from 1970 to 2009*. Based on analyses of *debates in German parliaments*, this chapter explores both how youth crime has been portrayed in politics in general and over the years, and what calls for intervention are and have been linked to that portrayal.[1]

An analysis of political debates has to consider two sides of crime as a political narrative: on the one hand, politicians have the space and scope to present their views and to pay only more or less attention to expectations from, e.g. the media and criminological experts (Dollinger et al. 2017c; Dollinger/Rudolph 2016). Politicians can advocate certain positions more strongly than others, put the emphasis on criminal policy or on alternative areas of action, etc. On the other hand, they are acting within the confines of path-dependent national specificities (such as the mass media landscape, the particularities of first-past-the-post or proportional representation electoral systems, welfarist traditions, etc.; Downes/Hansen 2006; Green 2008; Lacey 2008; Sutton 2004; Tonry 2007). These factors may not determine but they do influence political action. At least in democratic states, politics take place within a public, and that public gives or withholds from political players their fundamental means of (occupational) existence through dis-/approval and electoral success or failure. In their decisions, politicians are therefore well advised to consider the mood among the public, i.e. in the mass media and in the population.[2]

Parliaments are the places where both sides come together: politicians present their decisions to a public or an electorate with special expectations and interests. Parliamentary debates represent a revealing interface between politics and the public, even though the actual relevance of parliamentary debates in crime policy decisions varies from country to country. One key difference is that between so-called *working* and *debating parliaments* (Patzelt 2005). 'Working parliaments' are those in which legislative decisions are mainly presented and legitimised in plenary sessions, while the work on reaching the actual decisions is done elsewhere, for example in committees and parliamentary groups (a way of working that characterises the German Bundestag and the US Congress, for instance). By contrast, in 'debating parliaments', plenary sessions are much more important to shape and discuss policy decisions (an example is the British House of Commons). Despite this significant difference, the public is of great relevance *in both cases*. This is true for 'working parliaments' even though their decision-making processes are not always directly accessible to the public, for legislative reforms must then be justified to the public in parliamentary speeches. That need applies despite the significant influence of media on political action. Communication over the Internet and social media are of great significance to politics (e.g. Enli/Skogerbø 2013; Graham et al. 2016). However, it would be a mistake to conclude in the light of the importance of mass media and digitalised communication that parliaments had lost their function as an intermediary between politics and the public or of public oversight of the legislative process. Parliaments have been and still are a central arena in which politicians present their actions in public and allow those actions to be scrutinised (for Germany, see Burkhardt 2003; Burkhardt/Pape 2000; Dörner/Vogt 1995; Sarcinelli 2011). This is done in debates (including speeches) at which the public are present in numbers far beyond those in physical attendance: debates are broadcast, records are taken and, in the respective contexts, politicians must mobilise approval for a given position.

The following pages analyse debates from the German national and state parliaments; the main principle is that of the 'working parliament'. Analysing these debates reconstructs a form of political communication in which politicians turn to the public to justify their decisions or to criticise decisions taken by their political opponents. As this communication is public, it uses arguments and figures of speech that the public and in particular the group of voters addressed can be expected to understand, in other words that will meet with a positive response and legitimise political action (Zeh 1989). What is important here is less the decision-making itself and more how it is rooted in the semantics and narrative forms that the speaker assumes will be positively received and thus generate support for the political position in question by appealing to a (supposed) public common sense.

2.1 Parliamentary debates

a) Context

Some background information on German politics is first needed to put the parliamentary debates analysed below in context. One difference from other political systems is a strong focus on parties and their formation of coalition governments. German politics are shaped by the search for consensus rather than a 'winner takes all' system. Cooperation between different parties in the formation and work of governments has been a constant thread in German politics since the Second World War. With the exception of some brief periods resulting from specific situations, no government since the first post-war elections in 1949 has been formed by one single party at the federal level. Instead, the country has been ruled by coalition governments. These coalitions have often consisted of one large plus one smaller party needed to achieve a majority, and have less frequently been 'grand coalitions' or collaborations between the two largest parties, the CDU/CSU and the SPD (grand coalitions to date: 1966 to 1969, 2005 to 2009 and since 2013). Another key aspect is that the political system in Germany is to a large degree federalistic; the federal states have a considerable influence on the passing and implementation of laws. That is why Schmidt (2011, 41) calls Germany a "state of the Grand Coalition", as there is a "strong urge for cooperation" despite the competition for political ascendancy. Parties in government at a national level are often required to work together with the governments of the federal states represented in the Bundesrat, and those state governments are also frequently coalitions.

Lacey (2012, 16) points to one consequence of this structure, namely that in Germany, "single-issue pressure groups, notably those representing victims of crime", have relatively low chances of success compared to those in other national political systems. She believes the reason for this lies in the political relevance of special issues, which can, for example, be of great relevance to undecided voters. Their potential to decide elections can be decisive in countries with 'winner takes all' electoral systems; single issues can shape the parties' direction in the long term, as the example of crime policy in the USA strikingly illustrates (Beckett/ Sasson 2000). In Germany, by contrast, for the parties that have so far dominated the political scene and because of the usual need to form coalition governments – and thus to balance different interests on a range of political questions – crime is one issue among many. Crime is the subject of varying but never exclusive public interest; parties and campaigns in Germany with a strong populist agenda therefore face particular challenges (Dollinger et al. 2015a, 2017c).[3]

Nonetheless, this does not mean that German crime policy is not also subject to populist tendencies or that systematic trends towards harsher sentencing have not emerged over recent years. In fact, most penal reforms in the past decades have seen a move towards stricter penalties; liberalisation has been a much less common development (Schlepper 2014). Yet there was no comprehensive "punitive turn" like that which has characterised the USA in particular and to a lesser extent England and Wales (Dollinger 2011; Dünkel 2011; Heinz 2012). Firstly, a relatively high degree of continuity can be observed in Germany at the level of the judiciary, i.e. in the administration of criminal justice. Despite a certain fluctuation, the rates of imprisonment and the prison population have remained relatively stable overall when compared to what are in some cases dramatic changes in other countries (Dünkel/Geng 2013; Lappi-Seppälä 2014).[4] Secondly, stricter crime policy – not unlike that in other western countries – focuses on specific groups of offences and offenders, in particular on violent and sexual offences (Dollinger 2011; Dünkel 2011). Punitive changes of German crime policy have occurred, but while these must be taken seriously, they have not led to a general increase in the punitive nature of how the criminal justice system deals with (youth) crime.

b) Data

The following analyses are predicated on debates from six German parliaments. Two of the parliaments are national (the Bundestag or national parliament and the representative chamber of the federal states, the Bundesrat). Parliaments in four federal states were also examined to reflect the federal structure of German politics and the fact that individual states differ considerably in how they approach crime (for details see Heinz 2016, 315–395).[5] The state parliaments analysed were those in Bavaria, Hamburg, Schleswig-Holstein and, starting in 1990, Saxony-Anhalt. This selection represents a wide range of parliaments: Bavaria has traditionally had a relatively restrictive and Schleswig-Holstein a relatively liberal crime policy. Hamburg is a major city with the status of a federal state, and Saxony-Anhalt is one of the new federal states to join the Federal Republic of Germany after reunification in 1990.

With the exception of Saxony-Anhalt, the analysis was conducted systematically from 1970 to 2009, evaluating all debates on youth crime in the parliamentary records for the six parliaments listed above, 550 debates in total.[6] Debates on important statutory reforms in the field of youth crime up to the year 2012 were also reconstructed,[7] so that the analysis effectively extends to 2012. Alongside the parliamentary debates, a number of other documents (such as minutes of committee meetings, party publications and press reports) were also analysed where these were directly relevant to important debates.

It is worth starting with a few brief facts about the various parties: the largest conservative party in Germany is the CDU (*Christlich Demokratische Union*, Christian Democratic Union) together with its Bavarian sister party, the CSU (*Christlich-Soziale Union*, Christian Social Union). Over the period analysed, the CDU and CSU held the post of chancellor of Germany from 1982 to 1998 and 2005 to 2012. The SPD (*Sozialdemokratische Partei Deutschlands*, Social Democratic Party), a party to the political left, held the post of chancellor from 1969 to 1982 and from 1998 to 2005. As these two 'major' parties rely strongly on coalition partners, 'smaller' parties in Germany are also of key importance. Such smaller parties include the FDP (*Freie Demokratische Partei*, Free Democratic Party), with a programme focused primarily on economic liberalism, and the Green Party (*Die Grünen*; full name: *Bündnis 90/Die Grünen*). When the Green Party became established on the German political scene in the 1980s, it was relatively far to the political left. It subsequently became more centrist, taking on more moderate left-wing and alternative positions. The Green Party emerged from the environmental protection and civil liberties movement. Another smaller party is the Left Party (*Die Linke*). Founded in 2007, it is the product of a merger between the successor to the ruling single party of the German Democratic Republic and a splinter group from the SPD. The Left Party has a strongly left-wing programme (for a summary of German parties, see Decker/Neu 2013; Zehetmair 2004).

It should be noted that parliamentary debates are a very special type of material. The speakers in the debates get involved in controversies despite the fact that the parliament is primarily a 'working' one: these parliaments only simulate a 'genuine' decision-making process (Burkhardt 2003, 325; Patzelt 2005, 223). The speakers exchange opposing arguments, usually by reading prepared texts, and thus make a pretence of searching for the best, most appropriate decision through debate. In fact, as I said before the arguments are designed not to lead to an actual decision but rather to garner support for a given position and party. The speeches aim at obtaining public approval.[8]

2.2 Narrating crime in politics

The following analysis focuses on what central narratives are employed by politicians to connect youth crime and specific countermeasures. There is no further exploration of the differences between the individual parliaments, as the key point here is to ascertain distinctive and important narratives.[9]

a) Structural causes

The dominant political narrative on youth crime in the 1970s and 1980s is that of help and support. It comes with an explanation of youth crime as a product of societal problems and social circumstances that cause young people to be drawn towards criminality through little fault of their own (Baumann 2006; Dollinger 2014b; Reinke/Schierz 2010). Calls to deal with structural causes are a case in point: the individual offender cannot help social factors.

In extreme cases, politicians took this line of argument so far that perpetrators appeared free of all responsibility and punishment in general unnecessary or unfair. This specific narrative was rare compared to other 'social' narratives; it was primarily put forward by the Green Party in the 1970s and 1980s. The passage cited below is one example. It comes from a debate in the Hamburg Landtag (called the Hamburgische Bürgerschaft) in 1982. The debate concerned punks, a group of young people whose criminality had led to confrontations with other citizens and ultimately to a debate on the incidents in Hamburg's parliament. The speaker is from the Green Party, which was in opposition:[10]

Example 2.1

1   *Ebermann* GAL: Just a few remarks for those who today, once again, want a ceremonial celebration of
2   the state monopoly on violence.
3   (Prosch CDU: Haha!)
4   Acceptance of the supposed state monopoly on violence is not exactly being fostered everywhere. We
5   can see that the oft-cited state monopoly on violence is evidently not able to force business to provide

6   enough training posts, for example. Training posts are in many cases even better than social work
7   intervention.
8   (Kuhn CDU: You are advocating a state labour service!)
9   (. . .)
10 We would in fact welcome the full use of the state monopoly on violence if that finally dealt with
11 Hamburg's underworld. However, there could then be no more indulgence shown to one part of that
12 state monopoly, namely sections of the Hamburg police. (. . .)
13 One final point for those who refuse to understand that certain measures can in fact make using the
14 police arm of the state monopoly on violence wholly unnecessary, and that those measures must be
15 exhausted before we even consider the first police deployment. They can protest as often as they want
16 that youth policy cannot be made with truncheons; their approach will again and again bring about just
17 that.
18 (Applause from GAL) [HH, 1982, 10/4, 155]

The speech starts with an "orientation" as defined by Labov and Waletzky (1967, 32–33); in other words, the listener is given the basic thrust of what is to come: the speaker limits himself by announcing that he is making "Just a few remarks" (line 1). He contrasts his stance with other positions ("those", line 1), which he ironically refers to as wanting a "ceremonial celebration" (line 1). This is an 'ordinary' parliamentary debate and not a ceremonial meeting for a special occasion, so the irony is clear. The speaker uses that irony to communicate disparagement with a long history. Of the many meanings that irony can have (e.g. Hutcheon 1994), we are dealing here with adversative or oppositional use. From the speaker's perspective, there are people with whose arguments he claims to be familiar, as they "today, once again" (line 1), have something to say. He is thus adopting a position already established that opposes another, existing stance. This opposition and disparagement is confirmed and reinforced by an interjection[11] that acts as a special form of "turn-taking" (Sacks et al. 1974): a speaker from the CDU signals with a laugh ("Haha", line 3) that the ironic comment was addressed at him (or his party) and that he has understood it. As no joke preceded the interjection, "Haha" is itself ironic, questioning what has just been said and setting the interjector in opposition to it. Contrasting positions are negotiated and performatively created: a GAL politician and a CDU politician establish opposing stances. Their contrasting approach on youth crime is established before youth crime is actually explicitly mentioned, so this example illustrates that politics is to a great extent strategic self-presentation (Edelman 1971).

The issue explicitly addressed in the excerpt is not youth crime itself but, first and foremost, the state monopoly on violence, which is mentioned six times by the GAL speaker in this relatively short passage (lines 2, 4, 5, 10, 12, 14). The term is qualified in different ways: ironically as something that is unjustifiably celebrated (lines 1–2, 5), as something that is an appearance only ("supposed", line 4), as something that is employed only partly or in full (lines 10, 12) and as connected (line 15) to the police and "truncheons" (line 16) – in other words, something involving tough action. Clearly, we are dealing here with critical evaluations of the way in which the state employs its monopoly on violence.

A closer look at how the narrative develops reveals the following. At the beginning, the speaker discredits the monopoly on violence by describing it as flawed as it is not used to create the training posts that, it is claimed, would be a suitable response to the problem being debated (lines 5–7). Here, the speaker implicitly presents a striking catalogue of issues: the monopoly on violence does not apply to business and is therefore not appropriate. Social work measures are not ideal, either; a useful approach would be a structural measure for getting young people into work, namely increasing opportunities for training. Correspondingly, the speaker is placing the solution to the punk problem in the field of labour market integration. He is implicitly categorising punks – or offenders in general in the context of the debate – as people without access to professional training. The state and business appear to be failing them, and even social work, i.e. interpersonal supportive measures, are insufficient. Punks are thus, in the speaker's view, not fully responsible offenders, and their actions are not merely a result of their personality or history, for were that the case, social work would be the instrument of choice. Punks are instead victims of structural conditions. Generalised for youth crime as a whole, this means that an offence is not a question of malicious intent, the wrong friends, bad or irrational choices, hedonism or similar issues, but rather a consequence of misguided economic policy. The speaker links the "resolution" (Labov/Waletzky 1967, 39) of the punk problem, according to which economic policy and available training posts can prevent youth crime, directly to a negative assessment of the state monopoly on violence.

The second interjection (line 8), an ironic take on the speech from a conservative perspective, indicates that the speaker's position as a critic of the state monopoly on violence has become clear, and his explanation of and solution to the punks' violation of the law serve that position. The speaker continues by further discrediting state actions: he claims that the state is not only acting illegitimately, as it is not behaving sensibly towards the punks, but is also failing to make "full use" (line 10) of the monopoly on violence to deal with 'real' problems – "Hamburg's underworld" and even sections of the police (line 12). Ebermann explicitly attacks police action, the implementation in practice of the state monopoly on violence, for focusing on the wrong target group (the punks) and employing the wrong resources. The action of the police is described as senselessly severe, as illustrated by the use of "truncheons" (line 16) – an exercise of force that is patently unsuitable as "youth policy" (line 16).

A category-bound activity identifies a category-incumbent. If we apply this to crime, those who act in a morally reprehensible manner in the context of criminal law are offenders, and the innocents who suffer from such actions are victims (Watson 1976). In the speech above, the 'actual' offenders are the police or the state, and the punks are categorised as victims. The punks do not even need to be mentioned for this performative creation of an offender–victim relationship. It is enough to present 'misguided' action, of which a speaker here accuses established politics and the police associated with that establishment. He is reversing the roles: he places the punks in opposition to the police and the state, and in the same way, he places himself in opposition to the state or to the 'misguided' politicians represented by the interjectors. Finally, the "applause" (line 18) from GAL recorded in the transcript shows that the speaker is not alone. It defines him as part of a group; the speech therefore sets out first and foremost the contrasting positions of political parties rather than of individuals. In this case, the GAL or the Green Party is being contrasted, together with the punks, with state politics and 'its' police. The political outsiders (GAL or the Green Party) stand together with the social outsiders (the punks) against a violent state that is denying and perpetuating the 'real' structural problems of society by "again and again" (line 16) taking the wrong course of action.

As mentioned above, this position and its strong contrast to established politics is an exception in the political discourse. However, the radical nature of this stance is in fact limited by two points with which the speaker does not set himself in complete opposition to the criminal law categorisation of offenders and victims. Firstly, his reference to the "underworld" (line 11) recognises that criminality in the traditional sense does exist. Secondly, he also points to the need for preventive measures to avoid "using the police arm" (lines 13–14). He thus implicitly recognises the need for restrictive intervention following a failure to implement said prevention at least. He thus does not draw a complete contrast between criminality and restrictive action. He communicates to the listeners a minimum of conformity with traditional values, and it is those values than can make his narrative 'understandable' to a wider audience. Ultimately, this speaker too stresses the need to deal with those whom he regards as the 'real' offenders and to protect innocent victims. Yet, despite these limitations and in particular in light of the reversal of the categories of offender and victim detailed above, this position remains a minority stance in the overall discourse on the topic.

A much more common approach was an appeal for help for young offenders who were interpreted as victims of external factors, but factors associated less with brutal policy or police and more with abstract, social circumstances. The following example is a good illustration of this position. It comes from a debate in the German Bundestag in 1973 on drug-taking among young people. The speaker is Heinz Westphal, Permanent Secretary to the Federal Youth, Family and Health Ministry (*Bundesministerium für Jugend, Familie und Gesundheit*) and a member of the then-ruling SPD.

Example 2.2

1   Any debate today about the *drug risk* to which sections of our youth are exposed must also explore the
2   *social circumstances* without which addiction cannot be explained. Anyone who disregards those
3   circumstances will necessarily offer only a superficial response and be unable to make any
4   constructive contribution to solving the underlying issues that we are facing in the form of substance
5   abuse.
6   We know from many letters we receive that there is an underlying view that approves draconian
7   punishments, the establishment of work camps for drug addicts and even a macabre form of assisted
8   dying that would see addicts given free access to drugs because, so the argument goes, they will dose
9   themselves to death anyway. These are symptoms of an attitude that is intolerable for any society
10 claiming to be humane and socially minded; an attitude that is dangerous because it blocks any
11 understanding of how such deviant behaviour can develop. Yet that is the very question that we must
12 address in depth, and even a preliminary, open-minded look at the issue reveals circumstances of
13 immense importance to our society as a whole. [Westphal, SPD, BT, 1973, 40th Session, 2211]

The speaker is representing the federal government, and a particularly authoritative oratory is therefore necessary to underscore the status of competent
decision-making. The type of discourse in parliamentary debates with all their
controversies and the previous example, in which state authority is attacked,
illustrate the challenge here for a government representative and how he positions himself.

In the section cited, the speaker starts with a clear statement which colours
the rest of the speech: it is a debate about drug use, and he starts by giving an
explanation for the problem – the "*social circumstances*" (line 2). The speaker
does not detail where this explanation comes from and on what grounds it is
legitimate; he presents it as a simple fact. By so doing, he is also defining what
can be done to combat drug use, namely taking measures to deal with these
root causes.

The speaker is categorising himself as an expert: someone who knows both
the source of a problem already widely discussed at the time and what is to
be done about it. The implicit suggestion is that others do not. Defining a
social aetiology authorises the speaker to dismiss these 'others'. He does so relatively directly by talking about their "superficial" approach (line 3), but without
explicitly naming them. It is, however, clear to whom he is referring: in this
debate, a representative of the CDU had just attacked the federal government
for failing to do enough to deal with an alleged explosion in youth drug use.
The Permanent Secretary is using his speech to defend himself against such
accusations, as is standard practice in parliamentary debates. The speaker is
accusing the opposition of superficiality because – unlike him – it is not familiar with the 'complexity' of the problem.

He underlines the professionalism and 'in-depth' nature of his speech by
avoiding any elaborations or embellishments: the story is a nonstory; it is
stark and simple, without any personal stories that could be identified as
such. In other debates and speeches, speakers recount individual incidents
that they have experienced, for example, to present themselves as authorities

on the subject in question. References to experts and statistical findings are to this end also important in German parliamentary debates (Dollinger et al. 2017c) – unlike in some English-speaking countries in particular, where experts are more frequently criticised (Green 2008; Pratt 2007). Both specific experiences and references to experts or statistics can prove that a speaker is competent and well informed, yet Westphal makes no mention of such evidence of his authority. There is just one exception in his speech, which does not appear above, where he specifies a figure of "*0.5% of twelve and thirteen-year-olds*" as having experience with drugs (Westphal, SPD, BT 1973, 40th Session, 2211). This appears a relatively small number, and the speaker indeed gives that explicit assessment. By so doing, he is categorising himself as someone who is aware of the current extent of drug use, who knows that it is not particularly dramatic and who, furthermore, does not feel it necessary to cite specific authorities. His authority is primarily that of his official function; it allows him to speak as an expert who can rightly dismiss other positions and is able to make statements on the 'reality' of drug use. He is an expert politician.

This self-categorisation is strengthened by the use of the characteristic personal pronouns "we" and "us". Their relevance as an indicator of agency and group membership is considerable both in discourses on crime (O'Connor 2000, 2015) and in parliamentary debates (Burkhardt 2003, 406–412). However, its interpretation can be difficult, as the communicated membership is to a group whose limits are not clearly defined. It is, therefore, worth taking a look at the textual context of the first use of the pronoun in example 2.2 ("that we are facing in the form of", line 4). Drug use is presented as a problem facing an 'us'. Just before that, the speaker has pointed to general social circumstances that lead to drug use. He therefore appears to be using 'us' as a general reference to society, which causes and is affected by the drug problem (see also "our society", line 13), and as a member of which – and therefore as someone affected by the problem – he is categorising himself. The pronoun can hardly be meant to refer solely to the federal government for which he is speaking as Permanent Secretary, for he describes drug use as a social phenomenon. Drug use is an issue that affects everyone, including himself, but which the 'superficial' opposition cannot grasp in sufficient depth. What is needed to address the problem is, he suggests, an 'in-depth' understanding which he and thus the federal government has. This makes a different meaning of "We" (line 6) clear: here, the speaker is no longer referring to society, as he is talking about correspondence sent to an – unspecified – address or institution, i.e. probably the federal government. That government is in close contact with society ("many letters we receive", line 6), and this suggests that it is not only familiar with the facts, as outlined above, but is also aware of and able to assess what mistaken views on drug use exist. The speaker knows society; he is a part of it and yet he can act as a knowledgeable expert.

This takes us to the central help narrative: drug use is a social problem and one of society's "underlying issues" (line 4). It is therefore certainly relevant for 'us' (as a society) but, as the 0.5% illustrates, not dramatic (for 'us' knowledgeable politicians). What is, on the other hand, serious according to the speaker are demands for tough, even "draconian punishments" (lines 6–7) that are not appropriate for the problem – and of which he therefore takes a negative view. Such demands would only make the problems worse, as they are, like the recommendations of the opposition, founded on an ignorance of the 'real' causes of those problems. Here, too, the speaker is presenting himself as well-informed; able to speak with authority and point out the dangers to society of the opposition's position on dealing with an issue of importance "to our society as a whole" (line 13).

Almost incidentally in this powerful self-portrayal, drug use emerges as a problem that must be addressed calmly and above all with supportive measures. Tough intervention is rejected and described as a danger to society; in this respect, the speaker's attitude is not dissimilar to the previous portrayal of a police monopoly on violence that failed to address society's 'real' problems (example 2.1). In both cases, the speakers present not primarily the form of delinquency under discussion but the misguided and overly tough political action against it as the actual problem. Yet, in example 2.2, the speaker's central evaluation is directed at incorrect assessments by the political opposition. There is no dramatisation of deviance – dramatisation is in fact interpreted as a symptom of the opposition's mistaken approach.

This means that drug use as a form of deviance is described as a serious problem that needs political attention, but it is not a scandal and there is no moral panic. Instead, it is a social pathology requiring rational analysis. There appears to be enough time to address the issue "in depth" (line 12), as the situation is not dramatic. The problem does not appear to be escalating, and there is therefore ample time to consider the best measures to take. Such an interpretation takes the pressure off the government: if drug use arises from "*social circumstances*" (line 2) and societal developments, a government that has only been in power for a few years cannot be accused of failing to act faster and with greater force, for a society cannot be changed in an instant. In the case of example 2.2, the SPD had held the post of federal chancellor since 1969, prior to which the CDU had held it since 1949. It would therefore not be plausible to accuse the SPD of failing to take decisive action, in particular in the absence of a rapid escalation of the problem. Consequently, it is not swift, hard-line action that appears to be required, but rather careful consideration and on that basis 'rational' measures. Those measures should systematically address long-term, deep-rooted problems in society.

The social aetiology used in the speech to explain the drug problem underlines this stance. According to Westphal's sociopathological aetiology, drug use is not first and foremost a criminal justice problem but a structural one. He categorises the offenders (drug users) as victims (of society) and

demands that they be helped. With a phrase that is more strongly pathologising than "underlying issues", Westphal talks later in his speech about
drug use as one of various "social epidemics" (Westphal, SPD, BT 1973,
40th Session, 2212). He is therefore clearly advocating help and not punishment, as a judge could not reasonably treat a disease.[12] In keeping with
this line of argument, the excerpt does not include any explicit category-
bound activity of a criminal. According to the Westphal, the 'expert politician', users suffer social problems; they do not act and do not harm others.
They are affected by a disease, and that disease requires a doctor or, to
deal with the social disease, a psychologist or social worker, but not legal
professionals.[13]

Another example clearly shows the narrative reasoning for help for offenders. It is an unequivocal illustration of the predominant interpretation of youth
crime in the 1970s and 1980s as a social problem. It does not come from a parliamentary debate, but from the written response of the federal government –
at this point consisting of the SPD and FDP – to an interpellation from the
opposition CDU/CSU.[14]

Example 2.3

1   Where offences committed by minors are indicators of deeper, more serious problems of the young
2   person or in his or her immediate or wider social environment, the federal government believes that
3   the support options available from public and independent youth welfare organisations must be further
4   improved to combat the causes of delinquency and where possible render penal sanctions unnecessary
5   [Wolters, SPD, 1979, Printed Matter 8/3175, 17–18].

The excerpt shows an alternative to the tendency towards the pathologising
categorisation of drug use in example 2.2. Here, the writer points to social
(work) measures that he sees as particularly appropriate for the problem. It
is interesting that the narrative of youth crime presented is that of an issue
with social causes, and that the writer explicitly links this to "deeper, more
serious problems of the young person" or in his or her "social environment"
(lines 1–2). The author is thus distinguishing between 'ordinary' and 'more
serious' forms of youth criminality, and by exploring the latter in more detail,
he is placing it at the centre of the political debate. This is an example of the
political – as well as police and criminological – focus on 'persistent offenders', in other words young people who commit particularly serious and/or an
unusually high number of offences. The idea is that "if much of this offending
can be prevented (by locking them up, if needs be) then it is assumed that
this will have a reasonable substantial impact on crime rates" (Newburn 2013,
742). It is no coincidence that Newburn refers to the possibility of locking
up these young offenders, for in recent years, persistent offenders have repeatedly been the target of relatively tough measures, even if this has frequently
provoked criticism from criminologists (see examples 2.4 and 2.5 below; on

Germany, see Bindel-Kögel/Karliczek 2009; Dollinger 2014a; Walsh 2014; Walter 2003). The passage cited shares this focus, but clearly differs from demands for more punitive action: the serious crime raised by Hans-Georg Wolters is mentioned in the context of *avoiding sanctions* and not of potentially necessary severity. He defines specific forms of youth crime as meriting political attention, but does not justify this differentiation on the grounds of offences and their consequences, for example by pinpointing offenders as particularly ruthless, or in the light of tragic consequences for the victims of crime. Instead, the offenders are presented with the category-bound characteristic of *experiencing* "serious problems" (line 1) in themselves or their environment. Criminality is therefore not in itself to be taken seriously; it is merely an "indicator" (line 1) of other problems. As in examples 2.1 and 2.2, this turns an offender into a victim of circumstances. Addressing the "causes of delinquency" (line 4) is set out as a contrast to penal measures; social work support and sanctions are presented as opposites. Wolters thus shares what is (as yet) still the dominant interpretation in Europe of youth crime as a sign of personal and socialisation challenges (Dünkel et al. 2010b). He relates these problems specifically to persistent offenders and in so doing opens up an individual, social work option for help. Unlike in example 2.1, personal as well as structural measures are required, and unlike in example 2.2 with its tendency to pathologise, these measures are of a social work rather than pathological nature, as the problems are those of growing up and the social environment. Wolters does leave himself a get-out: "penal sanctions" should be rendered unnecessary *"where possible"* (line 4; B.D.'s italics) rather than strictly and absolutely. Nevertheless, he underlines the need for the decriminalisation of serious offences with a social aetiology and calls for help rather than punishment.

The focus on help for persistent offenders raises the following question: what is to be done with offenders who fall into another category that is not indicative of serious problems? If even persistent offenders are not to be punished, this leaves hardly any measures open for 'normal' offenders. Indeed, Wolters notes this elsewhere in the text: "the Federal Government is of the opinion that for many 'trivial' cases, the best solution can objectively be to avoid all state measures as far as possible" (Wolters, SPD, 1979, Printed Matter 8/3175, 17). Young people were ultimately, in the light of social causes, usually not themselves responsible for offences; the causes of their actions lay "in the adult world" (Wolters, SPD, 1979, Printed Matter 8/3175, 17). Wolters therefore appears consistent in his demand to address the causes and where possible avoid sanctions.

Wolters' position is part of a welfarist discourse on (youth) crime. At the heart of that discourse, delinquency represents *"social* problems, with social causes, to be dealt with by means of social techniques and social work professionals" (Garland 2001a, 47). Youth crime is a phenomenon on the surface that points to 'deeper' problems in society. Fighting youth crime means taking action against its social causes and not against individual offenders. Those who recount this narrative appear to see beyond the 'surface' of the mere symptoms and individual offences, and to be able to avoid dramatising youth crime: criticism and intervention should be directed at society and its injustices and not at youth crime itself. Demands for sanctions are not a legitimate consequence of the evil involved in crime; they arise from a superficial, poorly informed assessment of youth criminality. The enlightened, so the narrative goes, are able to initiate and implement the 'appropriate', i.e. effective social intervention to address the social causes.

The other narratives presented below only partly share this view or indeed contradict it in key areas. Nonetheless, the help narrative is an important point of reference that has hardly been entirely abandoned, not even by the other, in most cases more recent, and stricter discourses on youth crime that will now be explored.

b) Help and its exceptions

The 1970s and 1980s were largely dominated by a welfarist understanding of crime. Sanctions were to be reduced and, instead of punishment, sociopolitical and social work measures were to be employed. Even at that time, however, there were calls to at least not wholly disregard relatively tough measures, and this stance became increasingly relevant over the course of the 1990s (Höynck/ Ernst 2014; Lampe/Rudolph 2016).

There is a telling example from the Bundestag from the late 1980s, shortly before an amendment to the Youth Courts Law (*Jugendgerichtsgesetz*, JGG)[15] entered into effect in 1990. Conservative parties agreed to a liberalisation of the statutory provisions. However, they did not want to implement a comprehensive reform in this direction and the changes were therefore still relatively cautious. The reform did nonetheless involve a greater focus on non-custodial as opposed to custodial intervention (Heinz 1991). Individual, relatively harsh measures such as the option of remanding very young offenders in custody were particularly controversial, as is illustrated below. The speaker, Heinrich Seesing on behalf of the then-ruling CDU/CSU, starts by talking about education policy; he argues that school and teachers have an important role to fulfil in educating young people. He then continues as follows:

Example 2.4

1   In the same way, I must also address the questions of *youth welfare services, recreational activities,*
2   *careers choices* and *vocational training for young people.* Every German mark spent on these areas
3   prevents a much higher but nonetheless necessary financial commitment for criminal prosecution, the
4   execution of sentences, and probation services, to name but a few measures.

5 (Applause from the SPD and the GREEN PARTY)
6 (...)
7 Despite considerable efforts, there are, however, still young people (...) who come into extremely
8 serious conflict with the law. For them, we must look for ways in which *atonement* can be combined
9 with *preparation for a new life*. I believe that judges in the youth courts must have a wide range of
10 measures at their disposal. With very few exceptions, every person is different. Each young person
11 who has committed an offence will therefore respond differently to judicial measures. This places a
12 great responsibility on judges and institutional staff. I therefore do not want to rule out certain
13 measures from the outset. I personally am in principle also against *remanding in custody* 14 or 15-year
14 old boys or indeed girls who have committed offences or exhibited deviant behaviour. It is nonetheless
15 my experience that a limited period in custody can in individual cases in fact be a form of therapy, and
16 I say that quite clearly.
17 (Ms Nickels [GREEN PARTY]: But that is completely wrong, Mr Seesing!)
18 – There is really still much to consider. I think that we should take the time for that in the Committee
19 on Legal Affairs. I believe that that will also be worthwhile for the young people affected.
20 (Applause from the CDU/CSU and FDP) [Seesing, CDU/CSU, 1989, BT, 11/168, 12745]

The speaker first presents youth crime primarily as a problem of education, not just for schools but also for various institutions that work with young people (lines 1–2). In this respect, it is attributed similar categorical characteristics to those in the narrative of help in terms of structural causes (example 2.3). There is, however, a fundamental difference, which emerges in the use of "nonetheless" and "however" (lines 3, 7, 14). These adversative conjunctions illustrate a feature specific to this narrative: for the speaker, there is a subcategory of offenders that is distinct from other subcategories and that demands a particular form of intervention. Compared with the excerpt in example 2.3, it becomes clear that the latter also uses a subcategory of serious offenders and distinguishes them from 'ordinary' offenders. In example 2.3, serious offenders indicate a demand for help and support; in example 2.4, the opposite is true. According to Seesing, there is a "necessary [. . .] commitment" (line 3) to interventionist legal consequences such as imprisonment. He explicitly gives "*atonement*" (line 8) as a reason for dealing with these offenders: thus, a second, retributive objective is added to that of education or rehabilitation (but this objective is not yet the safety of society, as in example 2.5 below).

Seesing employs considerable argumentative effort to legitimise this distinction, using five different lines of argument to justify relatively tough measures against particular offenders:

- "Despite considerable efforts" (line 7): This places the use of tough measures in a temporal context. Retribution is necessary, but only if other options have been tried first. Help is therefore the priority and punishment has the status of an exception employed when supportive measures are not successful.
- "there are, however, still young people" (line 7): Punishment appears necessary in particular in the light of the distinct characteristics of certain offenders. The need for punishment is down not just to measures

implemented in vain but also to individual offenders. Punishment should be used not in general but for these specific offenders, in which cases it can be combined with rehabilitation ("can be combined with", lines 8–9).

- "a great responsibility on judges and institutional staff" (lines 11–12): Sanctions are not demanded automatically, as in explicitly punitive discourses (see point c) below), but rather as something that is to be employed with care by professionals. Punishment is not the norm, not even for specific offenders; it requires a careful assessment by experts of how offenders will respond to potential measures. In this regard, there is a revealing shift here compared to example 2.3, which calls on welfarist, social work professionals to deal with this specific subcategory of offenders. Now, the speaker is addressing criminal justice professionals and institutional staff; the responsibility for dealing with cases has changed.
- "I personally am in principle also against"; "It is nonetheless my experience that (. . .) in individual cases" (lines 13, 14–15): The speaker is not positioning himself as a strict opponent of supportive measures. While politicians across the world have, according to Wacquant (2010, 207), portrayed themselves as "stern 'crime fighters'" in recent years, Seesing is presenting himself "in principle" as an opponent of the tough measures specified. Only on the basis of "personal experience" – which legitimises him as narrator (Shuman 2015, 39) – does he know that intransigence is necessary "in individual cases". This also underlines the exceptional nature of restrictive action.
- "we should take the time"; "I believe that this will also be worthwhile for the young people affected" (lines 18–19): the coda to the narrative describes youth crime not as an urgent problem that must be addressed *immediately* with tough measures. On the contrary: there is time for carefully considered decisions. These decisions are, moreover, not to be aimed at the protection of the population or a notional need for revenge on the part of the victims, but at the offenders, "the young people affected". They are at the centre of the speech, and therefore despite a certain demand for tough action, there is no fundamental criticism of the welfarist approach.

These points show that, at the time of Seesing's speech, supportive measures were (still) the norm as a response to youth crime. As long as the speaker is talking about education and rehabilitation, he even – unusually – meets with the approval of the opposition ("Applause", line 5). Intransigence, on the other hand, must be carefully legitimised – and is disputed by the opposition (line 17).

Although the speaker is representing the ruling CDU/CSU, he does not make simple statements with the authority of official power, as is the case in example 2.2. Instead, the great argumentative effort that goes into the speech shows that Seesing is arguing against a powerful discursive trend. That trend demands the liberalisation of (youth) criminal law and requires a tough approach to be justified. Restrictive measures must be 'packaged', as it were, in a parcel of welfarism. Although there is a call for "atonement" (line 8), it is relativised; the speaker is "in principle" (line 13) against tough measures, and the tough option of remand is at the end of the excerpt no longer explicitly referred to as "atonement" but instead as "therapy" (line 15). The primary category-bound characteristic of offenders thus is and remains the need for help. It is with a tone almost of regret that the speaker nonetheless finds that measures do need to be tougher in exceptional cases.

c) The full force of the law

The next step up from demanding exceptions to the principle of help is the explicit call for tough measures as justified per se. Particularly since the 1990s, such demands were no longer sugar-coated, hidden in a complex system of arguments or presented as a regrettable circumstance, but made clearly and openly. In the 1970s and 1980s, adult 'drug dealers' functioned as a target of political calls for punitive action (Dollinger et al. 2012a). In the 1990s, there occurred a similar punitive stance in the discussion of youth crime, particularly pertaining to young "persistent offenders". They made it possible that the principle of the exception descibed above would not have to be entirely rejected, as repressive measures were usually not advocated for all offenders. They were mainly targeted at certain types of offenders or offences.

Calls for welfarism converge in the assumption that an offender is 'one of us', is part of 'our' society, and that he or she is not or not fully responsible for offences. Narratives of tough action turn this assumption around: "persistent offenders" with their basic characteristic of posing a threat to the public seem, by their very existence, require intransigence (example 2.5). Additional layers of punitivity were added with the attributes of being 'foreign' (example 2.6) and/or acting wilfully (example 2.7). Offenders who are foreign to 'us' and/or wilfully commit malicious acts deserve the toughest possible sanctions. In these cases, calls for tough and systematic intervention are strong and unapologetic. Welfarism appears in this narrative as a weakness.

The following example illustrates the category of "persistent offender". It comes from a speech in the Bundestag by Bosbach, a representative of the CDU/CSU, which in 2008 was governing in a grand coalition with the SPD:

Example 2.5

1   Educating people in non-violence and tolerance is very important for prevention – as is teaching
2   values, educating children in the best sense of the word. However, we also need to talk about those

3   who are persistent offenders, young people who have committed 50, 70, 100 offences and for whom
4   even the 98th meeting with parents, police and social workers [*Erziehungs-gespräch*] has no effect.
5   (. . .) There are unfortunately and incontestably cases in which even great efforts at sociotherapy are
6   not enough;
7   (Britta Haßelmann [BÜNDNIS 90/GREEN PARTY]: Why don't the judges do anything?)
8   the people in question must unfortunately be put behind bars to prevent them from causing serious
9   harm to others. That is the thing. [Bosbach, CDU/CSU, 2008, BT, 16/135, 14236]

The speech makes a clearer call for tough action than example 2.4, and that
action is to be reserved for a certain category of offenders who are explicitly
categorised as "persistent offenders" (line 3). Bosbach qualifies his strictness
with some regret ("unfortunately", lines 5 and 8). But – again differing from
example 2.4 – this reservation appears to be sheer rhetoric, as he ridicules how
extensively and how futilely well-meaning professionals are still trying to better
those young offenders who cannot be bettered with social measures ("the 98th
meeting", line 4).

Bosbach divides young offenders in two subcategories with two respective countermeasures: on the one hand, education is favoured ("very
important for prevention", line 1) to influence "people" (line 1). In an
approach that is characteristic of conservative positions on youth crime, the
focus here is on teaching values (lines 1–2), not on structural, social causes
or measures. Moral education appears able to prevent the emergence of
criminality. On the other hand, however, there is the criminality of "persistent offenders" whose existence the speaker assumes as a fact. In their
case, prevention or rehabilitation appear not to be sufficient or effective.
The specific predicate of these offenders is that they threaten the public;
restrictive measures therefore appear justified in order to protect the population, as "persistent offenders" seem impervious to 'soft' welfarist intervention. Bosbach equates frequent offending with a threat to the public that
demands tough action.

The opposition criticises this equation in an interjection (line 7); the respective turn shows that the blunt demand for repression has been understood and
is being disputed. It is interesting to note that the interjector from the opposition Green Party mentions "judges" (line 7): she is shifting responsibility for
measures against the category of "persistent offenders" from the legislature to
the judiciary, thereby suggesting that the answer is not tougher laws but a specific form of application of the law by the judges. Although this puts demands
for more restrictive regulations into perspective, it recognises the existence
of the category of "persistent offenders". By not explicitly denoting "persistent offenders" as a task for welfare professionals, as is the case in example 2.3,
Haßelmann too is presenting this category of offenders as a problem requiring penal sanctions. By comparison, Bosbach's demand is nonetheless fairly
drastic: according to him, there is a category of "persistent offenders" who are
resistant to education and require a tough response ("put behind bars", line 8),
in other words who are simply to be locked up as they no longer respond to

support. Corresponding with a central theme in punitive discourses (Garland 2001a), Bosbach combines this category with the activity of committing scores of offences and the characteristic of being unresponsive to rehabilitation or education.

Conservative politicians had argued in the past that the Youth Courts Law (*Jugendgerichtsgesetz*, JGG) should hardly be applied to young adults. They should be regarded not as requiring support but punishment. In the words of a speaker in 1997, politicians must avoid "a search for any kind of defect in every young person or young adult so that they can be sentenced under youth law" (von Stetten, CDU/CSU, BT, 1997, 13/203, 18288).[16] This was an interjection against a fellow member of the CDU/CSU who had advocated the systematic application of the JGG for young adults. Von Stetten rejected this call, arguing "that a 19 or 20-year-old who robs and murders is generally able to understand what he or she is doing" (von Stetten, CDU/CSU, BT, 1997, 13/203, 18288). Perpetrators therefore act consciously; they are not victims of the social. Accordingly, they can be punished. In 1997, such a call for intransigence was controversial within the CDU/CSU. Yet the similar position taken by Bosbach in 2008 hardly needed justification. Bosbach was at this time an influential conservative politician, and held in 2008, among other posts, that of deputy chair of the CDU/CSU parliamentary group in the Bundestag. With his speech, he is indicating that the position presented meets with approval not just from within the CDU/CSU but also from the public. There was no longer a specific need for careful explanation of such a tough demand. Although he qualifies his position with "unfortunately", he calls for intransigence and determination: "behind bars" is a dramatic phrase, and the expression "That is the thing" (line 9) presents a resolute political player. This player does not hesitate and does not justify himself; he is fully determined to implement a tough course of action. Here we are clearly seeing Wacquant's "stern" crime fighter, who was yet to emerge in 1989, in example 2.4.

Foreign offenders

There are a few early cases already in the 1970s and 1980s of foreignness being raised as a risk to safety. For example, in the Bavarian Landtag, where a speaker pointed to the "*flood of refugees from the Arab world*" (Schnell, SPD, 1972, BY, 7/37, 1927) and resulting insecurity for the population. Interestingly enough, this came from the SPD, although the CSU held the post of Bavarian minister–president throughout the period examined here and the CSU pursued, as one of its trademarks, a tough line against crime. Tackling this central aspect of the CSU's political positioning clearly appeared a profitable move to the SPD. The foreignness argument was, however, also used by the CSU: it too demanded restrictive action against (criminal) 'foreigners' (see for example Merk, CSU,

1972, BY, 7/37, 1933). These positions regularly denounced the liberalisation of criminal law and of the execution of sentences, and the respective punitive stances gained ground in the 1990s. This is reflected in example 2.6. by the Bavarian minister–president at the time, Edmund Stoiber, speaking in the Bundesrat in 1997. Stoiber's speech relates to a motion brought by the federal states of Bavaria and Hamburg entitled "*Strengthening domestic security*" (BR, Printed Matters 580/97 and 663/97). After discussing points including what was in his view the dramatic deterioration in the crime and security situation in Germany, Stoiber listed four demands; only that relating to youth crime is reprinted in full below.

Example 2.6

1   Today's motion from Bavaria is aimed at halting the growing rates of crime in the following areas and
2   thus offering citizens a safer life altogether:
3   Firstly: *the systematic deportation of foreign offenders!* (. . .)
4   Secondly: resolutely *combating the* huge *rise in child and youth crime!* We need to think about
5   whether the measures for preventing and combating youth crime as they have been implemented to
6   date are still effective. Of course we need to help at-risk young people, but clear boundaries must also
7   be drawn. Early intervention can in fact give young people more of a chance to change their life, to
8   gain a new direction, than if they get deeper and deeper into crime. Here too, we need systematically
9   to apply existing laws.
10   It is obvious that youth criminal law is currently being applied extremely broadly. This seems to be the
11   wrong approach, as evidenced by the *study on youth crime in Hamburg*, Mr Voscherau.
12   The content
13   – according to 'Die Welt'[17] from last Thursday –
14   can be summarised very simply: the number of violent juvenile offenders in Hamburg is
15   dramatically rising, while criminal prosecution appears increasingly lax.
16   We believe that for young people who are of age, indeed who have the full right to vote, youth
17   criminal law should only be applied in exceptional cases in which there are clear reasons for doing so.
18   We already presented a bill in the Bundesrat on this issue back in 1996. This is also mentioned in the
19   Hamburg resolution. Now, an agreement on the matter appears possible.
20   Thirdly: *better protection for women and children from sex offenders!* (. . .)
21   Fourthly: *not* trivialising or *decriminalising so-called petty crimes!* (. . .) [Stoiber, CSU, BR, 1997, 715,
22   p.338–339]

Help narratives were built by categorisations in which the roles of offenders and victims were largely reversed. Offenders were described as victims of society and in need of support. Society was not a victim of offenders, but the blameworthy cause of offences (examples 2.2 and 2.3). Here and similar to Bosbach's statements in example 2.5, we have a clear example of the opposite: offenders are actual offenders who pose a risk to others. Victims are people who have been seriously harmed by offenders. In the initial summary and orientation (lines 1–2), the speaker correspondingly categorises offenders as a growing threat. The development of crime rates over time indicates that – unless "clear boundaries" are drawn (line 6) – there will be an escalating crisis. Stoiber assesses crime as a serious risk that needs to be neutralised. Tough measures do not need careful consideration and sufficient time (as in example 2.4). They are, on the contrary, urgently needed. There is no weighing up of the pros and cons; instead, we have resolution, determination and the definition of limits.

Youth crime is one element of an overall threat to security in society. There is still a recognition that youth crime also indicates a need for help (line 6); however, clear criticism is aimed at the criminal prosecution process that "appears increasingly lax" (line 15). This criticism combines delinquency with a need for a tough response; leniency appears to aggravate the problem (Pearson 1983). Youth crime is placed in the context of social challenges – only these are no longer primarily problems of structural isolation and pressures on young people to which rehabilitation is the answer. Instead, the social problems now lie in a threat to the society's security posed by foreignness and serious offences, and youth crime is equated with these threats. There is such a thing as 'dangerous' (youth) criminality, which is set up in opposition to society and which the state must apparently fight (Steinert 2003). The *"systematic deportation of foreign offenders"* (line 3) who do not appear to belong to 'German society' and ought to be removed from it is symptomatic of this approach. Sexual crime as a serious form of violence also fits in with this threat narrative. It is this type of crime which legitimised increasingly restrictive criminal policy and penal intervention both in Germany and internationally (Ashworth/ Zedner 2014; Sack/Schlepper 2011; Simon 2007), above all in the context of the *"protection for women and children from sex offenders"* mentioned by Stoiber (line 20). The fourth point, the decriminalisation of petty crimes, appears like youth crime to be a serious threat to the general population. Clearly, so the message goes, strong political figures are needed who recognise this threat and act accordingly by not pursuing the 'lax' line of the past. Stoiber is positioning himself as an uncompromising and resolute protector of society as he links youth crime with a threat and with foreignness. Youth crime is part of an overall package of threats to security. In this package consisting of four points, it is coupled with foreignness, sexual offences and excessive laxity.

Personally responsible (foreign) offenders

In other cases, the argument of threat caused by youth crime is associated with the characteristic of 'foreign' offenders *acting wilfully*. Below is one example, which is, however, unusual in its explicitness. It is a question posed during a parliamentary debate. In the debate, Jürgen Meyer from the SPD is speaking on the question of a possible reduction in the age of criminal responsibility in Germany, which was then (and still is) 14. Meyer rejects the proposed reduction, and this stance is criticised in the interjection by von Stetten in the example below. Von Stetten links foreignness to personal responsibility and thus puts into words a particularly emphatic demand for harsh intervention.

Example 2.7

1   Dr. *Wolfgang Freiherr von Stetten* (CDU/CSU): Mr Meyer, are you trying to tell us that a thirteen-
2   year-old who steals has no understanding of right and wrong? We are already dealing with gangs of
3   Romanian children. In Frankfurt, we have Moroccan child gangs that peddle heroin. You can't say that
4   they have no understanding of right and wrong. Tell me how you are going to get these children off
5   the streets and protect the public from them if you are categorically refusing any type of criminal
6   sanctions against these children. [BT, 1997, 13/203, 18285]

The speaker places himself in clear opposition to "Mr. Meyer" (line 1) as the previous speaker. The latter had termed children who come to the attention of the criminal justice system as "victims of adults" (Meyer, SPD, BT, 1997, 13/203, 18285) who led children into crime. Von Stetten reverses this categorisation of offenders as victims by bringing up the criminal law argument of the knowledge of acting illegally ("understanding of right and wrong", line 2). Those who intentionally commit criminal acts are offenders; the (wilful) activity justifies the categorisation of the person, and therefore the children are offenders. Von Stetten takes this line of categorisation further as he not only mentions minor offences such as stealing but also ascribes three characteristics to the children: they operate in "gangs" (lines 2, 3), distribute hard, extremely dangerous and addictive drugs ("heroin", line 3) and are not German ("Romanian", line 3; "Moroccan", line 3). This turns the category "children" (line 3) on its head: usually, childhood is associated with "characteristics of innocence and naïveté" (Watson 1976, 63); common sense dictates that this category is, as Watson states, "a candidate for the categorization innocent victim". Von Stetten uses it differently, turning children into dangerous offenders by attributing criminal activities to them. These particular children appear not to require education or help; they are not innocents who must be treated with lenience or carefully integrated into society through education and socialisation. Instead, they are presented as a serious threat to the population; in light of their foreignness and their wilfully dangerous actions, they present a high risk to the general public. Without being integrated into 'our' society, they actively damage that society through culpable behaviour – something usually considered a feature of 'professional' criminal activity (Youngs/Canter 2012) rather than of the status of a child. Nonetheless (or perhaps precisely because of this), von Stetten stresses the specific categorisation of children in his speech by associating their delinquency with place categories such as major city ("Frankfurt", line 3) and "streets" (line 5), both of which are often associated with criminality (e.g. Bottoms 2012; Dinges/Sack 2000). Given these dramatic ascriptions, the speaker advocates repressive measures to address this situation, and at the same time implicitly accuses his political opponent of simply standing back and watching – because the latter rejects all "criminal sanctions" (lines 5–6).

One key element of the threat painted by von Stetten is wilful harm. In Meyer's account, which precedes von Stetten's interjection, children are passive and led astray by their parents. According to von Stetten, they are active: they take action and cause harm. Von Stetten does not present any causes of the illegal activities of the children, and they therefore appear to operate on their own initiative, of their own accord. A connection can be heard here being made between their activities and the status 'foreigner', the place 'major city' and the social category 'gang'. However, this additional information is not presented as an explanation that would justify or reduce the gravity of such behaviour in welfarist terms. These children appear to engage in criminal activity, to be quite simply malicious, because of "high levels of potency" (Youngs/Canter 2012, 246). There are no justifying circumstances or positive development possibilities. The dangerous children seem to threaten 'us' ("We are dealing with", line 2; "we have", line 3) and to merit punishment.

In this respect, example 2.7 is – beyond its atypical categorisation of dangerous children – formally typical: speeches that call for tough sanctions regularly connect people with apparently inexplicable or unexplained action that wilfully causes harm and thus produces offenders deserving of punishment. As regards responsibility, this tendency was suggested by the word "chance" (line 7) in example 2.6. A chance implies that support is (or has been) available, but has to be picked by a person. If s/he does not choose support, then it is up to him or her to bear the consequences. Correspondingly, an offence is presented "as an active choice on the part of the individual offender" (Robinson/Crow 2009, 121). When crime is committed, the individual offender is fully responsible, for crime is "the outcome of poor choices or decisions, and not the outcome of structural inequalities or pathology" (Hannah-Moffat 2005, 41–42). Those who repeatedly engage in criminal activity have not taken the supportive chances afforded to them, and can therefore be subjected to restrictive sanctions. After all, so the narrative goes, they have failed to change their lives and have retained their delinquent ambitions despite options of support. Bad choices seem to stem from "hostility or malice" (Komter 1998, 67). These offenders are not really part of society but in opposition to it, and act more or less without external, 'exculpatory' influence.

This point is clearly put by the following speaker who comes from the liberal FDP. "Convicted offenders are themselves responsible for their fate within civil society. We can only create the broad framework. Filling in the detail and ensuring that framework fulfils its objective is up to the person concerned" (Beckmann, FDP, 1985, BT, 10/181, 13758–13759). Offenders thus have themselves to blame for their punishment. Their central characteristic here is to decide *alone*; they are not social beings. If any explanation for their illegal behaviour is provided at all, it is an antisocial personality structure that makes tough intervention essential. In the case of sex offences and violent crime, this argument has been presented repeatedly since the 1990s, with specific 'types' of personality being associated with serious crime, thus paving the way for a call for stricter punishment. A speaker in a 2012 debate in the Bundestag on tightening youth criminal law had the following to say on this point:

Example 2.8

1   It is good that we currently have a relatively restrictive approach to detention in youth criminal law.
2   However, we do also need to see that we are dealing with a very wide range of offender personalities
3   and that the *personality structures of juvenile offenders* have *changed dramatically* over the years.
4   There is now an *increase in aggressiveness and brutality*. Despite an encouraging overall decline in
5   youth crime rates, the number of violent offences is rising. [Boddenberg, CDU, BR, 2012, 899,p.
6   330].

Here again, the speaker does not present any causes of crime but simply notes a temporal escalation ("over the years", line 3). There has in his estimation been a considerable change in the *"personality structures"* (line 3) of offenders. The rise in violence, which he ascribes to those personality structures, is presented as sufficient grounds for an exception to the restrictive approach to using youth detention. In this situation, demanding a departure from the principle of help appears logical, as already detailed above. Example 2.4 illustrated that exceptions from this principle were being justified even back in the late 1980s, when social support was the dominating principle in dealing with youth crime. Now, the situation is different. Intransigence is no longer "a form of therapy" for an individual offender as in example 2.4. Instead, Boddenberg establishes a narrative of threatening (not of threatened) youths as he links offenders to the category-bound characteristics of *"aggressiveness and brutality"* (line 4). Although indicating a willingness to show consideration, the speaker points out that tough action is legitimate. The message is that brutal offenders deserve harsh punishment. The (quasi-) reasons for their actions are to be found in their personality structures, for which and for the supposed increase in which no causes are mentioned, but which are associated with violence. The result is the justification of detention simply on the grounds of allegedly 'brutal' personalities.

d) *Readjusting on a 'tougher' level: offenders as the agents of problems*

The last example above takes us to narratives that have increasingly dominated the political discourse since the 1990s: narratives that continue the rhetoric of social support but in which measures are to be raised to a 'tougher' level not just in exceptional cases but across the board. The central term in German youth criminal law, 'education' ('*Erziehung*'), proves flexible enough to include both 'hard' and 'soft', repressive penal and supportive social measures. It is in itself largely meaningless, and certainly not to be confused with benevolent intentions for the well-being of individual offenders (Cornel 2018; Dollinger 2010). The flexibility of 'education' turned out to be significant in the realignment of political discourses on youth crime over the course of the 1990s, as most debates still talked of 'education' and help for juvenile delinquents – but were no longer welfarist to the same extent as in the 1970s and 1980s (Dollinger 2014b; Dollinger/ Rudolph 2016). Demands for security and victim protection became louder and could be compatible with a language of 'education' or 'rehabilitation' (see also Hannah-Moffat 2005; Robinson 2008). At least, welfarist language was not abandoned, and forthright demands for tough intervention and simply 'locking away' offenders as outlined in Chapter 2.2.c) did not come to dominate the discourse. They often emerged in combination with calls for other, 'softer' practices.

Help has still been demanded for many offenders since the 1990s. But these demands come together with arguments for boundaries, responsibilisation and confrontation. Youth crime is now less often explained with structural causes, and attributions of guilt to offenders as individual persons are a recurring theme in political debates. Offenders requiring containment and boundaries are no longer exceptions. Instead, youth crime has since the 1990s a quality that renders a confrontational and only selectively supportive intervention strategy necessary.

The speaker cited in example 2.8, Boddenberg, also argues along these lines. He refers explicitly to violent crime in order to justify particularly restrictive demands. But his speech also includes a call to take an educational approach to dealing with youth crime *and to implement education as confrontation*. Boddenberg's speech shows that demands for harshness (especially in the case of violence) could be coupled with a changed understanding of education. This new understanding was not exclusively thought of as repressive. It did not represent sheer harshness, but education could and should now be combined with greater severity than before.

Specifically, Boddenberg raises the issue of "*Warnschussarrest*" (literally "warning shot detention"): adding a period of youth detention to suspended youth custody sentences imposed on young offenders. The *Warnschussarrest* was impossible under law until 2013, when it was allowed following a statutory reform.

Example 2.9

1   With the Warnschussarrest *another educational measure in youth criminal law* is created which – I am
2   absolutely sure – the youth courts will use in a careful and targeted manner. We should at least place
3   that much confidence in the youth courts.
4   The Warnschussarrest should also *function as* – as some say – *a yellow card* that demonstrates to the
5   party in question unequivocally and in a manner that all will understand that they can soon expect a
6   longer period of detention if they do not change their behaviour. (. . .).
7   Moreover, the *Warnschussarrest* (. . .) allows not just a tangible but also an extremely *rapid response*.
8   [Boddenberg, CDU, BR, 2012, 899, 331]

In practical terms, the *Warnschussarrest* means harsher sentencing: offenders who receive a suspended prison sentence are additionally detained in a custodial institution. The term 'warning short' ('*Warnschuss*') itself indicates a relatively tough approach to offenders. In light of this intransigence, it is telling that Boddenberg does not disclose that the measure constitutes harsher sentencing. Instead, he describes the move as "*another educational measure*" (line 1) as if he were pursuing and simply complementing an existing – educational – intervention logic.

Boddenberg places responsibility for implementing these relatively harsh measures at the door of the youth courts (lines 2–3). The respective political debate is about criminal-political reform, but Boddenberg remains vague and uses the passive voice when portraying himself. An educational measure "is created" (lines 1–2). A hypothetical comparison illustrates the particularity of these expressions. Boddenberg could have said: '*Tougher action needs to be taken against youth crime. I therefore advocate the introduction of the* Warnschussarrest, *so that with my support young people can be set clearer boundaries*'. Although this wording reflects the sense of what he actually said, he avoids such a clear demonstration of decisiveness – and that in an area of criminal policy in which such decisiveness is often celebrated (see for example Beckett/Sasson 2000; Pratt 2007; Roberts et al. 2003). Boddenberg does not, it appears, assume that such activism would be rewarded by the public. He categorises himself not as an intransigent crime fighter but as a thoughtful politician as he depicts the *Warnschussarrest* as a mere continuation of the existing focus on the established educational principles of youth criminal law – principles whose actual implementation in practice should be left to the discretion of the youth courts (line 3).

This is a remarkably non-punitive narrative – that is nevertheless punitive in its thrust. The speech does in fact involve retributive, punitive attitudes and demands. For example, Boddenberg talks of a "*yellow card*" (line 4), in other words a clear warning like that common in soccer; an explicit threat of imprisonment is presented (line 6); Boddenberg also calls for an "unequivocal" (line 5) and "tangible" (line 7) sanction, giving the *Warnschussarrest* clear restrictive characteristics. The same applies for his description of it as an "*extremely rapid response*" (line 7), as this signals an immediate reaction to an offence with a negative sanction. This speed aspect – with which the parties in German parliaments have in recent years unanimously agreed (Dollinger/Rudolph 2016; Lampe 2017) – is equivalent to a fairly punitive narrative of youth crime.

Therefore, Boddenberg's narrative is ambivalent. He talks of education and avoids giving the impression of a bluntly punitive approach. Offenders are still deemed in need of education. Yet, he describes education as a confrontation and a relatively tough response. He calls for restrictive measures but does not categorise offenders as fully responsible and capable persons. Boddenberg argues as follows in his speech before example 2.9: "Young people specifically in some cases still lack the intellectual capacity to appreciate the significance of a suspended youth custody sentence" (Boddenberg, CDU, BR, 2012, 899, 331). He thus describes developmental deficits in these young people. However, these deficits are not a reason to provide the young people with help but are instead used to argue in favour of strict action and 'yellow cards'. He categorises juvenile delinquents as primarily immature people who *precisely because of that immaturity* require confrontation and sanctions but not per se welfarist assistance.

Another example provides a further illustration of this narrative. It addresses non-custodial measures as part of a speech warning against dramatising youth crime. The speaker recommends social policy instead of simple repression as a tool for preventing criminality. Nonetheless, he does not call for education as the opposite to sanctions, but demands at once "education and sanctions" (Meyer, SPD, BT, 1997, 13/3203, 18284). He describes the following as making "educational sense":

Example 2.10

1   For example, shoplifters could work for free in the shop they have robbed. (. . .) Graffiti sprayers
2   should remove their so-called artwork themselves. And through a greater use of offender–victim
3   mediation, offenders should be urged to *make amends for the harm they have caused* and in a face-to-
4   face meeting, if the victim consents, be confronted with the consequences of their actions. [Meyer,
5   SPD, BT, 1997, 13/3203, 18285]

Meyer argues against tightening the existing laws but still advocates a principle of confrontational and reparative punishment, which he qualifies as education. The offences he is speaking about do not appear to be caused by a lack of resources such as poverty or relative deprivation. The offenders in this narrative do not have the characteristic of being in need of, for instance, vocational training opportunities or other forms of support; they are not victims of society, otherwise the speaker could not recommend that a thief "work *for free*" (line 1; B.D.'s italics). The narrative does not call for the structural improvement of offenders' (social) problems; it is about their actions and experiences. Offenders are to make amends through their actions for harm caused (lines 1–2); an offence is the cause of harm for which offenders are to take active responsibility. Offenders are also to be "confronted" (line 4) with the victim, in other words to experience the victim's situation: interaction with the victim is to bring home to offenders the harm caused by an offence at a personal level. In any case, the focus is on the harm caused. An offender belongs to a category of persons who harm others and should either redress that harm himself or herself, or at least be made to feel the suffering of victims. The focus here is on responsibilisation and confrontation of the offender as an individual who has acted wrongly – irrespective of the resources that were at his or her disposal.

Social support is apparently not deemed necessary to deal with offenders. Instead, the speaker cites negative sanctions that are to have a noticeable impact. This understanding of interventions differs significantly from the positions and measures described in Chapter 2.2.a) above. Nonetheless, the 'new' confrontational sanctions have since the mid-1990s been considered a relatively lenient response to youth crime; they appeared an appropriate way of *countering* punitive responses to delinquency, as Meyer was arguing *against* the tightening of Germany's Youth Crime Act. Correspondingly, there has been a lasting change in the categorisation of young offenders. They are now young people who *cause* problems and who are to be held accountable for the neutralisation of those problems, whereas in the 1970s and 1980s they used to be young people *affected* by (social) problems.

Conclusion

This chapter looked at four different narratives to explore how youth crime as a political narrative has developed over time (*structural causes, help and its exceptions, the full force of the law, offenders as the agents of problems*). One significant finding from a comparison of the four narratives is the *flexibility* of the central categories of offender and victim. A naive assessment might assume that offenders are those who commit an offence and victims those whom the offence affects, and that politicians – cooperating with experts and the criminal justice system – have the task of establishing the most sensible measures in response. In fact, the narratives reconstructed here paint a rather different picture, namely that the central categories are by no means fixed.

- At the beginning of the period examined, *offenders* were victims of society. In the 1970s and 1980s, most debates did not centre on their acts; the focus was on their problems and pressures, for which an adequate form of social or structural support was to be provided. The actual offender was society, whose conditions gave rise to youth crime. Helping offenders was a goal in itself. Tough intervention was to be taken in specific cases but had the status of an exception. More far-reaching demands for a restrictive approach to youth crime could instead – as illustrated by example 2.2 – be used in the discourse as evidence of societal problems. This welfarist approach reflected a social aetiology of delinquency that placed social difficulties at the root of criminality problems. But over time, young delinquents gradually became individual offenders: they were made responsible for 'their' offences and the focus was consequently on punishing them. In the case of serious sexual offences and violent crime in particular, punishment could be restrictive in the extreme; in most cases, however, confrontations, warnings and the definition of boundaries swiftly following an offence were to have an 'educational' effect on offenders. Crime policy thus, from the mid-1990s, focused less on offenders' lack of resources and disadvantages and more on their sense of responsibility.

- *Victims* of offences were initially not a central subject of the political discourse. The position of victim was largely taken by the juvenile offenders (as victims of society). Gradually, however, victims of offences emerged more clearly as a category in their own right. They became a key argument in favour of responding to youth crime through personalised intervention, but that argument did not primarily centre on specific victims and their individual suffering. Instead, generalised victims were set up as "idealized subjects of the law" (Simon 2007, 77) in opposition to the guilt of the offenders, which became a central political focus. The victim employed discursively in this way is a general category of innocence which serves as a backdrop for social and political identification (Reiner 2007, 143): if offenders threaten 'us' and 'we' could all be victims, tough action against offenders appears justified. This narrative also rearranged the category 'society': society was no longer the offender that produced juvenile delinquents but the *public*, an actual or potential victim of crime and thereby an interested party directly addressed in political discourse.[18] In relation to the offender, the public has taken on the function of legitimising a change in the style of intervention against young offenders, as it had been or could be severely harmed by them.

There is thus no fixed definition of who is the victim and who the offender. Their positions were communicatively established through the attribution of pressures and problems, characteristics and activities. Those attributes are what make the categories of offender and victim 'understandable' and legitimise certain measures against crime, i.e. specifically in recent decades: increasingly tough and confrontational interventions.

Change in the discourses on this point was not sudden. What was initially an exception requiring specific justification – taking 'tough' action against offenders – gradually became more important across all parties. There was and still is no unequivocal consensus at the end of the period studied; divergent positions existed at the times of all debates analysed here. Nonetheless, a shift emerged over time, especially in the mid-1990s, and it significantly readjusted the meaning of youth crime. Ultimately, youth crime was increasingly dangerous. Bluntly repressive demands to lock young offenders away without perspectives of support remained an exception. When they surfaced, they were directed at particular categories of offenders (primarily 'persistent' or 'foreign' offenders in the context of sexual or violent crime). But the narratives became more punitive and confrontational altogether.

Youth crime tended to lose its welfarist appeal and more often 'required' uncompromising countermeasures. Offenders were seen with greater antipathy (Melossi 2000). They posed a risk to society (Garland 2001a; Pratt 1997), and their possible reoffending had to be controlled (Hofinger 2015, 145–152).

Relatively simple tools were employed to rearrange the dominant narrative on youth crime: offenders were increasingly presented as subjects with specific (e.g. 'brutal') or somehow 'foreign' individual personality structures. They were responsible for their actions, and for their behaviour there were few social causes. And, most importantly, this re-categorisation was narratively linked to serious harm that they inflicted on potential or actual victims (see also Loseke 2003, 85). The first narrative steps into this more punitive direction were oftentimes more or less cautious; parliamentary speakers had in particular to weigh up their position against what they guessed to be public expectations (see in particular example 2.4). However, the basic categorial structure that has to be operated by politicians is quite simple: *crime as a political narrative is moral communication in which individual responsibility for wrongdoing is either stressed or relativised in line with the desired discursive effects.* Adding to the discourse harm or possible dangers to – or, alternatively, a shared responsibility on the part of – society/the public produces a picture of youth crime requiring tough sanctions or, alternatively, social assistance.

Notes

1 Tonry (2007, 2) finds that "the determinants and characteristics of penal policies remain curiously local" (see also Muncie 2008, 2015). While an analysis based on a nation state will necessarily restrict how far empirical findings can be generalised, it allows an in-depth exploration of the specific situation.
2 This reference to the electorate indicates that there is a strong self-legitimising aspect to crime policy. Purely objective, 'rational' considerations are likely to be less relevant (Savelsberg 1987; Tonry 2013). In its extreme form, i.e. when political players make little or no reference to criminological findings, this is known as "penal populism" (Pratt 2007; Roberts et al. 2003).
3 Since the period of the analysis presented below, a new and decidedly populist party has been attracting more and more voters in Germany. Founded in 2013, the "Alternative für Deutschland" is right-wing populist to right-wing extremist and is promoting hostility towards migrants.
4 A long-term historical comparison, on the other hand, shows a significant reduction in custodial measures such as imprisonment in Germany since the end of the nineteenth century, coupled with a significant rise in non-custodial measures (Heinz 2014, 59).
5 For example, as of 31 March 2013, 39.64 people per 100,000 inhabitants were serving custodial sentences or were in preventive detention in closed or open prisons in Schleswig-Holstein. In Bavaria, this figure was 83.95, and in Berlin, 122.72 (see Heinz 2016, 384; Heinz 2016 also on the problem of the significance and comparability of the data).

6 The debates were initially examined by focusing on the rhetorical tools (symbols, meta-phors and special linguistic devices) used in each speech by the politicians to con-vince their listeners (Dollinger/Urban 2012). Findings from this first analysis provide an important backdrop to the narrative analysis presented here (Dollinger et al. 2017c, 2018; Dollinger/Rudolph 2016; Lampe/Rudolph 2016).

7 In 2012, the "*Gesetz zur Erweiterung der jugendgerichtlichen Handlungsmöglichkeiten*" ("Act extending the courses of action available to the youth courts") widened, among other things, options to detain young offenders and raised the maximum prison term for some offenders. The Act was passed in 2012 and entered into effect on 7 March 2013 (Dollinger/Rudolph 2016).

8 To be precise, the following pages analyse the publicly available *records* of the speeches rather than the speeches themselves. This difference can, however, be disregarded here as written records may result in minor alterations in form but not to changes in the meaning (see Olschewski 2000 for a more in-depth analysis of the respective difference).

9 The citations of the parliamentary debates contain the following information: the name and party of the speaker (if not specified in the excerpt), the year, the official record or session number for the parliament and the page number of the parlia-mentary record. The abbreviations of the parliaments are as follows: BT (Bundestag), BR (Bundesrat), BY (Bavaria), HH (Hamburg), SH (Schleswig-Holstein) and SA (Saxony-Anhalt).

10 The GAL (*Grün-Alternative Liste*) Hamburg is part of the Green Party.

11 Interjections are standard practice in parliamentary debates. They tend to interrupt the pre-prepared script of political theatre, but like speeches themselves also serve primarily strategic objectives (Kipke 1995).

12 Westphal later goes on to say that "the provision of help cannot and must not depend on whether or how far the needy party is personally responsible for his or her own distress" (Westphal, SPD, BT 1973, 40th Session, 2213).

13 Mixing social and pathological aetiologies is not unusual; it has occurred repeatedly in German discourses on criminality (examples in Baumann 2006; Becker 2002) and is equally common internationally (for example in positivist criminology following Lombroso's approach; see Brown et al. 2010, 193–234; Lilly et al. 2011, 15–38; Pfohl 1994, 101–168). Biological interpretations of criminality were, however, academi-cally deemed particularly problematic in Germany after National Socialist rule came to an end.

14 The interpellation was as follows: "Has the rise in youth crime caused the federal gov-ernment to take action, and if so, what action?" [Wittmann, 1979, CDU/CSU, BT, Printed Matter 8/3175, 14].

15 The JGG regulates how the criminal justice system in Germany deals with young offenders, i.e. with youths (aged 14 to 17 at the time of the offence) and young adults (aged 18 to 20). It does not define offences but does set out specific legal consequences for young offenders (for details see Eisenberg 2012; Ostendorf 2013). According to section 2 par. 1 JGG, the central tool for preventing reoffending is "education". The JGG was first implemented in 1923; a major revision came into effect in 1990.

16 The law states that the JGG is to apply if a young adult (aged 18, 19 or 20 at the time of the offence) is, in terms of his or her personality, equivalent to a youth, or if the act constitutes misconduct typical of a youth (section 105 par. 1 JGG). It is a matter of political dispute whether this is supposed to be an exception, or whether young adults should in general (or even never) be sentenced under the JGG (see Heinz 2008).

17 *Die Welt* is a German daily newspaper.
18 Jeff Stetson (1999) investigated how the media presented a death and describes how the category 'public' was gradually presented as the guilty party and one with a significant role in the case. Members of the public had failed to intervene when a woman was molested. She eventually pushed the attacker back; he then fell on rails and was killed by an approaching train. In the political debates explored here, the role of the public is rather different: over the course of the period explored, it was increasingly relieved of moral responsibility and addressed in the role of a (potential) victim.

3 Working with youths

Professionals

Professionals assume a significant position in discourses on youth crime, as they are working with youth crime 'on the ground'. In a way, they constitute youth crime on a daily basis as they interact with 'offenders' and categorise and process them correspondingly. Similar to politicians, professionals are also intricately connected to the contexts in which they are operating. On the one hand, professional action must achieve a kind of closure (Collins 1990). Professions, according to Collins, specialise in the ritualised provision of services. In competition with alternative approaches to a social problem, they can and must demonstrate specific competency if they are to be accepted as 'legitimate' problem-solvers. They monopolise responsibilities by demonstrating special skills that others do not have. Ideally, they are recognised for this, and their services requested and rewarded accordingly. On the other hand, professions must take account of politics and the public as they require support for their monopolistic resolution. Freidson (2001, 213–214) notes that

> professionalism is based on specialized bodies of knowledge and skill that have no coercive power of their own but only what may be delegated to them by the state or capital. They gain their protected status by a project of successful persuasion, not by buying it or capturing it at the point of a gun.

The key point here is not the recently widely debated question of whether we are currently – above all as a result of a change in political and economic management – seeing a general crisis of the professions (e.g. Freidson 2001; Otto et al. 2009; Timmermans/Oh 2010; Rogowski 2010).[1] The central issue here is the "project of successful persuasion" described by Freidson.[2] That project ensures political and public approval for taking action against a problem through a specific professional activity. Actual success in combating a social problem – however it could be defined and measured – is more or less irrelevant to political and public confidence in the professions (Best 2008). What is key is *faith in that success* and convincing politicians and the public that certain measures are effective and others not.

Hence the increasing numbers of people who have been imprisoned in western societies over recent years. Imprisonment is not a model for success as it is not a particularly effective way to reduce crime or to (re-)establish or maintain public safety in the long term (for the example of the USA, see Cullen et al. 2011; Jonson 2013; Travis et al. 2014; Western 2006). The increasing use of imprisonment was first and foremost a political decision tied in with cultural and public demands. There is a currently broad 'evidence-based criminology'-movement seeking to support criminal policy based strictly on valid scientific findings. Nevertheless, political decisions that are based on science and research do not appear to play a significant role in criminal policy, or are only relevant in exceptional cases (Case 2007; Smith 2015; Tonry 2013; see also Denzin 2011). In the area of youth crime, too, it is narratively conveyed ideologies and interests rather than 'concrete' successes or failures of particular programs that drive policy changes (Bernard/Kurlychek 2010). Politicians can obtain approval for their positions if they successfully tap into these ideologies and interests and present themselves accordingly.

From the perspective of the professionals and institutions that work with delinquents, the main issue is therefore not whether or not they are working well in preventing reoffending. They must *present* themselves particularly well by drawing on dominant ideological positions. Hasenfeld (2010, 409) summarises this situation as follows:

> Particular institutional logics, and their moral belief systems, become dominant when they resonate well in the public discourse as a better solution to the social crisis or problem they address, when they successfully delegitimize the opposing perspective, and when they gain the support of political elites.

Hasenfeld accurately stresses that professions or institutions do not only have an inherent "moral belief system" but must actively bring that system to bear. Professionals are not simply at the mercy of political and public discourses, but intervene in those discourses and communicate their positions and competencies as part of projects of successful persuasion.

In the context of crime, social work embodies the importance and implications of these projects in a particular way. Garland (2001a, 47) writes, on the subject of "penal welfarism" in the USA and the United Kingdom from after the Second World War until into the 1970s, that "social work became a growth industry, fed by the feedback loop of newly recognized problems in need of professional solutions". According to Rogowski (2010, 185), social work reached "its peak" in this period; it was then the subject of fundamental criticism particularly over the course of 1990s and given a new political direction towards more individualised, cost-effective programs. Social workers' discretion in how they dealt with cases was considerably limited in the process. Above all in the field of (youth) crime – and child protection, which also attracts great media and political attention – that discretion has in Rogowski's view shrunk significantly since the 1990s. There has been a growing focus on the manualisation of processes (for example with checklists and risk assessments), on cost reduction imperatives and on expectations that professionals will ensure safety and victim protection (e.g. Bradt/Bouverne-De Bie 2009; Burton/Broek 2009; Case/Haines 2009; White et al. 2009). Garland (2001a, 150) concludes that "welfare professionals have, since the 1970s, experienced a sharp decline in status and political clout". A focus on competition, self-help and personal responsibility has in Garland's view gradually delegitimised the established welfarist and social work positions. Instead, managerialist and socially exclusive logics of intervention seem to have come to the fore.

If one assumes that social work implements its project of persuasion through narrative profiling and case processing (Hall 1997; Hall et al. 2006; see also Baldwin 2013; Hall et al. 2014; Riessman/Quinney 2005), this does not appear to have been very successful over past decades. Other professions may have been more effective in tapping into political and public discourses through narrative self-positioning.

These assumptions require an in-depth empirical analysis, which can be conducted for Germany predicated on the data used below. It has to be asked *whether there has been a change in the predominant narratives on youth crime since the 1970s.* Social work appears to have been particularly affected by this (possible) transformation and is therefore at the centre of the following discussion. A comparison of social work narratives with those of other professions should be particularly interesting. The comparison below primarily analyses social work in relation to the police, whose status in the context of youth crime is evident. Social work epitomises a welfarist, supportive approach to youth crime, whereas the police symbolises law enforcement and penal action.

3.1 Professionals' journals

a) Context

For a clear understanding of the background to the following analyses, it should be noted that social work has a key role in institutional work on youth crime in Germany. The German Youth Courts Law (*Jugendgerichtsgesetz*, JGG), which still applies today with its key provisions unchanged, first came into effect in 1923. Since then, social work has been an established component of the criminal justice system, for example in the form of the youth courts assistance service (*Jugendgerichtshilfe*) (Kawamura-Reindl/Schneider 2015, 114–136). In criminal proceedings against youths and usually also against young adults, the social work institution of the youth courts assistance service must be involved. The main objective here is to provide social support for the young accused and to provide the youth court with information on his or her social circumstances and personality for consideration in its ruling (Trenczek 2018). Other social work, (youth) crime-related activities include work in probation services, social support in the avoidance of detention awaiting trial, social services during imprisonment, reintegration after imprisonment, offender-victim mediation, various other non-custodial measures (such as the supervision of work tasks) and crime prevention (for a summary, see Cornel et al. 2009; Dollinger/Schmidt-Semisch 2018; Kawamura-Reindl/Schneider 2015; Trenczek/Goldberg 2016). This is testimony to the welfarist approach that Germany takes to youth crime. The police are of course also key in the light of their role in the investigation of possible crimes and in criminal prosecution (Albrecht 2010, 171–202).[3]

In terms of the relationship between social work and the police, the more recent past has seen greater cooperation. In the 1970s and 1980s, conflicts were many and frequent, and social workers in particular appeared unwilling to enter into collaboration. Subsequently, however, various forms of cooperation in projects and institutions have increasingly emerged (Emig 2010; Möller 2010).

b) Data

The findings detailed here come from a project that analysed all publications on youth crime in a total of ten social work and police magazines for the years 1970 to 2009, four police magazines and six social work magazines.[4] All articles that directly addressed or in any way discussed youth crime were examined. A total of 403 articles in the police publications and 531 articles in the social work publications met these criteria.

Different magazines were deliberately selected to cover not just one specific trend in reasoning. All magazines were primarily practical rather than scientific or academic, usually with fairly short texts. The aim was to reconstruct how professions saw themselves with as close a relation to practice as possible.

The 1970s are a good starting point for analysis as penal welfarism was then at its height. Moreover, social work became established in Germany as an academic discipline in this period (Gängler 1998) and a number of magazines were launched that can be examined here.[5]

3.2 The social workers' and police perspectives

The focus below is not on individual magazines but on central narratives used by social work and/or the police. In each case, the period and profession from which the narratives come are indicated. As in the case of the political debates, my aim is again not to fathom the entire body of data but to provide an in-depth analysis of selected individual texts and passages.

a) Structural causes

In the 1970s and 1980s, the social work and police discourses were dominated by references to the social causes of youth crime (Dollinger et al. 2014a; Weinhauer 2003). Delinquency was not primarily caused by individual offender personalities but by young people's social circumstances. A mere recognition of social causes of youth crime is therefore of less interest in the following analyses than the different versions in which this approach emerged in the material analysed. The first version is particularly typical of the 1970s and 1980s and the position taken by social work. It presents structural (or societal) causes of youth crime as rendering individual help – which is in fact a key area of social work practice – largely obsolete. Social work thus declared itself to a great extent superfluous. The second version does not agree with this assessment; individual help appeared much more important.

The futility of individual help and the helplessness of the helpers

An example of the first version stems from a social work magazine dating from 1979. It describes the professional life of a social worker who works with juvenile delinquents. He had initially worked well with the police, but was then repeatedly confronted with police misconduct and violence against young people. When he stood up for them and in so doing upset the police, he was himself investigated. Ultimately, it became increasingly clear to him that the police wanted – if necessary with force – to use him as an accomplice to operate effectively and repressively against delinquency. The social worker, "Stoffel", wants to help young people but is reaching his limits. Above all, the police violence increasingly exercised against himself is putting him under pressure. The case study ends as follows:

Example 3.1

1   How can Stoffel say that he wants peace. – Quiet. – But that peace will not come because violence leaps
2   out at you; that not just your eyes but your head and ears hurt; your throat constricts.
3   *Do people in positions of force actually always realise the effect of that force before they use it?*
4   Stoffel is a policeman. A policeman of the poor. But he does not protect the poor. He works against
5   them.
6   He knows that objectively (!) his role is not that of help and is indeed not supposed to be. He occasionally
7   soothes his guilty conscience with targeted action on behalf of individual people or groups. He is
8   constantly making checks; he is a policeman. Actual policemen can only talk about their social
9   commitment; they cannot prove it. They're between a rock and a hard place. Because they are not by
10 definition bastards, their suffering in their role must make them helpless; vulnerable.
11 They are helpless but their role does not allow them to be helpless. They have to be strong if they know
12 what's good for them.
13 They only say who they are and all the things they can do. They are the law enforcement officers of the
14 public prosecution service, they don't need search warrants; they can make arrests, detain you.
15 The close connection between our roles, our tasks is at the root of our hate. We look at each other and
16 see ourselves. We cannot like what we see. (Kahl 1979, 37; social work)

This sequence is the end of a career history. Its outcome is described in a long, drawn-out resolution. The narrator presents an inside perspective by putting himself in the place of the protagonist, Stoffel. This happens right at the beginning: the narrator knows the mental processes that are going on inside Stoffel's head. These demonstrate a dilemma: a desire for peace hindered by force or violence. In addition, the narrator is a knowing expert who is able to pass objective judgement and can analyse not just Stoffel's situation but also that of the police. He can also see into the future, as he knows that the peace Stoffel wishes for "will not come" (line 1). The narrator has an in-depth understanding of social circumstances and the actions of the parties involved.

A characteristic feature of this example is the illustration of the tasks implemented by social work and the police, and the relationship between the two professions. As regards social work, Stoffel as its representative is portrayed as a victim: he is confronted with violence (lines 1–2) and cannot really help people. He also has a "guilty conscience" (line 7). Social work is thus in a difficult social position. But the story goes much further. Line 4 sets out a "complication" for social work (Labov/Waletzky 1967, 32). A general point was made above that professions engage in a project of persuasion to mobilise political and public support for their work. This is particularly true for social work, which often has to fight for its status in the face of more 'powerful' professions; social work depends on political requirements (Hall et al. 2006, 19). It can only operate if it receives 'ideological', legal and financial support from other, above all state players. For example, if politicians decide that young offenders are no longer to be educated or rehabilitated, this removes key avenues for social work action in this area. The categorisation of young offenders as people with a difficult history and the presentation of social work actions that can effectively address those difficulties is of central importance for social work. Stoffel, however, *cannot* help in this social work narrative, and this complicates the situation, for he is not a powerful helper but a "policeman of the poor" (line 4). He does not protect the poor but turns "against them" (lines 4–5); in other words, he is not only a victim of external restrictions and violence but also an offender. The category of "policeman of the poor" does signal a social backdrop to youth crime, for it appears primarily to be poor people whose criminality is addressed by social work. However, that work is described as police practice, and so not only is there no clear indication of help from social work, but social work practice is identified as an activity that is directed against those who actually need help. Social work is only associated with help for the alleviation of a guilty "conscience" (line 7), as social work in reality acts like the police and, in this sense as a category-bound activity, is constantly checking up on people (line 8). These activities legitimise the category membership: those who turn against the poor and make checks on them *are* police. As Stoffel undertakes these activities, he is a policeman; a specific form of policeman: a policeman of the poor.

Nevertheless, the police and social work are not fully equated with each other, for the author distinguishes policemen of the poor from "actual policemen" (line 8), creating two differing subcategories of police. The difference lies in their distinctive characteristics: social work is supposed to help, and a guilty conscience is the result of the inability to put that requirement into practice. The actual police, on the other hand, are associated with a demonstration of strength (lines 11–12). There are therefore differences between the subcategories. Nonetheless, police and social work do have aspects in common that place them both in the same category 'police', namely control, acting against subjects and a "role" (lines 6, 10) that is described as not helping.

A short (quasi-) list in the text is useful to further understand this categorisation: social work apparently helps *individuals* and *groups* (line 7). O'Connor (2000, 56 and 62) refers to the function of lists to communicate progressions and value judgements in stories of crime. Specifying individuals and groups may not be a full-blown list, but it follows this principle of evaluative progression, for individuals (at a social micro-level) and groups (at the meso-level) would logically be followed by society (the macro-level). Yet at that very level, Stoffel is not helping: his help or sop to his conscience in the form of "targeted action" (line 7) happens only at the micro-level and meso-level. Society remains open; no help is provided here despite the reference to poverty in the category "policeman of the poor", indicating that social work's police role is at a societal level, as poverty is an abstract societal category. Not only individuals but also "the poor" (line 4) in general as a social category are portrayed in the text. It is precisely at this important level that Stoffel is unable to help, and this appears to be a shortcoming in his professional activity. In fact, Stoffel uses force, and this explains "his guilty conscience" (line 7): he is not fulfilling his central responsibility, which is to deal with the social causes of poverty. In this respect, he is similar to the "actual policemen" (line 8), as they too are unable to help. They may "talk" (line 8) about it, but they cannot "prove" (line 9) that they are actually helping; ultimately, they are themselves "helpless" (line 11). The 'actual police' might give a show of strength, but in light of the social causes of youth crime or poverty and the help needed at this macro-level, the police and social work are in a similarly helpless position. They exercise the same function, i.e. social control, but they do not help. Therein lies their "close connection" (line 15). Both are helpless and bound by far-reaching social or political structures – and in the case of the police explicitly also the structures of the public prosecution service (lines 13–14) – that prevent real help.

Interestingly enough, the author describes this relationship between the police and social work as the cause of "hate" (15). Indeed, he describes the police in the text before the passage quoted as violent towards Stoffel; in his case, they cause clear suffering. According to the author, Stoffel appears to know that he ought to be helping at the societal level but that this possibility is "objectively (!)" denied to him (line 6). Beyond his own suffering, this could explain the "hate" as awareness that social work should be providing support but cannot in the light of its societal function.

Altogether, the author uses a complex series of categorisations. He defines the 'real' social functions of social work and the police, and also duties that they ought *actually* to be fulfilling instead. He too defines their relationship to each other by describing the professions both as offenders and as victims. They are offenders as they exert control and violence. And they are victims as they have been assigned abstract social functions that dictate their actions and leave little scope for 'genuine' help. These functions preclude a substantial change in their predicament. The coda to the narrative (lines 15–16) does not contain a resolution of the problem but the joint ("our", "we", lines 15–16) observation of social work and police that, given their close connection, they do not like each other and have no reason to be content. That is the essence of the (social work) story. Another key message is that interpersonal help is ultimately irrelevant in the face of the potency of society. Stoffel only salves his conscience when he helps individuals and groups, but in that very act of help he is failing his actual duty of support at a societal level: that support cannot be provided because of social work's irrelevance on a structural macro-level. Social work with individuals and with groups remains futile. Social work is, as another social work text from the same year puts it, a mere "puppet show" (Die Redaktion Sozialmagazin 1979, 32). In other words, it is a simulation of help that actually ought to be provided at a societal level.

Applied to the comments by Hall et al. (2006) mentioned above on social work's need to legitimise itself through categorisation appropriate to its actions, it is striking that social work is not expressing itself in a way that could justify its activities. On the contrary, social work presents itself as helpless. This is the position of an explicitly critical social work, according to which "many or most social problems come from the structure and organization of society rather than from individuals' behaviour. It follows that the appropriate response is social change to eliminate the source of the difficulties" (Payne 2014, 321). In relation to example 3.1, this means: as youth crime has social causes but social work cannot help at a societal level, social work is ultimately unnecessary or even damaging, as it only reproduces or complements police work but does not 'really' help.

This self-referred de-legitimisation is typical of social work narratives in the 1970s and 1980s (Dollinger et al. 2012a, 2015b). Based on the data analysed here, it cannot be determined why social work was so critical not just of the police but also of itself. Yet one point worth considering is that socially critical neo-Marxist positions were common in the German social work sector's definition of itself and its role at that time (Hammerschmidt et al. 2017, 19–32; Thole 2010, 38). Those positions were connected to a politicisation of social work and a strict criticism of personal, individual help, of traditional institutions and of modern society as a whole.[6]

Help despite social causes

Another version of the social work and also police narratives drew other conclusions from societal analyses. Here, too, social problems were causes of delinquency. However, this did not lead to calls for an end to interpersonal measures. Socio-structural conditions were criticised in the context of social work, but social work could counteract these conditions by providing support for individuals and thus partly alleviating social problems. This narrative denounced unemployment, educational inequalities, poverty and disadvantage, discrimination, a lack of opportunities for emancipatory development, etc., and argued that social work had to and could at least partially address these issues (Dollinger et al. 2012a). In the police, social causes were conceived of differently – primarily as problems of a value shift and symptoms of the breakdown of traditional values, an erosion of established family structures, negative influences from the mass media, etc.: in other words, factors largely pertaining to conservative cultural criticism. Social work, by comparison, attached much more importance to economic problems. There were overlaps as both criticised modern society, but in their detail the two positions differed, also relating to the conclusions drawn from the criticism. Within the police, the approach was authoritarian: education or re-education was to lead juvenile delinquents back into the established value system and thus restore order and security (Busch et al. 1988; Weinhauer 2000, 2008). Social work, on the other hand, in some cases, considered methodical approaches to interpersonal help. These frequently remained vague, however, and were rejected by some authors who called instead for a show of solidarity with young people in the fight against institutions such as the police and the criminal justice system.

The following example from social work revolves around this point: a critical consideration of interpersonal support. It is a first-person narrative, which tells of the daily work of a (social work) supervisor in a juvenile prison ("*Betreuer*"). It recounts short leave ("*Ausgang*") from the prison that she undertook with a young detainee ("Pimo"), during which the young man suddenly disappeared. He later returned to the prison, and the supervisor then engaged in in-depth discussion with him and tried to provide support. In the process, she reflects on the fact that she learned during her academic studies that prisons and personalised measures do not really help, but tend to make the situation worse (as outlined in example 3.1). This knowledge from studies and theory is inserted as quotes from books in the narrator's text in short, italicised passages, as can be seen in the example below. The passage is the end of the story told by the narrator.

Example 3.2

1   Pimo is a person who's serving a sentence here, who by accident or not is here because of his social
2   "misconduct".
3   *"The criminal justice system today needs the 'soft' technique of social work to supplement disciplinary*
4   *isolation (which still is standard practice). That technique seeks to address individual cases by*
5   *programming them; seeks further to pursue the individualisation and isolation of social problems*
6   *already set down in criminal law at the level of treatment".*
7   I do not deny that I do sometimes use techniques, you could also say work methodically. My work is

8   not to be equated with technique. I am not always "soft"; my "softness" is perhaps more like a bit of
9   empathy. (. . .)
10   Critical analysis is always very easy, they taught us that for long enough at the FU.[7] But who teaches
11   us to live with the Pimos?
12   I may not be addressing social problems, but I can't abandon the Pimos either . . . (Spitczok von Brisinski
13   1981, 8; social work).

The first person makes the narrator visible as a person involved in the activity of help. She appears authentic as she has direct experience (Shuman 2015). Yet the excerpt does not start with her, but with "Pimo", who is presented as a "person" (line 1). The passage does not run 'Pimo is serving a sentence here . . .' or 'Pimo is an offender who . . .'; instead, the category "person" is used, a category that is in itself trivial as it applies to everyone. Explicitly employing the category highlights it as noteworthy, however, and it takes on an interactive function. Being human, a person, is of primary importance, while the "misconduct" placed in quotation marks – as a quote or as a distancing device – is secondary and is associated with "by accident" (line 1). The orientation of this text section thus categorises Pimo primarily as a person and only secondarily as an offender.

The subsequent quote comes from an academic publication and defines social work as a "'soft' technique" (line 3) that addresses individual cases "by programming them" (lines 4–5), in other words, does not see them as individual people. This quote defines social work's role as pursuing the logic of criminal law, categorising social workers as subordinate to and bound by criminal law. Criminal law and social work appear to form a pair that follows the same standardised logic but employ different practices, as social work is a "'soft' technique". In this partnership, social work is attributed a will and a comparatively high activity status: social work is not occupied or forced by external powers; it "seeks" [German original: "will", literally 'wants'] (lines 4, 5) of its own volition to pursue or reproduce the criminal law logic. This logic is narratively discredited, for it is aimed at handling individual cases 'by numbers' ("technique" and "programming", line 4–5) and demands "isolation" (line 5). This handling must necessarily be judged negatively from a social work perspective in light of the profession's interest in humanity and integration (e.g. Holland/Scourfield 2015; Hugman 2008). In the quote, social work is an agency of the criminal justice system that, of its own accord, entails social isolation.

In the following paragraph, the narrator outlines her own position. She does "sometimes use techniques" (line 7), so she does through this activity describe herself as part of the negatively evaluated category 'social workers as agents of criminal law'. However, she defines the nature and function of her work differently from the quote. She qualifies herself as a social worker as not acting purely with technique but (also) with empathy (line 9). As for the function of her activity, she cites not the pursuit of isolation but rather help for Pimo and the individuals that he represents ("Pimos", line 12). The narrator thus resists the categorisation of interpersonal social work as a *mere* reproduction of social exclusion. Social work can in her narrative help individual people; it can act compassionately and should do so, otherwise it would – irrespective of any social problems that might continue to exist (line 12) – "abandon" (line 12) those people. Interpersonal help is thus not unproblematic but is still useful and necessary. With her advocacy of help, she positions herself in the context of "penal welfarism". Unlike in example 3.1, the measures advocated represent *necessary* individual help – beyond academic reflection and interventions on a societal level.

In the police, too, help for individuals despite social problems is qualified positively. However, both this understanding of the problems and the concept of help differed from social work positions in the 1970s and 1980s. The motif of a "Don Quichotte" (Lazai 1985, 231), used by a police writer to describe police work on youth crime, is typical. In the light of social causes, practical intervention by the police for individual young people appears of little use in the long term, and yet individual cases are an important starting point for practical work. Such a position is in itself similar to the social work narratives illustrated in example 3.2: there are social causes of youth crime that do not invalidate interpersonal measures. Help for individuals is necessary despite the social challenges, even if the profession in question appears unable to address the actual causes of the problems at the macro-level. Yet despite this (superficial) similarity, there are considerable differences between the police and social work. The example below highlights those differences on the basis of relevant categorisations. It is the start of an article in a German police magazine. The text describes a case in Switzerland of a juvenile delinquent from an immigrant background.

Example 3.3

1 **Introduction**
2 We report below on a case that could happen not just in Zurich but anywhere in Switzerland where the
3 children of foreign workers cannot assimilate. Fortunately, however, it is not an everyday occurrence.
4 Our youth services have been facing problems like this for years. We are constantly having to conduct
5 major investigations into children and young people from immigrant families, and those investigations
6 clearly show that the children of many migrant workers are left too much to their own devices. They
7 lack above all the guidance and direction of adults who have authority without being overly
8 authoritarian; people who have time and understanding for the problems of their children. In the case of
9 migrant workers, where both parents often work full time, this is frequently lacking. What is more, the
10 language barrier prevents the children of such families from making the friends they need and want
11 either in school or on the street or in the park. These children must feel excluded by society and
12 ultimately inferior. As they cannot take their problems home, the young people get drawn into crime as
13 they seek to find friends and gain their respect. (Casparis 1978, 123; police)

The article starts by giving the readers an orientation and a judgement: the place categories "Zurich" and "anywhere in Switzerland" (line 1) suggest that the case reported is ubiquitous, at least as regards Switzerland. The report is "on a case" (line 1), but that case is generalised and not presented as an isolated incident. As it could happen "anywhere in Switzerland" (line 1) – and moreover probably anywhere in Germany, as the article appears in a German magazine – the author is presenting a general issue. If a case could happen anywhere, it must indicate generalisable patterns, and those are what the author is discussing. This is associated with an evaluation: it is "fortunately [. . .] not an everyday occurrence" (line 3), i.e. although it could happen anywhere, it still has the status of a certain exception. The case is to be viewed negatively; otherwise, its rarity would not be fortunate.

The subsequent details give the reader the typical features: the pattern of the specific case. The reader is briefed to see the case as the author sees it, namely as a symptom of a long-term societal problem facing Switzerland – and one which the country has to date clearly been unable to resolve, but to which there is a solution (known to the author). The long-term dimension implies that problems have apparently been occurring "for years" (line 4) and "constantly" (line 4) confronting the police – and the author as a knowledgeable and affected party ("our", line 4) – with issues of crime committed by young offenders.

The author is aware of the causes: young people become delinquents because they are foreigners, because their parents do not bring them up 'properly' and because they are excluded by friends; in their search for social recognition, they then get "drawn into" (line 12) crime. The delinquency described is thus a social problem, for it has its roots in the difficult shared existence of 'foreigners' and local Swiss people, yet the author does not name structural problems such as poverty, unemployment or institutional discrimination or racism that would particularly affect 'foreigners'. Work is certainly discussed, as it is given as a cause of parenting failings – this fits in with the fact that 'being foreign' in Europe at this time was often associated with the demand for labour (Melossi 2015, 51–52). However, work is not the deciding aetiological factor in the narrative. Youth crime is instead culturalised: it is caused on the one hand by a lack of parenting and supervision skills on the part of 'foreign' parents (lines 6–9), and on the other by language-based problems and a related problem of recognition for the young people (lines 9–12); the focus is therefore on cultural difficulties. Those difficulties are the basis for a "victim" narrative in which an offender is "alienated from others who are nonetheless significant to him" (Youngs/Canter 2012, 240). This narrative raises a dilemma: the young people are seeking recognition that is denied to them because of circumstances beyond their control. As they do not receive adequate guidance and do not have a good command of the local language, they become delinquents. As offenders, they appear relatively weak, for they "get drawn into" (line 12) delinquency. They are not determined, malicious creatures but rather victims of circumstance; the circumstances are largely linked to their 'being foreign'. The category 'foreigner' is thus associated with the young people's difficulties (lack of guidance and language skills) and those difficulties with criminality.

Despite social problems, the main problem is not society. Instead, the central issue lies with the 'foreigners' and their non-Swiss characteristics and linguistic shortcomings.

The author implicitly presents a solution to the problem of 'foreigner' crime. The young people in question are in a difficult situation. To deal with that situation, strong — but not excessively strict (lines 7–8) — authority is needed that will give the young people guidance and treat them with "understanding" (line 8). The young people must also learn the language. Otherwise, they will be unable to resist the temptations of delinquency as they appear incapable of producing this power of resistance themselves. The commission of youth crime is associated with weakness.

As in example 3.2, despite underlying social problems, the author is calling for measures that can be implemented at an interpersonal level. However, the self-presentation of this police author is very different to that in the social work example 3.2. The author in example 3.2 is highly self-critical; she justifies herself by explaining her desire to provide inter-personal help despite socially induced problems. The police focus is differ-ent: it communicates clear, deterministic circumstances. The police author presents himself as someone who can confidently report on general case patterns. He is familiar with the problem of 'foreigner' crime and can "clearly" (line 6) place it in context. He claims to understand the social and subjective situation in which the delinquents find themselves, and his references to parenting as "guidance" (line 7) and to language learning sug-gest maxims that could deal with youth crime. The essence of example 3.2 was that you had to "live with the Pimos" and show them "empathy". In example 3.3, the police do not put forward such a perspective of empathy and having to cope with the problems in the long term. Instead, the police offer an opportunity to overcome youth crime in the case of 'foreigners'. Social work's message to the reader is pessimistic, as the problems can-not be overcome, but it includes a call for sympathy with the offenders as victims of society. The police, on the other hand — as later would social work, which to a certain extent adopted this position (see Chapters 3.2 d) and e) below) — demand stricter measures (i.e. upbringing or education as "authority", "direction" and "guidance") and connects them with the vision that crime can be overcome.

In keeping with this approach, the author argues towards the end of his article that even highly delinquent young people "can be brought onto the straight and narrow through suitable educational support and strict but correct guidance" (Casparis 1978, 126). The problems of the 'foreign children' or the problems that they cause could therefore be resolved — provided the 'foreign-ers' behave like the Swiss, in other words stop being different and "assimilate" (line 3). This narrative claims a solution to problems of criminality but not for the recognition of difference.

b) *The negative power of the organisation*

In the 1970s and 1980s, many representatives of the police and social work assumed that youth crime had social causes; more so than the police, social work presented interpersonal measures as relatively futile. Another important difference between the professions at this time was the specific focus on organisations. Like structural causes, organisations represented external criminogenic influences on young people. However, organisations are, as it were, closer to the individual than society is; with their representatives they interact directly with young people. Differing from the police, social work argued that organisations had a central role in the injustices and disadvantages that youths and young adults were confronted with. Young people appeared largely defenceless, at the mercy of the power of the organisations.

An example from a social work magazine published in 1979 illustrates this point. The edition focuses on youth detention, and the excerpt below is part of a story told over nine pages. The story's two protagonists, Heiner and Charly, have their say at length, notably through their own written notes, as the paragraph below explains. The author named provides a commentary on verbatim quotes from the two young men. The following excerpt introduces the nine-page story.

Example 3.4

1   **No *Umschluß* for Heiner and Charly**
2   Charly and Heiner have become friends in prison and that friendship has come with big plans: they
3   want to change. Prison stinks. It only brings them disappointment, loneliness and violence. They
4   experience that once again when the institution stops allowing their friendship. Their intimacy is hard
5   to supervise. Because the other prisoners and the wardens consider them "gay pigs", they are
6   separated. By destroying their hope for survival, the prison 'rehabilitates' Heiner and Charly for
7   reoffending. This sets the seal on their criminal careers.
8   Using diary entries, personal histories and essays, Hannelore Cyrus, who taught Heiner and Charly in
9   prison, reconstructed the 'prison biographies' of the two young men. (Potting 1979, 21; social work)

The title (line 1) provides a summary and an orientation: two named persons are being denied something. "Umschluß" is when one prisoner is allowed to be locked up with another in his or her free time. This requires the consent of the prison staff. The title does not indicate who exactly is withholding this consent or why. We simply learn that Heiner and Charly – obviously prisoners – are confronted with the decision that they cannot spend free time together; that they are being denied something and, in the context of the title at least, for no reason.

A further categorisation of Charly and Heiner then follows in the first paragraph of the subsequent text: they have "become friends" (line 2) and are people with "big plans" (line 2); in other words, they have social ties and actively make decisions. This agency is associated with a desire that must appear legitimate and sensible from the point of view of intervening institutions: "they want to change" (lines 2–3). As they are referred to as prisoners, a desire to change must be a desire to lead a law-abiding life. They do not want to be imprisoned any longer, for "prison stinks" (line 3). Readers of the magazine are thus being given a positive evaluation: a friendship has formed between two people who want to end their involvement in crime and get out of prison.

What is holding them back is their adversary: the organisation 'prison'. It exhibits characteristics and actions that do not hinder reoffending or render it impossible, but in fact encourage it. The prison has two reasons for the "Umschluß"-ban: firstly, Heiner and Charly are "hard to supervise" (lines 4–5) when together; in other words, the prison is seeking a perfected form of social control. Secondly, the prison is discriminating by considering the friends as "gay pigs" (line 5; "schwule Säue" in the German original) – an extremely derogatory term – and separating them on those grounds. The prison is thus failing to fulfil its role of facilitating desistance and rehabilitating offenders; in fact, it "sets the seal" (line 7) on the two friends' recidivism. This failure is down to measures that must appear particularly negative from a social work perspective, for the prison appears to be a discriminating and purely controlling organisation. It has no 'legitimate' reasons for the way in which it deals with the two friends, but destroys their will to live and their hopes. The prison prevents a future free from crime and further imprisonment. Two young people who are positively categorised as friends and active subjects are thus placed in opposition to a morally dubious organisation – an organisation that is, moreover, extremely powerful, as its decisions can effectively destroy the friends' will and future.

The author appears just as helpless as the two friends. Here again, social work's implicit self-categorisation is telling. The author from the social work sector explores the case of two people who are referred to by name both in the title and right at the start of the text that follows; they are presented as individuals facing an anonymously operating and powerful organisation. Social work is thus an institution that gives a voice to clients who are silenced by organisations. The author allows the two young men to express themselves by reporting from their "diary entries, personal histories and essays" (line 8). The information is presented in the magazine not by a professional social worker but by a teacher, as the category-bound activity of teaching tells the reader (line 8). Nonetheless, teaching is an educational activity and is being cited in a social work magazine to present the perspective of clients. Social work is thus directly associated with clients; it knows them well and is aware of their interests and their needs. Such needs and interests appear to be authentically reported in the magazine because the teacher, as the readers are told (line 8–9), taught the two friends herself. She is therefore in an allegedly excellent position to tell their story as it is. Social work is presenting itself as an institution with a 'genuine' interest in clients: an institution that listens to them and that can justifiably and authentically take issue with the friends' predicament, caused by the prison's superior strength. Yet social work cannot change that predicament. Although it can make the friends' wishes and needs clear, this does not change anything. The "seal" appears to have been set on a lifelong career of crime for Charly and Heiner despite the investment by social work (line 7). Social work is thus an authentic, committed and client-focused but – when faced with the powerful organisation of the prison – also a helpless institution. Individual support does appear to be possible, as the friends are determined to change their current situation. In practice, however, that help is useless as it is nullified by the criminal justice system as represented by the prison. That system is a barrier to clients and to social work.

c) The positive effect of cooperation

So far, we have looked at positions from the 1970 and 1980s. While there were some areas of overlap during this period, social services and the police largely adopted different approaches (Dollinger et al. 2013, 2015c). Cooperation with the police and criminal justice system was correspondingly rejected by social work. In this context, Feltes (2010, 30) refers to collaboration between social work and the police as the "story of a 'dysfunctional relationship'", although he notes a lessening of the tension and numerous partnerships in practice in the more recent past (see also Bannenberg et al. 2005; Emig 2010; Kessl 2011).

Issues such as the 'fight against repeat offenders', demands for early prevention or calls to bring together different professions in local networks for fighting crime have more recently met with an increasingly positive social work reception. This development has not happened without criticism, but since the mid-1990s – which also saw a significant shift in political discourses on youth crime (see Chapter 2) – social work has been increasingly prepared to work with the police and criminal justice system to promote the safety of society.

The question of cooperation was, however, not an entirely new one for social work. As we saw in the political sphere, discourses do not simply abruptly change. Instead, previously marginal opinions become predominant (and vice versa). In politics, this development became evident regarding demands for offenders to be considered and treated as offenders (i.e. who caused harm and were not primarily victims of social problems). Exceptions from welfarist measures of support and help that initially applied to only a few delinquents gradually became the model for a greater willingness to sanction overall. In the professions, we can trace a similar historical progression. In the 1990s, there occurred a generalisation of demands that social work had previously rejected firmly or advocated only in marginal positions. This applies in particular to demands for cooperation and 'tougher' measures against delinquents.

An early social work text on the question of cooperation is revealing in this regard, although or precisely because this position was still a marginal one in social work at the time of publication in 1973. The author was a probation officer and the text was entitled "Cooperation between the police and probation services".[8]

Example 3.5

1   Probation services are not an island of social romanticism and soppy sentimentality, nor is the police
2   service a barracks for hierarchy-obsessed automatons and puppets, neither a state within the state nor a
3   society of supermen. A 'pragmatic consensus' ought to connect the two institutions, as their common
4   function is to 'wash society's dirty linen' (. . .). The focus should not be on the institution but on the
5   people – and a criminal is also a person. He or she is often slowly but surely reduced by the outside
6   world to the status of subhuman.
7   Returning to social and humane objectives should not just be the prerogative of the probation service,
8   it would also be fitting for the police. Today, as everything is being called into question and for the
9   most part rightly so, all parties should seek to change how they see themselves. (Baumann 1973, 32–33;
10 social work)

The excerpt starts by categorising probation services and the police by rejecting certain characteristics. For the probation service, the author rejects the notion that it is a purely romantic and emotionalised institution (line 1); in other words, the author sees this as a possible, but incorrect, perception. The author also protests against an incorrect categorisation of the police, namely that it is a collection of "puppets" (line 2) or "supermen" (line 3).

This non-categorisation categorisation leaves open the question of what the two professions do stand for, a question that the author answers by citing a common point of reference, clearly suggesting cooperation. He does so using a social positioning that already appeared in example 3.1: as a "common function" (lines 3–4), the author connects the two professions with "society's dirty linen" (line 4). In other words, they both work with marginalised groups. A characteristic of both police and social workers links them. The author in example 3.1 related the same finding to the exercise of social control and rejected cooperation on this basis. In example 3.5, the author reaches a different conclusion, defining a positive projection – looking after the "people" (line 5) – as a common feature. He justifies this reading through drastic characterisation: offenders are the victims of external circumstances; they are reduced "to the status of subhuman" (line 6) by "the outside world" (lines 5–6), i.e. through no fault of their own.

The term "subhuman" ("*Untermensch*") was in Germany a feature of National Socialist discourse and therefore taboo in the period after the Second World War (Urban 2014). Anyone who used it could, whatever their intention, expect to cause a storm of protest. The author's evaluation is therefore stark: offenders are treated very badly – they are reduced to the status of "subhuman" – and whoever treats people like that appears not far removed from National Socialism. This sharp criticism of the then-current approach to youth crime comes with the observation that currently "everything is being called into question" (line 8) and "for the most part rightly so" (lines 8–9). Society or at least society's approach to offenders is thus presented as extremely flawed in its form and focus. Building on a willingness to change that situation, the police and social work could cooperate by placing "people" at the centre of their work.

These "people" are connoted as badly treated creatures in need of help and not as offenders; the author thus takes a social work perspective from which he presents an option for potential cooperation between the police and social work. Implicitly, he is ascribing both professions the ability to demonstrate a willingness for change in practice as cooperation on the basis described would not otherwise be feasible. A positive option is therefore set against harsh criticism of current society. The author is placing himself – including the police and social work – on the side of those demanding criminal policy reforms that focus on the well-being of the person and not the punishment of offenders.

It is insightful to compare this narrative with a positive assessment of cooperation by social work at a later point to illustrate the change in categorisation. Cooperation with the police was still criticised (Dollinger et al. 2012a, 77), but from the 1990s on, it became more broadly acceptable, and the in some cases sharp distinctions drawn with the police in example 3.1 gradually disappeared. The following example illustrates this shift. The text was printed in a social work magazine and calls for the prevention of violence and racism to be taken seriously as a duty of the youth welfare services. Such an approach, the author argues, is more effective the more . . .

Example 3.6

1   (. . .) the various youth welfare service organisations collaborate in an institutional network and on a
2   practical, cooperative basis both with each other and with other bodies (social services, the police and
3   justice system, schools, organisations representing migrants and asylum-seeker centres) and join
4   together to combat racist sentiment and acts. (Hafemann 1994, 9; social work)

The author argues that youth welfare services need to change, describing them as an institution that is currently not sufficiently well networked either internally in terms of individual youth welfare service organisations (lines 1–2) or with other institutions (lines 2–3). Youth welfare services appear fragmented and better integration is necessary. Integration means working with other institutions to implement a common project to prevent racism. Youth welfare services are thus a body that has, like others, a duty to work for the good of the general public and that must cooperate. Cooperation is to be effectively implemented in practice; youth welfare services are being presented here in terms of their role of reducing deviance. They are legitimised if they are able to provide the relevant services and coordinate provision with other bodies. This cooperative process takes place at multiple levels: at the level of institutional networking (line 1), of actual working practice (line 2) and of general "sentiment and acts" (line 4). Cooperation is thus to be fostered both horizontally (in reference to different professions and institutions) and vertically (in terms of practice, institution and culture) so that deviance can actually be prevented, and youth welfare services are a key player in this interaction. This key player exhibits the activity to fight side by side with other institutions against delinquency, which is qualified as intolerable per se. Delinquency is not a symptom of structural or social problems that social work has to tackle by siding with young people who would be excluded by powerful institutions. Now, social work is working with and within, no longer against, these institutions. It is fighting *against deviance*, not explicitly *for people*.

In individual texts, this re-categorisation of social work as a cooperative and effective crime-fighter was taken one step further by explicitly linking it to domestic security objectives. They served as an envisaged common ground on which cooperation of social work with the police and the criminal justice system could be implemented. Klug (2003, 35), for example, wrote in a social work magazine to call for more risk assessments by probation services, "for they allow better risk detection. This would make an important contribution to public safety". In this vein, social workers were categorised as professionals who can play an important part in promoting safety and security. While social work in the 1970s and 1980s stood largely on the side of young people, demonstrating solidarity with them and working to combat a police and criminal justice system that behaved aggressively and intrusively, these calls for cooperation now place social work on their side, demonstrating solidarity with potential victims of crime and working against offenders in order to protect public security (Dollinger/Rudolph 2016).

From a police perspective, social work was in some cases criticised for inaction, but it was also called on to engage in cooperation. One example from a police magazine shows the cooperation expectations of the police. The article addresses the issue of "crash kids", children and young people who drive stolen cars, speed and in some cases end up in chases with the police. The text ends by asking what needs to be done in future to deal with the problem of crash kids.

Example 3.7

1   In the area of supervised activities offered by the Youth Welfare Office and independent providers, we
2   have seen a lot of changes towards greater flexibility. Nonetheless, most youth leisure facilities are
3   still, as before, closed at the weekend. Late in the evening or after midnight, it is unfortunately often
4   only staff from the youth protection arm of the police who are working around the main train station,
5   for example, more or less as social workers. What we need above all is to widen cooperation between
6   all relevant authorities and institutions, for neither the police nor other bodies can solve such problems
7   alone. (Leven 1997, 55; police)

At the start of the excerpt, the author outlines a development over time: there have been "a lot of changes toward greater flexibility" (line 2). Social work – represented by the Youth Welfare Office (*Jugendamt*) and independent providers – was therefore previously (more) rigid and is now providing more flexible services. However, the development is not perfect, for facilities in some cases remain "closed" (line 3). There is a negative evaluation in the assessment of this development, for the police have "unfortunately" (line 3) to intervene if social work services are closed. The police are filling a gap that should actually be covered by social work.

The author specifies places and times as categories to describe this short-coming in cover. There is the "main train station" (lines 4–5) and its surrounding area, and there are specific times ("at the weekend" line 3; "Late in the evening or after midnight", line 3) that have to be covered by professional actors. Crime in this assessment occurs in specific places and at particularly late hours, i.e. outside of 'normal' office hours, which means a wide range of "authorities and institutions" (line 6) become involved in the fight against crime.

Activities linked to these categories of places and times are not specified. We would expect police work to be dealt with by the police, whether at midnight or at any other time, and at the train station or elsewhere. The same applies to social workers and other professionals; there are no further details of the work expected from them, either. As a matter of principle, the various activities do not coincide, for the author *critically* notes that "staff from the youth protection arm of the police" (line 4) have to deal with things that are actually the responsibility of "social workers" (line 5). In other words, the police are not per se competent in all areas and cannot for example carry out all social work tasks themselves. The police are, however, shown as recognising gaps in provision that are important for youth crime work. The police are aware of the needs and can detail institutions such as social work to cover those needs, and can also if necessary and exceptionally take on the latter's role. They only do this "more or less" (line 5), in other words not as well as the body that is actually compe-tent, but at least they are carrying out that body's duties. With this knowledge and these supplementary activities, the police force is a fundamentally well-informed institution that is able to control and assess cooperation between different players.

At the heart of this cooperation organised by the police is the prevention of crime. In example 3.5, the central aspect of institutional cooperation was pre-sented differently, as it were from a social work perspective: cooperation was all about the 'people', who were to be protected and supported as human beings (and not as offenders). In example 3.7, on the other hand, the communicative reference is crime prevention, which must be implemented without gaps in service provision.

This shows that cooperation does not simply mean different professions or institutions working together. In fact, collaboration between different professional groups often involves divergent and competing narratives that do not simply exist in parallel. Cooperation means conflict or confrontation: a battle for dominance between specific professional categorisations of a social problem (e.g. Buchna et al. 2017; White/Featherstone 2005). When parties cooperate, that cooperation can involve the establishment of specific narratives that favour particular forms of action and delegitimise others. As the examples above illustrate, social work initially insisted on its socially critical narrative, whose central arguments the police did not share. This difference weakened significantly over time, as illustrated in example 3.6, as social work took on a cooperative approach to addressing youth crime. The police interpretation of youth crime ultimately dominated calls for cooperation. Social work adapted to these calls. *The 'people' in question became 'offenders' who had to be controlled and prosecuted or whose occurrence should be prevented.* Other aspects that had long been a police concern also became more evident in social work in the course of this convergence: the responsibilisation and confrontation of individual offenders, and if necessary tough action against them.

d) Accountability

In the 1990s, relevant sections of the social work sector moved away from an insistence on the social causes of delinquency that rendered help but not punishment necessary. A 'tougher' approach to offenders was now to be taken by social work, too. Not only did this facilitate cooperation with the police, it also led to a considerable change in how social work narrated crime and depicted itself as an institution dealing with crime. Although socially critical voices within social work remained (Dollinger et al. 2012a, 2015b), this was a significant shift from the welfarist discourse that social work represented (Lutz 2010; Ziegler 2005), as the following example illustrates. It is a social work text in which the author criticises social work for its (alleged) position, namely over-emphasising the social causes of crime and underestimating the personal responsibility of offenders.

Example 3.8

1   By taking responsibility, offenders can reflect in-depth on the suffering they have caused and thus
2   become less likely to reoffend. Victims are given a real opportunity for redress that would not
3   generally be offered by criminal proceedings.
4   Alongside offenders' need for help, which is to be assessed, another broad and problematic issue is
5   increasingly being recognised. Help for victims of crimes. Social work has long failed fully to
6   recognise the need for victim support and has completely neglected this area. (Kipp 1994, 50; social
7   work)

The excerpt begins by categorising the people with whom social work deals in the rehabilitation service for offenders and ex-prisoners (*Straffälligenhilfe*):

"offenders" (line 1). They are not "people'", as in examples 3.1 and 3.5, or specific individuals who suffer from sanctions, as in example 3.4. Instead, the category "offenders" is used: these are people who have violated the law and are now to be categorised accordingly in criminal law terms. Social work adopts this criminal law category and – in accordance with the criminal law approach and common public interpretations (Watson 1976; Stetson 1999) – qualifies an offender as someone who causes "suffering" (line 1). An offender is not the victim of circumstance, but someone who harms others and produces victims of his or her acts. Social work thus now accepts and reproduces the cultural and legal connection between offender and offence.

The same applies to the duty that follows from this categorisation and which the political discourse in the 1970s and 1980s already assigned to social work (see Chapter 2): preventing reoffending. If offenders cause harm, it appears reasonable to call for the prevention of that harm by working with offenders – in other words not simply with "people", but with people with the characteristic of being "offenders". This contention, which social work had long criticised or at most only given tepid support (see example 3.2), is now also recognised in the field. *Action against offenders is needed.* How this can be achieved in practice is left fairly open in the excerpt; however, it does call for "taking responsibility" (line 1) and corresponding reflection by offenders. Restrictive measures could be used, but so could 'traditional' supportive social services. In all cases, offenders are responsible for their actions and, e.g. by reflection, must answer for them to reduce the risk they pose to other people.

The offender is now contrasted with the category "victim" (line 2); the *standardised relational pair*[9] of offender and victim is here – as common sense would imply – no longer reversed as in older social work texts that presented offenders as victims of social problems. Offenders are now people who cause suffering and thus produce the category "victim"; victims are people who have suffered and therefore are entitled to receive help. In the light of their responsibility for their actions, offenders are not by definition in need of help; that need "is to be assessed" (line 4). No assessment is, on the other hand, required for the victims of crime: they are by definition sufferers and therefore have a right to support. This apparently opens up "another broad and problematic issue" (line 4) for social work. The moral readjustment of the categories of offender and victim in this approach broadens the scope of social work activities, for certain offenders could (probably) still be helped or at least brought to a sense of responsibility, and at the same time, victims have now also become social work clients. The author strongly criticises the fact that this field of social work has, as he believes, to date been "neglected" (line 6). He can back this criticism up from a moral perspective with the assumed suffering of the victims: suffering legitimises social work, for "redress" (line 2) for victims has apparently yet to be provided through the criminal justice system.

That categorial arrangement implies a critical assessment of the current role of the criminal justice system (as ignorant of the needs of victims of crime). Yet unlike in earlier social work texts, that role is not fundamentally called into question or denounced as unjust (see examples 3.1, 3.2, 3.4 and 3.5). On the contrary: just like the criminal justice system and the police, social work too is now fighting youth crime. The criminal justice system is only criticised here for ignoring redress for victims, which has the advantage of allowing social work to fill that gap. Social work can thus operate in harmony with the criminal justice system and complements the latter's work. It is able to do so thanks to a re-categorisation of offenders as "offenders"; their previous categorisation as victims of social problems is replaced by a categorisation that is in keeping with categorisations by the public and the criminal justice system. Social work has in other words become a 'legitimate' partner in the cooperative fight against youth crime.

In this categorisation of offenders, they are linked to the category-bound activity of producing suffering, and they are now also linked to the moral characteristic of having to take responsibility for that suffering. This interpretation was already widespread within the police, which is hardly surprising: it is a core principle of criminal law that offenders only become 'deserving of punishment' when they are responsible for their actions. In the case of youth crime, this attribution of personal responsibility to individual offenders appears to have become increasingly relevant in recent years (e.g. Cavadino/Dignan 2006; Moore/Hirai 2014; Phoenix/Kelly 2013). In German social work, the approach started to become established as outlined from around the mid-1990s.

As Ward and Kupchik (2009) note, a corresponding focus on accountability can mean different things. It can imply a call for rehabilitation or, in the predominant trend in recent years, it can represent a punitive approach. The corpus of data analysed here reveals the growing importance for social work of the accountability of young offenders. They were now, according to a social work text from the corpus, "themselves (. . .) responsible" (Morath/Reck 2002, 316) for delinquency and for the success or failure of intervention. In line with Ward and Kupchik, such an ascription was, however, not associated per se with a desire for a tougher approach. There is an important social work tradition of focusing on supporting people and carefully seeking to recognise and develop their personal responsibility (Payne 2014, 243–270). This approach is not necessarily punitive but geared towards help. In the context of criminal law, however, it is easy to link personal responsibility to calls for 'tough action'. Social work also adapted to this trend, for from the mid-1990s on, it increasingly called not just for the personal responsibility of offenders to be recognised but also for restrictive steps to be taken against them.

e) Traditional and newfound severity

In the light of the police's authoritative understanding of measures against youth crime, a certain severity was always present, at least implicitly. It could also be advocated quite clearly and openly, as the following examples illustrate. The first takes us back to 1971, showing *the historical continuity* of these demands within police texts. The issue of severity will then be explored on the basis of two more recent examples from the police and social work.

In the older text, the author describes ways of tackling youth crime. He calls for comprehensive measures, which he illustrates using the example of a police station that has a night staff of eight. Two remain in the station and two go, in uniform, on patrol. Thanks to these last, "locals who are out on the streets at night and meet two policemen on the beat (. . .) feel safe and secure" (Stümper 1971, 396). Yet the policemen on the beat – like their two colleagues in the station – could do little to actually prevent crime. The same is not true for their four other colleagues, about whom the author writes as follows:

Example 3.9

1   The two plain clothes observers will have more of a preventive (and not just repressive) impact. It is
2   much easier for them to pinpoint and arrest an offender. A repressive success does not just
3   (potentially) act as a deterrent, but it also effectively takes offenders "out of circulation" for a while if
4   they are remanded in custody or indeed receive a custodial sentence. During that time at least, they do
5   not commit any criminal offences. We can simply note here as an objective fact that the considerable
6   reduction in the execution of custodial sentences resulting from statutory changes to remand and the
7   reform of criminal law is therefore removing not just repressive but also preventive options. – The last
8   two officers, who are in charge of a youth club, ensure – if we take a naive and idealistic view – that
9   the young people, who are often bored and at a loose end, are occupied and learn to occupy each other,
10   and therefore do not commit crimes. The last form of deployment would therefore seem the most
11   likely to succeed. (Stümper 1971, 396; police)

The text describes the relationships between the police and (potential or actual) offenders in terms of the effectiveness of police measures. How the police are organised has clear consequences; plain-clothes police officers are linked to a deterrent effect (line 3) and above all neutralisation (lines 3–5); the effect associated with police officers who are in charge of a youth club is, on the other hand, that of occupying young people and thus preventing crime (lines 9–10). The author does not require stories in the conventional sense of the word to justify his conclusions; in a nonstory, instead, he recounts his clear and direct view of the facts in which cause and effect are directly connected. Those facts ascribe varying crime prevention effects to a specific visibility and specific activities of police officers. Together with the four other police officers who are mentioned before the excerpt (two police officers for the organisation of the station and two police officers in uniform on patrol), the story is about comprehensive and effective crime prevention by the police. In this clearly organised arrangement, organisation, public reassurance, repression and preventive police work complement each other. Each of these activities is directed at a different target group: the organisation at the police itself; the uniformed patrol at law-abiding citizens; the plain-clothes officers repressively at delinquents; the youth club police officers preventively at not-yet-delinquents.

The category 'police' thus has four subcategories with subcategory-bound tasks, targets and effects. Overall, the police can implement all necessary actions for combating youth crime; as a category, it is associated with the characteristic of an effective fight against youth crime, and the four subcategories contribute to this fight with different skill sets. Criminal policy reform trends, on the other hand, upset the balance. It should be remembered here that the trend in criminal policy at this time was towards greater liberalisation (see Chapter 2). The author criticises this, for his story at its heart is proof of the need for repression: it seems necessary to take some offenders "'out of circulation'" (line 3). If this repressive police activity is limited – by a politically induced restriction on activities that the author defines as established subcategory-bound police practice – the police can no longer operate effectively. Intransigence is one of their core competencies.

The police can also take on social work activities. Stümper does not demand cooperation with social work, as police officers can supervise youth clubs at least well enough to prevent the respective young people from committing offences. This is in line with trends in other police texts, which in some cases accuse social work of being too reluctant to intervene (Dollinger et al. 2012a). Thanks to a clear structure and clearly defined range of competencies, the police appear able to respond to and prevent youth crime using both preventive and repressive measures.

Severity is described as necessary and competently employed by the police in the fight against youth crime. On this point, we can see a thematic continuity in police texts, as another example illustrates. Before the passage cited below, the author outlines the options open to non-police institutions for responding to youth crime committed by those under the age of criminal responsibility.

Example 3.10

1   *Case: A child below the age of criminal responsibility engages – professionally – in pickpocketing or*
2   *robbery or goes on the rampage with a gun*
3   This case obviously relates to a persistent or serious offender. Action from the competent authorities is
4   required here on the grounds of prevention and protection of the at-risk child alone, as well as to avoid
5   further offences. In such cases, custodial measures pursuant to section 42 subsection 5 SGB VIII
6   [German Social Code Book VIII; B.D.] are permitted, even in opposition to the will of the legal
7   guardians and if necessary also (initially) without a court order! (Ogrodowski 2008, 54; police)

The author starts by describing a "case" (line 1); in other words, he is qualifying the general as a specific case. He is also telling a nonstory, for he does not provide any details, any specifics of an offence or event or any further information on social relationships, for example. The case in lines 1 and 2 largely consists of information about the child and the offences committed by that child. For example, the author reports that the child is below the age of criminal responsibility, which under German law means under the age of 14 at the time of the offence. He also paints a picture of the child's criminality: the child is acting "professionally" (line 1), in other words repeatedly and with the objective of obtaining money. Types of offence are also given: theft, robbery and going "on the rampage with a gun" (line 2). The conjunction "or" (lines 1, 2) does not indicate an escalation of an individual case; the author is listing different types of offence committed by one ("A", line 1) child. As we are, according to the author, dealing with one individual case, it is irrelevant whether a child comes to the attention of the authorities as a result of thefts, robberies or by going on the rampage. In each instance, we have a specific type of child, namely a "persistent or serious offender" (line 3) with whom one of the three types of offence is associated. It is irrelevant which specific type of offence a child commits; for each of the types specified, a child is a "persistent" or "serious" offender and can be dealt with accordingly, and this means intervention "from the competent authorities is required" (lines 3–4).

As regards cooperation, the author writes that not the police but rather the "competent authorities" need to act – which alludes to social work, for the SGB VIII (lines 5–6) is a central piece of legislation for the German social work sector (Jordan et al. 2012; Rätz et al. 2014). Section 42 subsection 5 SGB VIII regulates *Inobhutnahme*, a serious measure that allows youth welfare services to remove a child from its family temporarily and place it e.g. in a social services care facility (Trenczek 2009). Irrespective of whether or not this is legally possible in the way described by the author, he is clearly calling on social work to make use of this option for "persistent or serious offender[s]". If a child is a "persistent or serious offender", which can be the case in light of a wide range of offences, such tough measures are possible. As the author emphasises – see the exclamation mark at the end (line 7) – such tough measures can be taken simply following a decision of the youth welfare services, i.e. even against the wishes of the parents and at least temporarily without a court order. The categorisation "persistent or serious offender" – in other words a category used in criminal law and crime policy (Walter 2003; see also Chapter 2) – legitimises tough social work measures, and the police call on social work to make use of those measures.

A last example of calls for severity refers directly to the social work side. Here, too, the category of "persistent offender" is associated with demands for a more restrictive approach. Over the course of the 1990s, social work became increasingly willing to deal with young offenders more restrictively than before and to confront them with the suffering of victims to reduce reoffending (Dollinger et al. 2012a). The following example shows a social work training method for violent offenders (Anti-Aggressiveness-Training; AAT). At the centre is the "hot seat": other participants and the social workers form a circle around a young person and confront him or her with negative assessments to try and make him or her change the way he or she thinks (Weidner/Kilb 2010).

Example 3.11

1   To us, a 'hot seat' is always successful when the participant is really pushed to a limit. On the question
2   of the victim in particular, it is important not to settle for too little too soon. The young person will
3   only find a way out of violence if he or she is able to feel genuine empathy with his or her victim. That
4   is why it is key on this point above all not to let up until a genuine breakthrough is evident. To achieve
5   that breakthrough, it is often necessary to put the young person in the HS [Hot Seat; B.D.] in such a
6   position of distress that he or she feels just as vulnerable, humiliated and helpless as his or her earlier
7   victims. Only then does the "penny drop", only then do participants transfer in their head the
8   helplessness they have experienced to how the victim must have felt. The participant breaking down in
9   tears at this point, as often happens, is a good signal for the group that they have now really got
10   through to him or her.
11   **Example:**
12   Kemal, a 15-year-old Turk, had to take part in AAT because – even before reaching the age of
13   criminal responsibility – he had over a long period extorted money from and beaten up many of his
14   fellow pupils. For a long time in the hot seat he simply grinned and appeared unmoved. This changed
15   when he was so intimidated – including with gestured slaps in the face – that he left in tears. A few
16   minutes later he returned and said "the way I behaved, that wasn't human; no human being behaves
17   like that". He had understood what he had done to his victims. (Morath/Reck 2002, 319; social work)

The passage begins with an evaluation: the training method described is presented as "successful" (line 1) under certain circumstances. At the centre of the description is a specific categorisation of offenders or training course participants in relation to victims and the people running the course: offenders are categorised as people whose resistance must be broken. They are to be "pushed to a limit" (line 1). Various different issues are raised to this end, as the "question of the victim" (lines 1–2) is not the only one but is presented as key. The criterion for success in working on this question is that the offender is turned into a victim (lines 5–7). Victims are people who feel "vulnerable, humiliated and helpless" (line 6) as a result of an offender's actions. The group reverses these roles by making offenders victims of the group and forcing this victim experience on them.

Where offenders in earlier social work texts were victims of society (see examples 3.2 and 3.4) and social work was itself a victim of society in its desperate fight for these offender–victims (see example 3.1), the relation between the various parties has now changed. Offenders are once again victims, but victims now purposefully created by social work, and social work is working – as it were cooperatively – with other institutions to prevent reoffending.

The training method appears successful when offenders are systematically degraded and turned into victims. Empathy or solidarity with the young people (as offenders) does not appear necessary here; on the contrary, the author argues in favour of intransigence: you cannot stop the humiliation until you are sure as a professional that the young person genuinely feels just as humiliated "as his or her earlier victims" (lines 6–7). Social work is thus deliberately repeating the result of a crime, now directed against the offender, to break that offender's alleged psychological resistance. How the training session progresses or develops offers a way of measuring its success: a participant "breaking down in tears" (line 8) appears to be a good indicator that the goal has been achieved.

The example given in the text is supposed to offer further legitimisation for this view. It shows how tough and confrontational the social workers are as they employ actions including "gestured slaps in the face" (line 15) to turn the offender into a victim. Here, too, tears are a clear sign that the intended change of heart has taken place: the young offender appears to have become first a victim and then repentant. Through intransigent severity, social work appears to have initiated a sudden conversion that blurs the categorical boundaries: although Kemal has been a persistent offender "over a long period" (line 13), he suddenly becomes a victim, a category which he then leaves by showing remorse. He describes himself in his earlier offender role as "no human being" (line 16) and in so doing appears to prove his awakening and moral renewal. He is transformed from a non-human (offender) to a humiliated human being (victim) and then to a new, remorseful person who recognises his own failings (a successful participant in the training course).

Where social work had previously sharply criticised the criminal justice system for not taking offenders seriously as people and reducing them to the status of "subhuman" (see example 3.5), this reduction is now evident here too, albeit in different circumstances and with a varying thrust. Here, it is initiated by social work and implemented by the young person himself, who retrospectively qualifies himself as unworthy of the term human and has already left this category by the end of the story. A tough approach and confrontation by social work appear to have enabled this move. The question of why Kemal became a persistent offender is as irrelevant here as criticism of society or the police. This type of social work has departed from those earlier positions to instead 'effectively' employ tough tools to deal with offenders. Social work here is successful because it is repressive.

The text is an exception in the very restrictive approach that it demonstrates. It was unusual for social workers to go so far as to systematically humiliate young people and even employ suggestions of physical violence against them. What is characteristic of the discourse, however, is that a tough approach and confrontation are favoured and earlier socially critical social work positions are called into question. Criticism of society and empathetic, client-centred approaches did in part continue within social work. Yet the social criticism was overall reduced or suspended; there was a greater focus on the use of effective methods and preventive measures, and certain professionals called for tough action against offenders and for offenders to be confronted with victims' suffering. In the context of the social work discourse, this was a marked change and resembles earlier demands by police and politicians for repressive actions against 'persistent offenders' (Dollinger et al. 2015b, c). Social work was thus joining the fight against offenders with a clear punitive focus.

Conclusion

In the four decades after 1970, there occurred significant changes, particularly in the social work sector. In the 1970s and 1980s, social work clearly criticised society and its institutions, including the criminal justice system and the police and indeed also social work itself for its role in work with juvenile delinquents. Social work appeared to be in a similar situation to that of the young offenders: rejected by society and lacking realistic options or opportunities to improve its position. Real opportunities to help could only come from structural reforms, but those were a question for politics and not social work. Social work thus tended to categorise itself, like offenders, as a helpless victim of circumstance. Where a rehabilitative approach was nonetheless to be taken to individual delinquents, this required a particular justification. The heyday of "penal welfarism" referred to at the start of this chapter was, in the view of social work, therefore anything but a golden age (Dollinger et al. 2012b). It was narrated as a time of repression that did not take social work positions seriously (even when these were advocated in politics at that time; see Chapter 2).

The police did in some respects share this criticism of society. For the police, too, youth crime was often a question of social problems. However, unlike that of social work, the police's criticism related primarily to cultural challenges that could be addressed with targeted interpersonal measures rather than to structural problems requiring political solutions. The police voiced much less self-criticism on this point than social work. Where social work frequently called itself and its control function into question, social control was for the police not a problem but in fact necessary to contain problems of criminality: delinquents needed supervision and a firm hand. If social work did not want to cooperate with the police to achieve this – and it generally did not in the 1970s and 1980s – this attitude was met with criticism from the police.

The relevant categorisations and self-positionings of the two professions subsequently changed. The police increasingly focused on cooperative prevention under their management and targeted action against 'persistent offenders'; they also advocated *Diversion* (not prosecuting, or the discontinuation of formal proceedings) for less serious offences (Dollinger et al. 2012a, 82–92). This did not represent a fundamental shift from their earlier positions. Social work, on the other hand, in some cases entirely reversed its categorisations of offenders and victims, taking a new position in relation to delinquents, victims and the police or the criminal justice system. In particular, it came to regard offenders as personalised offenders, in other words as people responsible for their actions who caused harm to others and were therefore no longer to be seen as 'people' but as 'offenders' (and treated restrictively as such). Victims of crimes also emerged as important figures in this context. Where offenders had once been victims of society, victims were now a group in their own right that deserved support from social work; a new client group. This stance was no longer that far removed from police and criminal justice system positions. Cooperating with the police, social work could now fight youth crime and seek to contain its negative consequences. This was a substantial departure from earlier social work narratives. The narratives and categories now dominant were broadly that of the police (Frehsee 2010). They had largely been adopted by social work, as offenders were now to be addressed directly and victims protected. From the 1990s, these objectives could be pursued cooperatively. In some cases, this even involved drastic measures that were now also taken by social work against 'persistent offenders'.

An increasingly tougher approach to youth crime, as reconstructed for politics in Chapter 2, was therefore not a development imposed on social work from the outside. In fact, social work itself established positions closer to those of the police and to the newly emerging political consensus on tougher action on youth crime. Had change been forced on social work by external actors (as social work had complained in the decades before the 1990s), social work would probably have taken issue with it and set out alternative demands, but the reverse is actually true. From the 1990s, social work increasingly categorised offenders as offenders threatening society rather than as victims of society. Delinquency was now to be addressed in partnership with the police and the criminal justice system by engaging in methodical, preventive and cooperative action directed at offenders. The well-being of the individual delinquent was not irrelevant, but it was only one optional focus alongside the central point of reference, the safety of society. From the 1990s on, social work not only abandoned former models of work on youth crime but also adopted police approaches. This transformation allowed social work to draw directly on narratives that had also become hegemonic in politics. These narratives made youth crime a threat to the social.

Notes

1 Nor is it relevant here whether the two groups examined in more detail below, the police and social work, should be termed 'occupations' or, as a subset (Leidner 2010, 421), more specifically as 'professions'. I prefer the term profession solely in favour of a consistent terminology.

2 This project of persuasion would surely be affected by a (possible) crisis of the professions. Yet, persuasion represents an *essential* task for professions which is indispensable to fulfil if they are to be equipped with the authority and discretion to deal with social problems.

3 The police force in Germany is bound by the duty to uphold the law, the "*Legalitätsprinzip*" by which it has no choice but to investigate wherever a crime is suspected. A decision not to punish a crime can be taken by other bodies such as the public prosecution service, but not by the police.

4 Titles of the police magazines: *Deutsche Polizei, Der Kriminalist, Bereitschaftspolizei heute* and *Kriminalistik*; titles of the social work magazines: *Sozialmagazin, Archiv für Wissenschaft und Praxis der sozialen Arbeit, Pädagogik extra/Sozialarbeit* (later *Extra Sozialarbeit*, then *Sozial Extra*), *Blätter der Wohlfahrtspflege, Theorie und Praxis der Sozialen Arbeit* and *Bewährungshilfe*. A description of the magazines can be found in Dollinger et al. (2012a, 33–37).

5 Similar to the political debates in Chapter 2, each article was first examined for specific rhetorical devices (symbols, metaphors, etc.; see Dollinger/Urban 2012). The results of this first analysis form the basis of the analysis below. I used the former findings to select relevant texts and re-analyse them according to the principles described in Chapter 1.2. For results of this first analysis see e.g. Dollinger et al. (2013, 2015b, c).

6 At the same time, the welfare state in Germany was still under construction. It was not until the mid-1970s that symptoms of a crisis were diagnosed in that construction process and gradually became significant in the provision of welfarist services (Doering-Manteuffel/ Raphael 2012, 47–48; Wehler 2008, 265–266). In the field of youth criminal policy, welfarist approaches were – as discussed in Chapter 2 – still broadly supported until the mid-1990s (see also Lampe 2016). Social workers could therefore still assume, despite their fundamental criticism, that jobs and resources would not be permanently reduced – a situation that was later to change. Prior to this change, the self-critical narratives placed social work in a "penal welfarism" context, but only insofar as penal welfarism is defined in socio*political terms* and not insofar as it is conceived of as socio*educational* and requiring *interpersonal* action. What social work aspired to motivate was radical social change, not support for individuals.

7 "FU" refers to a German university, the *Freie Universität Berlin*.

8 It should be noted that the probation service in Germany has a strong social work footing (Kawamura-Reindl 2018).

9 A "standardised relational pair" is two categories grouped together with specific interrelated characteristics or associations. These can be mutual rights and obligations (Silverman 1998, 82) or, as in the very particular case of offenders and victims, specific forms of (non-)agency and (lacking) guilt/responsibility.

4   Being a delinquent youth

Young defendants recounting their cases

There are similarities in the previous analyses: we can see comparable trends in the political and professional narratives. There are narratives of benevolent support and of severity, which involve different categorisations and dominate at different times. Each type of narrative explains and evaluates delinquency differently and demands different countermeasures. In recent years, more emphasis has been placed on restrictive measures in both political and professional narratives. The next key step is now to reconstruct the extent to which narratives observed so far are also relevant to the people at the centre of narratives on youth crime: the (alleged) offenders.[1] This chapter *uses interviews with defendants to reconstruct their narratives*. Its central question is how the defendants portray themselves and 'their' offences. It is to be expected that offenders will use narratives that are also relevant to other persons and institutions when presenting their actions and portraying themselves. It would be a mistake to see offender narratives as purely personal, isolated accounts. We should recognise that offenders are part of a culture. When presenting offences, they need to reference culturally available interpretations of crime. They are able to do so because narratives on crime are broadly culturally established 'interpretation packages' that can be used by all individuals and modified for their purposes. The following pages now reconstruct in detail how offenders do so, i.e. which narratives they use to describe themselves and the acts of which they stand accused.

As in the preceding chapters, preliminary remarks can be useful. In principle, offenders have often been 'forgotten' by criminology as far as their own views and narratives are concerned. In the context of criminal investigation and criminal law, the accounts of a party charged with an offence are of key interest, but generally only with a narrow focus on resolving a case and establishing the truth of individual narratives. Individual narratives are similarly of little interest in 'classic' criminology, which often bases its work on statistical factors that (allegedly) define people's thoughts and actions. People thus tend to become "crash test dummies" (Case/Haines 2009, 25) whose own views are largely irrelevant to an analysis of influencing factors. As already described in 1.2, a limitation also applies to a large extent to 'critical' criminology, in the context of which individual narratives have tended to be (more or less) disregarded

(Presser 2016). Despite its interest in the social construction of what is a contingent reality of crime (Lilly et al. 2011, 229), the primary focus of critical positions is on structural conditions that damage people or cause processes of criminalisation. A genuine interest in individual narratives is therefore secondary, and those narratives are largely not taken seriously in themselves. A few schools of criminology, in particular the Chicago School, were interested in narratives and in some cases placed them at the centre of their analyses (Bennett 1981). However, narrative studies in criminology remained an "exception" (Aspden/Hayward 2015, 236). Recently, though, there has been a growing interest. For example, research has found how offenders understand 'their' criminality in the context of possible desistance processes, i.e. focusing on the chance of a future without reoffending (Maruna 2001; Rajah et al. 2014). Linguistic practices used by prisoners to describe and explain their actions have also been reconstructed in detail (O'Connor 2000, 2015). Individual types of offences such as drug use and drug dealing (Sandberg 2009; Dickinson/Wright 2017), violence (Andersson 2008; Toch 1993; Presser 2008; from the victim's perspective Meyer 2016) and sex offences (Victor/Waldram 2015) have also been addressed in this context (for an overview, see Presser/Sandberg 2015b). These and other examples demonstrate that interest in individual narratives in criminology has recently grown. This chapter draws on this trend. At the heart of the analysis are narratives of young defendants who were interviewed in the context of their trial.

In interviews, narratives are tailored to the situation and to the interviewer. They are interactive performances as those involved adapt to each other as an audience; this also means adapting to people who might later hear or read the interview (Atkinson/Delamont 2006, 167; Clifton/Van De Mieroop 2016, 8). This interactive orientation applies to all social situations, including trials. Here in particular, the narratives and self-presentation of the parties addressed depend greatly on context: the narrators are largely being addressed as (potential) offenders and portray themselves accordingly.

Whether or not someone has 'really' acted criminally is irrelevant to this study (see also Sandberg 2010); what is of interest is that person's self-presentation with regard to a trial. It can be assumed that young defendants often do not 'really' understand the role of judges or public prosecutors in detail and the exact structure of a trial (Miner-Romanoff 2014; Redding/Fuller 2004; Rajack-Talley et. al. 2005). According to Butler (2011, 111), young defendants often display "naiveté and immaturity" in court even in the face of a potentially tough sentence, because they do not understand proceedings. Nonetheless and irrespective of what is probably a usually limited legal competence, they still develop narratives that present them as a specific category of person (or offender). Institutions expect certain types of narrative (Gubrium/Holstein 2009; Polletta et al. 2011), and people draw on these perceived or anticipated institutional expectations. Criminal proceedings are a very particular type of institutional procedure and have a particularly significant influence on narratives (Arnauld/Martini 2015; De Fina/Georgakopoulou 2012, 131–135; Ewick/

Silbey 1995; Olson 2014; Scheppele 1994; see also Brooks/Gewirtz 1996). Communication is structured accordingly (Atkinson/Drew 1979; Komter 2014; Licoppe 2015).

This chapter analyses primarily not communication during court proceedings but the narratives of defendants before and afterwards. The particular situation of a trial leads the narrators – possibly influenced by their lawyer and other (in-)formal advisors – to employ what they see as a suitable form of self-presentation to achieve a positive judgment for them (Dollinger/Fröschle 2017). The corresponding form of strategic narrative is not to be understood primarily as intrapsychic and intentional; it is an interactive performance that only makes sense within the particular context and in the light of specific expectations (Heritage 1990/91). That context and those expectations are in this case not just the interview situation, but the trial as an exceptional event before or after the interview.

4.1 Interviews with defendants

a) Context

German youth criminal law affects the narratives of young defendants in the context of a trial from two different angles. On the one hand, the young defendants are in court charged with an offence (or multiple offences). The formal circumstances of an offence and any criminal antecedents are key criteria in a legal decision (Albrecht 2010, 224–226). On the other hand, the court also judges the personality of the defendant. The demand for rehabilitation – or in Germany 'education' ('*Erziehung*') – is associated with a strong focus on the person of the delinquent, which is why the German Youth Courts Law (JGG) is referred to as "*Täterstrafrecht*" (criminal law based on the person of the offender; Laubenthal et al. 2015, 2). Legal consequences or sanctions are supposed to be tailored to the offender's specific personality to make reoffending unlikely. A defendant's need for support must be determined during the trial so that punishment is not the main or not the only aspect of a judgment. Instead, the judgment and legal consequence(s) are targeted at prevention and rehabilitation in the offender's particular case (Ostendorf 2013, 30–34). Despite the obvious particular self-portrayal of defendants in a trial, its aim must therefore be to *obtain authentic information about the person of the defendant.* This information can be based on the defendant's own statements and/or on assessments of other people who know or can render an expert opinion on him or her (Dollinger/Fröschle 2017; Komter 1998).

Against this background, a trial presents a revealing starting point for research: narratives from defendants are highly significant in a trial, are assessed by the court and can potentially lead to tough sanctions (Arnauld/Martini 2015). The following analyses seek to show how young defendants position themselves in this complex situation, in which they face the challenge to narrate 'their' offence(s) and themselves.

b) Data

The data used in this chapter was collected in 2016 in three stages.

- The *first stage* was a qualitative interview with youths or young adults who were about to stand trial. The purpose of this interview was to get to know the young people, and in particular how they saw themselves, their offences and the other people and institutions with whom they had come into contact in the context of crime. They were also asked about their family, friends and expectations of the upcoming trial.
- The *second stage* was an observation of the trial. The main purpose here was to reconstruct the interaction between the professionals involved and the defendant, and a key focus was on the defendant's self-portrayal.
- The *third stage* was a second qualitative interview with the defendant shortly after the trial. This interview was used primarily to reconstruct the defendant's experience of the proceedings. The defendants were asked to give their assessment of the proceedings overall, of the actors involved and of the judgment.

Both interviews were transcribed in full and extensive field reports were drawn up for the observation. The data was first evaluated using computer-assisted coding, which inductively assigned code to content on the basis of the material. This method identified key sections of the interviews in which interviewees gave important narratives on themselves, other people, their understanding of crime and the institutional approach to dealing with crime. These sections were then evaluated in more detail drawing on the principles described in Chapter 1.

The study focused on changing categorisations over time.[2] The basic idea was to establish (possible) transformations in the defendants' narrative self-categorisation and categorisation of others before and after their trial (Dollinger/ Fröschle 2017). The time frame of the data (a few days, weeks or months before and after a trial) differs significantly from the data used in Chapters 2 and 3 (with a time frame from 1970 to 2009/2012). I will therefore not concentrate on actual changes of the defendants' categorisations. Instead, this chapter presents a cross-section of central narratives used by the interviewees in the social situation of the interview to relate their history and their offences.

A total of 15 men between the ages of 15 and 21 were studied; all had been under 21 at the time of their offences and were standing trial under the German Youth Courts Law. The offences varied widely and included violent offences, drug offences, sex offences, theft, robbery, driving without a licence and fare-dodging. Considerable difficulties were experienced in gaining access to the defendants. Contact was made through the youth courts assistance service (*Jugendgerichtshilfe*), social work facilities working to avoid detention on remand (*Untersuchungshaftvermeidung*), district and regional courts and remand and youth detention facilities. It was finally possible to recruit the 15 people and convince them to take part using a voucher as a small incentive. One key selection criterion was that the persons in question were facing a non-suspended youth custody sentence, i.e. imprisonment. This criterion was set to ensure that the potential sanctions were significant for the interviewees; that the cases did not simply involve minor offences or might be eligible for *Diversion* (a decision not to prosecute, or the discontinuation of proceedings). Most of the interviewees were not just in court for one single offence; they had already faced a range of charges and had several years' experience of the police and criminal justice system. The majority had already gone through a number of court proceedings and experienced a range of sanctions.

4.2 Principles of penal welfarism and the struggle for mild punishment

The following analyses are not aimed at providing a description of individuals. They look instead at narratives that were used to characterise oneself, other persons and offences. The main difference is that varying and indeed contradictory narratives can be used for one and the same individual, as narratives are diverse and context-dependent. This is hardly acknowledged in biographical research, for example, which ultimately assumes that there is *one* person to portray (see Atkinson/Delamont 2006; Bamberg 2004, 356).[3] Such a presupposition is not necessary here. The focus is on narratives in the face of a potential prison sentence, not on the reconstruction of biographies.

One important finding is the 'naturalisation' of punishment. The interviewees did not question the fact that crimes had to be followed by institutional interventions. A second is that 'sad stories' served a decisive function in the narratives to achieve a mild sentence. Both reflect fundamental principles of penal welfarism: the defendants recognise that punishment is necessary; however, that punishment is to be lenient and allow for the fact that the interviewees bear no or little responsibility for the offences in question. External causes have led almost automatically to a criminal career. In accordance with principles of penal welfarism, crime is a fact for which there must be consequences that are determined in a fair trial based on the rule of law; those consequences are to be adapted to the problems of the individual offenders. Offenders are to benefit from interventions and be guided to a position of conformity with support tailored to them. Punishment can therefore take on a friendly guise as a social and supportive intervention. These core principles of penal welfarism are reproduced in the narratives of the interviewees.

a) Self-evident criminal careers and 'natural' punishment

The interviewees repeatedly argued that they did not deserve a tough sentence. However, they did not dispute that punishment is in itself necessary following crime, including in their case. A telling example is the following story by a young adult aged 21 who had already been imprisoned for earlier offences. Just before the passage cited, he says he did not receive support from the youth courts assistance service. The reason he gives is that "I never really wanted to be helped either, let's put it like that" (RV, Int 1, line 901). He is then asked about his court-appointed defence counsel, and responds simply that he "should do his job" (RV, Int 1, line 908). The interviewer goes on to ask the young man about the offence at the centre of the upcoming trial:[4]

Example 4.1

1   I: Yes. So tell me, why- what's the trial coming up actually about. It's scheduled for November, I
2   think, or two hearings, that's what you said, right?
3   RV: Mmm.
4   I: Em, so what are they about? I mean, what happened and how is it that you em-
5   RV: Yeah, I don't want to say because eh (.) yeah, if I'm honest, because I would like- I mean (.) if,
6   no, I won't, cos' it's not come to court yet and I've not been done hard for it yet and so at the moment
7   I'm (.).
8   I: Okay. You don't have to talk about it-
9   RV: Yes.
10   I: But of course I'd be interested em (..) are you afraid at all about what might happen? I mean, why
11   don't you tell me? (4)
12   RV: I'm afraid of going down for a long time.
13   I: You're really afraid?
14   RV: Mm-hm (*affirmative*).
15   I: Oh damn (.) but you've come to regret things a bit now, haven't you? (..)
16   RV: Yeah, sure, but (4) hey, if I'm honest, I think it's all fuckin' great, yeah. You've got, if I think
17   about it, get up in the morning, work, blablabla and the same all day every day, then [untranslatable
18   fragment] me I've got variety, I (.) I found it fuckin' great, find it great, it is great, that's it, (.), right?
19   Life, like that, but it's got to stop some time, right? Anyway and (.) actually you never really want to
20   stop.
21   I: Mmm.
22   RV: Taste it once, you come back for more.[5] That's the way it is.
23   I: Mmm.
24   RV: [untranslatable fragment]- I can't say any more. It's like that. [RV, Int. 1, lines 907–944]

The start of the interview is revealingly difficult. With the first turn (lines 2–3), RV does not take on the speaker position offered to him, so the interviewer starts anew. Once again, RV does not respond to the actual question. Such a reaction is socially dispreferred; a question is normally followed by a meaningful answer (Sacks et al. 1974). RV acknowledges this expectation, for he immediately connects his refusal with an explanation ("because", line 5): he justifies his position on the interviewer's question. As the reason for his unexpected response, he attributes to himself a characteristic: he qualifies himself as "honest" (line 5), a trait that is socially preferred. In an interview, the person interviewed is expected not to lie but to be honest. A first, socially undesirable reaction is thus being more or less neutralised with a later hesitant ("I mean (.) if, no", lines 5–6) self-presentation, but one presented as authentic and with positive connotations.

This start illustrates the dilemma of strategic communication and (in-) authenticity in the context of a trial. It is as if the judge is present at the interview, for RV purposefully withholds information that has "not come to court yet" (line 6). He communicates that he sees the interview as an arena in which something could come to light that might later work to his disadvantage. For him, there are two aspects to consider: responding to questions in the interview and at the same time focusing on the upcoming trial, in whose outcome he has a huge interest. He chooses to focus on the trial, while seeking to communicate a positive personality trait. In doing so, he qualifies the trial as something negative that is to come: he expects to be "done hard for it" (line 6) (in the German original to get a "*Kelle*", i.e. a tough sentence). Such a sentence appears beyond doubt, as he tells the interviewer that he has "not been done hard for it *yet*" (line 6; B.D.'s italics): he does not mention the possibility of escaping sanctions.

Alternative forms of self-presentation would be conceivable in RV's situation. For example, he could argue that the trial will finally give him the chance to show remorse, or he could present himself as a young person with problems whose need for help will hopefully be recognised. He could also set himself up as an 'average' man who is at a loss to understand why he has been charged, as he has done nothing or hardly anything wrong. By their very absence, these and other alternatives illustrate the particular identity category RV narratively gives himself. It is that of a criminal who is shortly to be punished. As a consequence, he is careful about what information he reveals – an interactive practice similar to the information control by a stigmatisable person described by Goffman (1963). Such a control makes sense if a person assumes s/he has a stigma that others could discover and reveal, in this case 'really' being a criminal deserving of punishment (or at least very probably being defined as one). RV consequently assesses the trial as a threat and deals accordingly with the interview: it is better to be (more or less) impolite during the interview (and to mitigate this with a socially acceptable explanation, namely that he is "honest") in order to be sure not to incriminate himself further for the future trial. He reinforces this division into a time before and after the trial – and thus puts his rudeness in the present social situation of the interview into perspective – by presenting his current non-cooperation in the interview as temporary ("not [...] yet", line 6; "not been done [...] yet", line 6; "at the moment", line 6). The message is that he will be able to talk freely again when the hearing is over, but that the risk of self-incrimination through the interview temporarily prevents him from opening up. The categorisation that RV is recounting for himself is therefore one of a delinquent who has not yet received his – deserved – punishment.

The interviewer shows understanding (line 8) and changes the subject to the question of emotionality, and more precisely fear (line 10), which RV then confirms. "Regret" (line 15) ultimately introduces a new issue. RV's reaction relates being "afraid" to the upcoming judgment, while he links "regret" to his acts. Here, the 'naturalisation' of punishment comes into play. It becomes clear when RV paints a picture of a delinquent enjoying his career who is forcibly stopped by punishment. In response to the interviewer's question, he hesitates: after a relatively long pause lasting four seconds (line 16), he then drops his cautious approach. Following another appeal to his honesty, he provides further specifics of his self-categorisation as an offender. That category does not contradict the category of the criminal shortly to be punished, but instead provides that criminal with a motive: fun. RV clearly finds "delight in deviance" (Katz 1988, 312; see also Maruna 2001, 82), in what is for him an exciting activity. While Katz (1988, 312) describes being "stunned by [delinquents'] shame" when they are "under arrest", this is not the case with RV – who is already in prison for earlier offences at the time of the interview. In fact, he clearly recounts that delinquency not only used to but in fact still does excite him. He gives a list that refers to three different times – "I found it fuckin' great, find it great, it is great" (line 18) – and this progressively shows his criminal inclination more and more strikingly. "I found it fuckin' great" would still fit with an alternative self-categorisation in which he describes himself as remorseful, for example, as it provides a motive for *previous* delinquency. With "find it great", however, he is presenting himself as just as interested in crime *in the present* as he was in the past, and thus defining himself as deviant. He emphasises this image with "it is great", a general statement that crime is fundamentally fun, and in so doing gives himself a potential motive for crime *in the future* as well: it is in itself exciting. As another interviewee puts it, it is specifically the relatively serious offences above all that are "FUCKIN' great" (BK, Int. 1, 182).

RV does not categorise himself as a repentant sinner who was once stupid or led astray but has now come to his senses and 'learned his lesson'. Presser (2008, 14) talks in this context of a narrative of "reform" as a "return to moral decency" (see section b) below). The interviewer offers him such a categorisation by talking about "regret" (line 15). RV at first briefly agrees, but he goes on to contradict ("but", line 16). He therefore rejects that categorisation that is common and to be expected in the context of a trial, instead categorising himself as a 'for-kicks criminal' by claiming to enjoy engaging in crime. By rejecting the proffered 'repentant sinner' category, he puts himself in the position of a (potentially) lifelong delinquent, a target of preference in penal discourses (see Chapter 2). Lifelong delinquents are young people who repeatedly harm others for no 'forgivable' reason, e.g. because they enjoy it or find it exciting. With the saying "Taste it once, you come back for more" (line 22), RV describes his delinquency as a type of automatism fuelled by fun: delinquency follows from delinquency (see also O'Connor 2000, 54). Using a saying makes further justification for criminal action appear unnecessary, for sayings appeal to common sense and generalise a specific situation (Silverman 1998, 96). Based on the common sense expressed in the saying, RV rejects a conventional moral standard of remorse; this standard and its associated lifestyle appear boring ("the same all day", line 17), while his life as a delinquent offers "variety" (line 18).

It is atypical for the interviews that RV does not show remorse, but similar to the other interviewees he contrasts his continuous offences with the fact that you cannot always be a criminal ("but it's got to stop some time", line 19). This is presented as a given with no further justification. It appears self-evident, even though the need for "it" to "stop" is in opposition to his narrative of ongoing criminal excitement. Bodies that make it "stop", in other words the police and criminal justice system, are thus institutions that 'naturally' confront him and threaten him with sanctions. He does not criticise or question these bodies or the respective professionals' work; he presents it as a necessity, for "it's *got* to stop" (B.D.'s italics). Careers in crime must therefore logically end. In the coda (line 24), this narrative of a 'for-kicks criminal' at odds with the inescapable end of a criminal career is presented as a fact and further details appear unnecessary.

A comparison with another example is insightful. It is also unusual but, concerning remorse, more in line with expectations than RV's narrative. It is on the one hand unusual because unlike the other interviewees, the young person in question, KL, describes his life as largely free from problems. Most of the others, including RV, report numerous difficulties in their personal histories. On the other hand, KL's story is not an unexpected one before a trial as he employs the category 'repentant criminal' (or 'sinner'). Based on that categorisation, he also describes a 'naturalisation' of punishment, as the following excerpt shows. Before the passage cited, KL has described the commission of a range of precisely planned offences committed with friends. According to KL, the police said that they would not have discovered him; it was his mother who informed the police of his involvement in crime after finding money and a weapon in his room. At the time of the interview, KL stood charged with multiple property and violent offences, some involving the use of a weapon.

Example 4.2

1   KL: Huh- and then- then I thought (.): If my mother hadn't done that, we might have I mean I'd
2   maybe- maybe we'd (.) I'd maybe have still been at home, see?
3   I: Mmm.
4   KL: But now I also reckon I mean I'll say it myself: actually I'm glad she did that, because who
5   knows, maybe we'd have said after like: come on, that's not enough or something or we'd have been
6   like on a roll: come on let's do some more.
7   I: Mmm.
8   KL: And then suddenly T. [*name of a co-offender*] says like, suddenly he says: come on, we're doing a
9   bank. Let's rob a bank, somewhere quiet where there's no one around (.) or, I dunno, let's go to a
10   casino. I mean like totally eh totally-
11   I: Yes.
12   KL: stupid stuff (.) and then- a casino or something, that's like no way, really, if you- I mean, how're
13   you supposed to nick something and how many security guys and stuff but we'd have been on a roll:
14   Yeah come on we'd think, what're they gonna do, they won't get us anyway Then we'd just have gone
15   into that casino (.) then they'd have caught him or something and then he'd have been screwed and all
16   the rest of us and all. Right and then with the casino hold-up, we'd all have been done for a few years,
17   four years or three years easy.
18   I: Mmm.
19   KL: Right, and so I reckon now: this way I've at least a chance of a suspended sentence, right.
20   I: Yes, yes.
21   KL: So this way I've still got a chance to get out of the (.) out of the shit we did (.) if I'd like- My mum
22   wouldn't have done it, I don't think (.) if we'd like done something again or again and then we'd have
23   thought: come one, they'll never get us, we've done it so often before. We- we would have and
24   thought they- How're they gonna get us? We're too smart for them or something. Like the way you
25   think at that kind of moment, right?
26   I: Mmm.
27   KL: Yeah, but actually they always get you in the end.
28   I: Mmm.
29   KL: Doesn't matter how, they always get you (..) and so I'm really grateful to my mum that she did
30   that.
31   I: Mmm.
32   KL: I mean, who knows what else might've happened (..). [KL, Int. 1, lines 1467–1501]

The interview was held in a social work facility providing an alternative to remand. KL had previously received what in his view was an extremely tough sentence of several years' imprisonment. He was now appealing against this sentence in the upcoming hearing. The place category "at home" (line 2) is therefore a stark contrast to his current situation. This suggests a reproach to the mother, who was the author of his current, difficult situation (lines 1–2). Up to this point in the excerpt, he categorises himself as a criminal (or a member of a group of offenders, considering the plural "we", lines 1–2) who has been caught and sentenced following external intervention – a lifelong criminal who would likely have continued to offend had he not been stopped.

This changes with a re-categorisation using the adversative connectors "But now" (line 4), which introduce a significant break in the narrative. Where the mother had previously predominantly influenced the end of his career, his self-categorisation and activity status now change. Maruna (2001) talks here of a "rhetoric of redemption". One characteristic of that rhetoric is the presentation of an external influence as a key turning point in the narratives of delinquents who have been able to end their criminal careers. This influence is presented not simply as something from the outside, independent of the person of the offender, but as the trigger or revelation of an internal force within him or her (Maruna 2001, 96). That force makes the narrator active and visible in his or her own agency. In the example with KL, the shift introduced by "But now" reflects just such a development: a strong self that is able to become active thanks to the external influence of his mother. In line 4 alone, where "But now" appears, KL refers to himself five times in the German original ("ich" three times, "mir" and "selber").

RV and KL both – like most of those interviewed – suggest an automatism of repeat offences, RV with the phrase "fuckin' great" and KL with the "roll" (line 6). Both are working on the assumption that a criminal career develops following its own internal logic. The significance is not, however, the same in both cases, for unlike RV, KL demonstrates a shift towards remorse. Pushed by his mother, he is now *himself* "glad" (line 4) that the "roll" has been interrupted. He is thus categorising himself as now a reasonable person who is distancing himself from his earlier actions and experiences remorse. In his narrative, the previous identity he narrates differs from his current narrating identity (see also Brookman 2015, 220; Presser 2008, 63–64). Through his new identity, KL categorises himself as a 'repentant former criminal', and from *this* position he now paints the picture of the automatism that leads to ever more serious crime; this is, however, driven not by himself but by a fellow offender ("T.", line 8) who appears to have led KL into his career in crime (Dollinger/Fröschle 2017). This allows KL to portray an escalating criminal career, his own involvement in that career and what is from a current perspective a plausible disparagement of that activity, all at the same time. The 'repentant former criminal' can explain that his offences were "stupid stuff" (line 12) that are in "no way" (line 12) acceptable. Thanks to his mother and thanks to his own remorse, he now apparently has the "chance" (lines 19, 21) to change. The term "chance" itself once again suggests his agency: he himself now appears able to take his life in hand in a positive way. He can therefore agree with the moralist stance of his mother and the probable moral expectations of the legal professionals who will rule on his case in the trial, for they all, including himself, abhor his earlier actions.

This new narrative self-categorisation is associated with a condemnation of the previous 'lifelong criminal' in two ways: firstly because of the sanctions and the serious consequences for himself ("we'd all have been done for a few years, four years or three years easy", lines 16–17), and secondly on the grounds of the harm he would have caused to others ("who knows what else might've happened", line 32). He talks about this harm in depth and with great regret in both interviews. The first aspect is functional and the second moral. O'Connor (2000, 43) draws on the work of Charles Taylor to refer in this context to a "weak" and a "strong evaluator". The former relates to consequences and the latter demonstrates a person capable of moral reflection. RV's narrative and KL's functional focus on his career in crime are weak evaluations, while KL's moralising is a strong one. The latter evaluation may be an attempt to appear particularly remorseful in court in order to achieve a lighter sentence – as the offender has *already* learned and accepted *for himself* that crime is bad. A tough sentence would thus be unnecessary, at least from a rehabilitation perspective.

The naturalisation of punishment becomes apparent in both cases; RV and KL both convey that punishment is inevitable. As another interviewee put it despite considering his own earlier sentences far too tough, "of course you have to be punished, right?" (BK, Int. 1, 1073). Another interviewee, after recounting positive experiences with drugs, admitted "It's crap, but (..) everyone has to be normal" (JH, Int. 1, 815); in other words, everyone must find their way to a 'normal' life despite the appeal of drugs or delinquency, and punishment is part of that process of normalisation. You are, according to KL, "actually [. . .] always" (line 27) caught. This is very similar to the statement from RV that "it's got to stop some time". RV's statement is, however, from the perspective of the self-categorised 'for-kicks criminal' who regrets that a criminal career cannot last. KL, on the other hand, naturalises punishment in his status as a 'repentant criminal', a moral individual who is glad to be able to leave crime behind him. RV is positioning himself in the world of delinquent values that remain important to him, and KL in the world of lawful moral standards. In both cases, however, punishment appears normal and unavoidable.

b) Sad stories

The analysis so far demonstrates the relevance of moral communication in the defendants' self-categorisation, particularly in the context of the upcoming sentencing. In one case (RV) this means rejecting, in the other (KL) acknowledging established moral values. Another important aspect is how the narrators present their own upbringing or childhood and personal history. This, even more, relates to the question of how the narrators portray individual agency or restrictions imposed upon it by external factors as they were growing up.

A key theme in the narratives is that of a "sad story". Goffman (1961/1991, 140) uses this term for the presentation of a life story as a collection of negative influences. If people's actions go against prevailing values and norms, those people could be well advised to argue that they were not themselves responsible; that they were the victims of "circumstances beyond their control" (Rajah et al. 2014, 292) that have led to their criminality. This narrative accepts that crime is something negative and admits involvement in it. However, it makes "excuses" (Scott/Lyman 1968, 47) to reject full responsibility for that involvement. In accordance with the prevailing moral standards enshrined in criminal law, the narrator categorises himself as a 'problem criminal' by admitting delinquent behaviour and associating crime with negative characteristics. At the same time, however, he suggests his options were limited by attributing to himself characteristics that, on a continuum from strong to no agency (Bamberg 2012, 106), clearly tend towards minimal agency. This allows the narrator to reject responsibility, as something beyond his control has led him to engage in delinquent behaviour. It also reduces a potential accusation of guilt, which is of central importance in an (upcoming) trial. The interviewees recounted three different versions of the sad story with regard to agency:

- **Suspension of personal responsibility:** Minimal to no agency in the light of difficult circumstances dominates this narrative. Those circumstances appear to have a continued impact in the present, meaning that crime is still attractive. The narrators do not fundamentally distance themselves from the corresponding motives.
- **Self-accusing suspension of personal responsibility:** Here too, negative circumstances are important in the explanation of criminality. However, the narrative presents retrospectively at least a degree of individual input associated with current remorse and self-accusation.
- **Deliverance from the sad story:** This sad story suspends personal responsibility but includes a change: narrators previously could not help their actions, but later or in the future they do have or anticipate that agency.

I describe the three versions below. They indicate different moral and agentic narrative focuses, although overlaps are quite possible.

Suspension of personal responsibility

IU provides a striking example of the first version. The interviews with him took place in a prison for young offenders. He had been charged with a range of property offences, driving without a licence and drug offences. The following passage is the start of the first interview.

Example 4.3

```
1    I: (. . .) Em and to start with I would of course first like to ask, (.) HOW did it come about that you are
2    here?
3    IU: (Clicking his tongue) (.) 'Cos of alcohol, right?
4    I: (Interrogatory) Hm?
5    IU: I started going downhill because of alcohol.
6    I: Mmm.
7    IU: (Thoughtfully) Yes. Lost my job. Ended up on the dole.
8    I: Mmm.
9    IU: Lost my family because of that.
10   I: /Mmm.\
11   IU: /Friends.\ (.) Yes. (..)
12   I: Start at the very beginning and tell me about it all.
13   IU: (Hesitantly) Fff:: yeah I started having problems in (.) two thousand and twelve.
14   I: Mmm.
15   IU: After my grandpa died.
16   I: Mmm.
17   IU: That just pulled the rug from under me. (.) And then alcohol, drugs too.
18   I: Mmm.
19   IU: The wrong friends. (.) And then more and more there was this KICK. (..) and more and more money,
20   see?
21   I: Mmm.
22   IU: Yeah, and more and more. (.) There were cars too. (.) No licence. (.) (Breathes in audibly) Yeah.
23   (. . .) (getting quieter) Then that was the way it was. [IU, Int. 1, lines 5–28]
```

IU has a clear response to the interviewer's question about the background to
his current imprisonment: "alcohol" (line 3). The interviewer and IU check
with each other that a serious problem with alcohol is really meant: IU first
seeks confirmation himself ("right?", line 3), and the interviewer confirms that
there is uncertainty on the meaning ("*hm?*", line 4). This interaction illustrates
the relevance of the interview situation and the presentation of plausible reasons for the clearly bad situation in which IU currently finds himself – in
a young offenders' prison. He does not describe offences or issues in early
childhood, but an issue that is associated in common sense with a life of problems, namely alcohol (dependence). With "started going downhill" (line 5) he
is indicating gradually escalating problems and, with the status of an alcoholic,
he is categorising himself as a 'problem offender': someone who was driven to
delinquency through circumstances (more or less) beyond his control. He is a
victim of alcohol.

   IU consolidates his categorisation as a victim in the passage in two ways apart
from the alcohol consumption: firstly, he is apparently facing a wide range of
problems. He did not just become an alcoholic, but alcohol also caused him
to lose his job and end up "on the dole" (line 7) (in the German original,
"Hartz IV" [basic unemployment benefit], a welfarist programme to cover his
basic needs). He also recounts that he has lost family and friends, key aspects
that, according to common sense, are important to any person. Secondly, he
explains that his excessive alcohol consumption is the result of a difficult experience, the death of his grandfather (line 15). As someone who has lost nearly
all social relationships and is not to blame for this – the death of his grandfather

had a traumatic impact that he tried to overcome through excessive drinking – IU represents more or less the classic case of a 'problem criminal'. He communicates problems and burdens that are 'textbook' for this category, and makes sure in the interview that the interviewer understands them in this way. What does not emerge are narratives underlining personal agency and responsibility. Only twice, through the personal pronoun "I" (lines 5, 13), does he himself become visible as an actor, and this in the context of being driven downhill (in German "abrutschen", literally 'slipping down') by outside forces. Everything else seems to happen automatically: problems and alcoholism lead directly to long-term and escalating criminality, which manifests itself in drugs, a search for a "KICK" (line 19), the possession of "more and more money" (line 19–20) and driving without a licence (line 22). IU is heavily involved in crime, but this is not his fault. The coda (line 23) closes the narrative; for IU, telling this problem story is sufficient explanation of why he is in prison.

IU's narratives throw up some contradictions. Later in the interview, for example, IU says that he has "always been a problem- a problem child" (IU, Int. 1, line 1048). This does not fit with the story of problems starting in "two thousand and twelve" (line 13) – when IU was a youth – for if the above story were true, he would have had a family, friends, work and the grandfather who was so important to him before he started going downhill. The reason "pulled the rug from under me" (line 17) indicates that a sudden event has led to a cascade and escalation of problems, which in that case could not always have been part of his life.

It is also worth mentioning a second point that affects the consistency (or the communicated authenticity) of the problem story: the fact that IU himself states that he made it up. On this point, here is a passage from the interview with IU after the trial, in which he has received a relatively tough sentence with which he is not happy and which he wants to appeal.

Example 4.4

1   I: (...) But this alcohol issue, I'd like to talk about that with you again, because it was- it was mentioned
2   AGAIN and again in the trial, right? Your lawyer raised it too. *(Smiling) You're grinning. Tell me about*
3   *it.*
4   IU: *(Smiling) Yeah because I'm grinning, huh? Because I- I know* what happened and is- what's a lie,
5   see?
6   I: Yes. (.)
7   IU: Yeah. And I know what I said, not to the court either, right?
8   I: Yes.
9   IU: The- this alcohol, this- it's complete rubbish.
10 I: Mmm.
11 IU: I- we – me and my lawyer- I'm not stupid, you know.
12 I: Yes.
13 IU: He says, he says right: "There's this-". When I came in. We met outside as well before, and he says
14 to me: (.) "You're going to [*name of a prison*]. That's definite. I'll keep representing you, but there's
15 this treatment section. If you want out of here, go in there and tell them some story". (.) Well and I
16 thought to myself, well I don't take drugs. You can see I don't take drugs.
17 I: Mmm.

18   IU: Well, then I've got an alcohol problem right. Recently I've drunk a lot of alcohol outside, downed
19   up to two bottles.
20   [. . .]
21   I: Yes, yes. Because- I'd have asked again, because this alcohol and drug thing was, I mean I think the
22   judge did say at the beginning something like "I've never heard anything about this", or something?
23   IU: Yes no, I've drunk alcohol for a long time, right?
24   I: Uh-huh.
25   IU: But not as excessively as it was described in court.
26   I: Yes.
27   IU: And about the drugs (.) Tried drugs once, right? My lawyer says: "Yes", where we took a break. Em
28   he says: "You- you take amphetamines too, right?" I say: *(shocked) "What?"* He says: "You take them,
29   it's obvious!" I say: "Oh right, yeah sure, I take them, right?" And he goes: "What'd you take? PEP?" I
30   go: "Yeah, PEP, PEP right". I knew what he wanted from me then. And we'll get that accepted in the
31   appeal and then we'll try *(swallows)* well for alcohol there are no provisions, no treatment provisions.
32   [IU, Int. 2, lines 900–961]

At the start of the first interview, IU categorised himself as an almost stereotypi-cal 'problem criminal'; this now changes. When asked by the interviewer about the alcohol problem that was also discussed at the trial, he now describes it as a strategy to have the court assess him as in need of help and thus treat him more leniently. The problem story was, at least as far as alcohol went, incorrect or "complete rubbish" (line 9). IU thus re-categorises himself from 'problem criminal' to 'manipulator'. We could therefore dismiss the problem story told in the first interview as a lie or pure strategy. IU was also described by the public prosecutor as a manipulator during the trial; the prosecutor said he had the "impression that he [IU] is relatively manipulative" and "a great actor" (field protocol). The impression of a contrived story that is also emphasised by the judge (line 22) may have contributed to IU receiving a relatively tough sen-tence. From the narrative perspective taken in this study, however, the question of whether IU *actually* has a difficult history and became a delinquent because of a series of pressures is irrelevant. It is not IU's 'real' biography that matters, but rather the impression he creates, and *every* sad story is ultimately an interac-tive achievement.

Nevertheless, a closer look at the relationship between 'staging' and the prob-lem story is revealing. Although in example 4.4 IU places the emphasis on staging, he sticks with a sad story that he recounts in *both* interviews. Even in the second interview, after he has admitted or recounted staging his alcohol and drug issues, he continues to describe himself as experiencing problems. When he explains that staging, in the excerpt above, he says that he has "drunk a lot of alcohol outside" (line 18). The question of whether he could be categorised as an addict is left open, but at other points in the interview he also describes himself as someone who drank a lot of alcohol and for that reason repeatedly came into conflict with those around him. He explains that an exaggerated account was presented at the court hearing (without explicitly naming him-self as the person giving that account; "not as excessively as it was described in court", line 25). However, he still recounts excessive alcohol consumption, thus reiterating the category-bound activity of a troubled person. In this regard, even when categorising himself as a 'manipulator', IU does not present himself as an independent actor. The actual actor is his lawyer, both for the alcohol story ("He says, he says right", line 13) and for the drugs story ("My lawyer says", line 27). IU is executing the lawyer's instructions. When the interviewer later asks how he sees himself, he responds that he "didn't get the support" (IU, Int. 2, 1178) he required and that he had needed someone who gave him "a kick in arse more often" (IU, Int. 2, 1183). Also later in the second interview, IU recounts that he had "caused a lot of problems" in his life and been in "lots of institutions" (IU, Int. 2, line 1058). He does not rate his future chances as particularly good; in light of the tough sentence, he anticipates further offences (IU, Int. 2, line 1271). These examples show a dominant narrative of problems: the narrator presents himself as someone who experienced difficulties early in life and has since been deeply involved in problems that are – like the strategic decisions of the lawyer – an external factor defining his behaviour. He is a 'problem criminal' whose issues have previously led to (and probably will continue to lead to future) offences. Individual responsibility is continuously suspended: responsibility for the category-bound actions of this 'problem criminal' lies with the problems and not with him. Despite all contradictions, this is the gist of IU's narratives.

Another brief example illustrates this category of a 'problem criminal' discharged of personal responsibility. It comes from RV, from whom we already heard above, who talked about his life story as follows at the start of the first interview.

Example 4.5

1   RV: My family was (.) addicted to drugs and so that's actually kind of why I ended up taking drugs.
2   I: Mmm.
3   RV: And because the drugs had to be paid for somehow right that meant first crime to feed the habit
4   and in the beginning- it started with harmless theft.
5   I: Mmm.
6   RV: And ended up with robbery. [RV, Int. 1, lines 24–31]

Here, too, the central category is that of a 'problem criminal' who is destined for crime by circumstances beyond his control. The drug-addicted family is the reason for his own drug consumption: RV is a member of the category 'family'. He defines that category as drug-addicted (line 1) and he, as a member of the category, thus has this characteristic. This means that he *is* drug-addicted, which in turn sets in motion a "path down" (O'Connor 2015, 190; related to drug use) that leads to drug-related crime ultimately involving robbery. There is no freedom of choice and no scope for subjective considerations; drug use is transferred from the family to the narrator who is forced ("had to be", line 3) to obtain financial resources by illegal means.

This self-categorisation by RV – like that of IU, although he discloses a fabrication of this categorisation – is a version of a sad story in which individual responsibility is suspended. Such a 'problem criminal' acts without agency, i.e. without making his own decisions and without personal responsibility. This is evident in both the narrated person and in the present narrator, as neither responsibility nor remorse for wrongdoing surface in the interviews.

One category with an important role in this self-categorisation is that of a 'persistent offender', which also emerged in political debates (Chapter 2.2) and professional magazines (Chapter 3.2). In the latter cases, its primary function was to justify calls for 'tough' measures. Persistent offenders are offenders who cause serious harm to others and supposedly cannot be prevented from engaging in further crime without strict intervention. It may at first appear surprising that the young accused categorise themselves accordingly, yet this happened repeatedly in the interviews. The category was adapted to fit sad stories. One striking example is the following passage, which comes from the first interview with RV.

Example 4.6

1   RV: Well I never really- I was difficult even at nursery. I kept running off there too and (.) well
2   because of the- my mum, because she was a single mum she didn't cope with all that.
3   I: Mmm.
4   RV: Then we got help from youth welfare services and I refused everything and (.)-
5   I: Mmm.
6   RV: Like and so on. Yeah what d'you want me to- Did my first crime at twelve.
7   I: Okay.
8   RV: So I wasn't even criminally responsible.
9   I: Yes.
10 RV: At thirteen I was already a pres- persistent offender. I reckon it (.) was because of that. [RV, Int.
11 1, lines 84–95]

Here too, RV portrays himself as a 'problem child'; he "was difficult even at nursery" (line 1). With the word "even" he is describing himself as permanently "difficult", and he has an explanation for this which lies in his family, specifically with his mother: she was a "single mum" (line 2) and could not cope. With "I refused everything" (line 4), he attributes to himself a certain degree of agency; however, this is put in considerable perspective by the age category 'child', the mother who cannot cope and the characteristics of being difficult and in need of help. His criminality results from this self-categorisation as a 'problem child' who does not receive genuine help. In the coda to his narrative, he provides an explicit explanation for his status as "persistent offender" (line 10): his problem status (line 10). He is a "persistent offender" who is the product of difficult circumstances. A drug-addicted family and a single mother who cannot cope in this case fulfil the same communicative and moral function. Unlike in types of sad story in which there is redemption, it is characteristic of this narrative of RV that – as described above ("Taste it once, you come back for more. That's the way it is"; example 4.1) – his status is still shaped by his problems, even at the time of the interviews.

Self-accusing suspension of personal responsibility

Other narratives modify the problem history. One version allows a culpable 'I' despite that individual facing considerable problems. The following example illustrates this narrative attribution of guilt to the narrator. It comes from LE, who was interviewed in a prison for young offenders and had been charged with burglary, theft and driving without a licence. I cite a relatively long excerpt to show the timeline recounted by LE, the associated problems and his categorisation of himself as an offender.

Example 4.7

1   I: So you, you're originally from [*city in western Germany*]?
2   LE: Eh, I was, I was born in [*another city in western Germany*]. And
3   I: Okay.
4   LE: Over eh (..) the last few years I've been in eh, moved to a lot of institutions. And I was in foster
5   families as a child.
6   I: Mmm.
7   [. . .]
8   I: And that was, was that an institution, right?
9   LE: That was, that was an institution. In [*northern German state*] I was with a foster family and in
10   [*city in western Germany*] I was in a foster family too.
11   I: Mmm.
12   LE: Eh (. . .), yeah, in group homes[6] (.). Then I finally went to the next stage of group home in [*city in*
13   *western Germany*].
14   [. . .]
15   I: Mmm. *(Writing noises)* (..) Okay. And how is it that you, em, ended up in different institutions?
16   LE: My mum was very young when I was born, sixteen years old.
17   I: Mmm.
18   LE: Eh, she (.) had problems with her family HERSELF.
19   I: Mmm.
20   LE: And (.) finally gave me away when I was six (..) to the youth welfare services, see?
21   I: Okay.
22   LE: Eh (. . .)
23   I: And that's when you first went into /an\
24   LE: /That's\ when I first /went into an institution\
25   I: /Went into an institution\.
26   LE: Exactly.
27   I: Okay.
28   LE: First to a group home. And JUST afterwards to the first foster family.
29   I: Mmm.
30   LE: It didn't quite work out.
31   I: Okay.
32   LE: And personally I didn't like it in terms of eh- The chemistry just wasn't right.
33   I: Mmm, mmm.
34   LE: Though I was still so young e:h.
35   I: Mmm.
36   LE: And the e:h- The second foster family, the (.) MUM got very ill, the foster mum. And so
37   unfortunately that wasn't possible any more. Em (..) right, then I was e:::h in homes for difficult
38   children, then in NORMAL homes.
39   I: Mmm.
40   LE: Eh I was in PROJECTS. At [*seaside region in Germany*] for example, just to get away, to recover
41   a bit from, from this (.) from all the mess that has happened.

42   I: Mmm.
43   LE: E::h (. . .), yeah, and then the institution in [*another region in western Germany*] went bust.
44   I: Mmm.
45   LE: Things were actually pretty GOOD there. I went to school.
46   I: Mmm.
47   LE: That was just before I did my middle school leaving certificate.
48   I: Mmm.
49   LE: And, yes, then they went bust. And eh, eh then I ended up in [*city in western Germany*].
50   I: Okay. And you just said em home for difficult children. What does that mean?
51   LE: Yeah, before, eh when puberty started, it was very difficult with me. I, I was at a special school
52   for kids with behavioural problems.
53   I: Mmm.
54   LE: Eh I had t- tantrums a lot. You could say I was very QUICK-TEMPERED.
55   I: Mmm.
56   LE: Em (. . .), yeah, social interaction wasn't perfect. To be honest, it wasn't working at all. So no
57   friends really. The others found it REALLY HARD to put up with me.
58   I: Mmm.
59   LE: That's how the, the, the staff saw it too.
60   I: Okay.
61   LE: I lived in a family-like home and eh (..), yeah, it didn't work at all just because of my behaviour. It
62   didn't work, see?
63   I: And how was it from YOUR point of view? I mean, because you said how the staff saw it (.)
64   /was it like that.\
65   LE: /Yeah, at that point\ I thought of course eh, everything, it's everyone else's fault. It's RUBBISH
66   of course and eh I'm a nice boy, right?
67   I: Mmm.
68   LE: But looking back, the older I GET, the, the more eh it's clear to me what I (.) really did wrong and
69   eh (.) how I ACTUALLY behaved.
70   I: Mmm.
71   LE: Eh:::m (4) I mean I'd say that they, that they were right- I mean the staff, yes. I mean it's, now I
72   see it like that too, yeah, I accept it, yeah.
73   I: Mmm. And how do you explain it? I mean (..) how did it happen?
74   LE: The tantrums and stuff?
75   I: Yes, I mean (.) –
76   LE: That's hard to say. I mean I definitely had (.) a serious attachment disorder, because I was always
77   living in different places and saw a lot of VIOLENCE, even as a kid. I reckon it (.) was because of
78   that. [LE, Int. 1, lines 97–201]

At the start of the passage, the interviewer asks where LE comes from (line 1). LE not only names a place but also provides the interviewer with an "orientation" (Labov/Waletzky 1967, 32) on who he is (lines 4–5). This orientation categorises him in a number of different ways. If we apply the references for orientation employed by Labov and Waletzky (*"person, place, time,* and *behavioral situation"*), LE does not initially name any persons other than himself and in particular not his family, but rather "institutions" (line 4; German *"Einrichtungen"*), in other words, social work facilities outside his birth family. Places are also relevant, for LE mentions not just two cities but also the various different institutions as places where he has stayed, clearly showing how often he has moved. The timeline covers LE's entire life from childhood almost up until the present: As a child, he was "in foster families" (lines 4–5), which he formulates in the plural, and over "the last few years" (line 4) in many different institutions. This signals forms of social work accommodation and ongoing challenges when he was growing up. He had no home in the classic sense of the word as a place where a child grows up in the constant care of his or her parents. Instead, he categorises himself as a person growing up in changing social, institutional facilities without respective relationships and with problems requiring him to be cared for by strangers.

LE goes on to communicate a reason for his stays in institutions (as to his 'behavioural situation'): the fact that his mother could not cope. He immediately excuses her by citing her youth (line 16) and a number of problems with her birth family (line 18). The stress ("HERSELF", line 18) emphasises that she bore little responsibility for her problems but was faced from an early age with difficulties of her own. LE is thus part of a long and unbroken line of family problems. Those problems continue in the institutions. After each change of accommodation that is supposed to resolve the current problems, new difficulties emerge in an ongoing vicious circle. A detailed analysis of this process does not have to be undertaken here. However, in terms of the particularities of this type of sad story, it is worth noting that LE communicates both a lack of and the presence of personal responsibility. He associates himself with numerous problems, a mother who was unable to cope and with multiple changes of institutions. In some cases, he was unlucky, for example because one foster mother became "very ill" (line 36) or because one institution "went bust" (line 43). Nonetheless, he still blames himself. The narrator's position is one that condemns his own self in the past: he was "very difficult" (line 51), "QUICK-TEMPERED" (line 54), someone it was almost impossible to "put up with" (line 57); he also portrays his earlier self as unreasonable (lines 65–72). His assessment of this earlier self is clearly negative. He even underlines this negative view of himself in the past by citing the opinion of the staff, i.e. institutional figures of authority, and thus providing evidence to support his self-denigration (lines 59, 71–72; see Scott/Lyman 1968). He categorises himself as a 'really' difficult child or difficult youth, as highlighted not just by child or youth care professionals but also by his older, mature narrator self – a narrative persona created through the very act of self-criticism. The use of a pathologising diagnosis ("serious attachment disorder", line 76) and the reference to his childhood experiences of violence (line 77) leave the interviewer no opportunity to see him as anything but a 'problem child' whose behavioural difficulties and criminal actions are an almost automatic product of his life story.

This divergence between the narrating self and the narrated self is not unusual in offender narratives. However, it takes on a particular form in the context of the sad story. LE clearly categorises himself as a 'problem criminal' in whom externally induced difficulties have produced delinquency. In his case, however, this does not consistently lead to his moral exoneration; in fact, LE pinpoints the problems depicted as lying in his individual personality and recounts in detail how difficult he was. Other people therefore *rightly* had trouble with him (e.g. "because of my behaviour", lines 61). Moreover, although he expresses current understanding and describes himself as someone who has matured with age (lines 68–69), this does not lead him to an optimistic view of the future. In neither interview does he state that he now has sufficient resources and potential to overcome his sad past and move in a positive direction. For example, he describes his involvement in delinquency with the words "It's an ENDless cycle" (LE, Int. 1, 294). Delinquency is therefore to be expected from him in the future. What is more, LE claims similarity with groups of people who are often disparaged – also by the interviewees in this study, whose self-categorisation frequently distances them from those whom they consider, by their own standards, 'worse' people. Yet in the case of LE, he recounts that he was once housed in a "homeless shelter" (LE, Int. 1, 359). The people there "were just people like ME, each had his STORY, one had come out of jail, one was maybe a drug addict, another had been kicked out by his wife" (LE, Int. 1, 363–365). He is aware of the stigmatisation of those living in homeless facilities, yet he identifies himself with them.

A change to his negative view of himself is provided by the prospect of training in prison (LE, Int. 2, 361–363), but at the same time, he claims to need imprisonment as he would otherwise become delinquent again (LE, Int. 2, 527). He is in fundamental need of help as he does not manage on his own (LE, Int. 2, 790–803), and he firmly rejects the attitude that "it's everyone else's fault" as "RUBBISH" (line 65). In a process similar to that used in recent programs and training courses for responsibilisation (Phoenix/Kelly 2013; Rajah et al. 2014; Robinson/Crow 2009, 121), LE's focus is on the impact of his own actions. His acceptance of a degree of agency tempers his self-categorisation as a 'problem criminal' who is not responsible for his difficulties. However, the options open to him do not extricate him from his problems. He *is* a person in need of help, facing difficulties, who in the light of his own agency can plausibly recount and regret that he previously acted wrongly, although he was himself only in part to blame for his problems.[7] The story is thus a self-accusatory one that does not give a consistent, exonerating victim narrative, as the narrator is at least in part an offender who acted wilfully. In keeping with this narrative, LE found his relatively tough sentence fair, as he apportioned himself a relatively large share of blame (LE, Int. 2, 407).

Deliverance from the sad story

Alongside the two versions of the *sad story that suspends personal responsibility* and the *sad story modified by self-accusation*, there is a third version: that of "*moral redemption*" (Presser 2010, 433; B.D.'s italics) – the development of positive options for action following a negative past. This narrative is that of a difficult life involving a series of problems, but also a life in which the narrator has overcome all obstacles or at least believes he or she can leave behind the obstacles in the future. In the face of this self-categorisation, it can appear unnecessary to impose tough sanctions on the person in question as he or she is not responsible for his or her problems (and offences). Interventionist measures overall, for example custodial social work institutions, also appear useless as the offender already seems to have extricated himself or herself from earlier difficulties (see also Emerson 1969; Maruna 2001).

The interviewees repeatedly presented narratives of growing maturity and improvement that had already begun at the time of the first interview. Some young people, recounts YE for example, "just don't get it (. . .). Yeah they just keep on smoking or fighting" (YE, Int. 1, 361). He, however, "can't be doing with it any more" (YE, Int. 1, 364), i.e. he has apparently understood that crime and violence have to stop. Measures taken against his delinquency thus appear irrelevant as he has himself already decided to end his delinquent career. He categorises himself as a 'matured former offender' who has been released from a criminogenic past.

The situation is similar when offenders categorise themselves as 'persistent offenders' as part of a sad story and qualify this as their previous status. BC – who is facing charges including property and violent offences, some involving the use of weapons – explicitly categorises himself as "a PROBLEM CHILD" (BC, Int. 2, 341) and also as a "persistent offender":

Example 4.8

1   I: Okay. But how often have you been charged before?
2   BC: I've been charged a lot. I used to be a persistent offender.
3   I: What does that mean?
4   BC: That means (.) you've- I mean persistent offender well you've got to do a lot of SHIT to become a
5   persistent offender. And at fifteen I was (.) the well like the policeman said to me the worst in [*city in*
6   *western Germany*].
7   I: Mmm.
8   BC: Of my age. [BC, Int. 1, lines 1028–1035]

The "problem child" became a "persistent offender" (lines 2, 4); a transformation which BC qualifies as particularly dramatic for – as attested by a policeman – he was even "the worst" (line 5) in his town. However, BC does not connect this latter category with a demand for punitive measures. Instead, he twice associates his status with a relatively young age (lines 5, 8): he was frequently delinquent at a young age. As a "problem child" and a particularly young person, he bore little responsibility for his acts. He thus uses the category 'persistent offender' to explain why he has been charged so often, but not that he rightly received tough sanctions. The subcategory '*young* persistent offender' communicates his incomprehension of what is in his view too tough a sentence that was imposed on him. In the second interview, he describes this recent sentence and refers to an earlier sentence that had been handed down to him when he was 15:

Example 4.9

1   I: Mmm. (.) But what do you think, how was it that aged fifteen you already /got [. . .]⁸\?
2   BC: /I was a persistent offender\.
3   I: Oh, right.
4   BC: But all the same, huh? That they, I, I've got I still don't understand that outcome today, why at

5   fifteen, I'd never been on probation, once had community service, weekend detention, and then
6   straight after that prison.
7   I: Mmm.
8   BC: No idea why I got [. . .].[9]
9   I: Mmm. (.) Do you know why, were there any reasons given, can you remember?
10   BC: No, can't say.
11   I: Mmm, mmm. (.) Okay.
12   BC: DOESN'T MATTER what reasons they gave, there's no reason for that. A fifteen-year-old [. . .],[10]
13   he could get ten complaints against him and go before court and say, it's normal, he's young right?
14   He's young. [BC, Int. 2, lines 607–622]

The interviewer shows with "already" (line 1) that a custodial sentence of several years appears unusual for a young person. A harsh sentence is depicted as inconsistent with young age. From BC's perspective, being a "persistent offender" is relevant in this context, for he provides this category as a response to the inconsistency (line 2). With the adversative "all the same" (line 4; German original: "Aber trotzdem"), however, he makes it clear that he does not accept the sentence and "still" does not understand it "today" (line 4). To express his incomprehension, he associates himself with two characteristics: on the one hand, the minor nature of his previous convictions (line 5), which are in contrast to a tough prison sentence ("straight after that prison", line 6). This suggests that previous criminal law professionals had not seen him as particularly deserving of punishment, in other words that he was a fairly harmless offender. This is, on the other hand, emphasised with the reference to his young age at the time ("young", lines 13 and 14). The essence of this narrative is that although he was a "persistent offender" at an early age, he was a young boy who was punished too severely. This punishment, as he reiterates throughout the interviews, had a lasting negative impact on him (for example BC, Int. 2, 594–595). But he does not categorise his *current* self as a "persistent offender" – as shown by the past tense used in example 4.8 ("used to be a persistent offender", line 2) and example 4.9 ("I was a persistent offender", line 2). He is no longer a member of that category, and the justice system treated him unfairly by imposing too harsh a sentence on him. BC is indicating that had he received a more lenient sanction, his development would have been more positive.

With this narrative, BC does not express an explicit deliverance from delinquency to a law-abiding lifestyle. However, he presents a route towards that redemption implicitly, for BC has – for whatever reason – left the status of persistent offender behind him and is now being hindered in his positive development by an unfair justice system. The link to deliverance remains fairly hidden, but it is the very implicit nature of the reference that can be revealing (Sandberg 2016). BC uses an age category to criticise his repressive treatment by the criminal justice system, thus indicating that he could have been a 'normal' youth had he been treated fairly. This produces contradictions. For example, BC describes himself on the one hand as particularly bad (example 4.8, lines 5–6). On the other hand, he portrays himself in the manner discussed as not deserving harsh punishment, as an unfairly treated young offender. Whether BC's use of the respective category-bound characteristics 'young' and 'only minor previous convictions' succeeds in neutralising this contradiction between drastic actions and an offender not meriting harsh punishment is not a matter for discussion here. What is key to the analysis is that he categorises himself as a problem child and young offender who was too harshly punished and *intrinsically* has the potential for positive development.

Another example demonstrates more clearly the change over time in self-categorisation as "*diachronic identity navigation*" (Bamberg 2012, 103) and the new agency that this can demonstrate. KX provides the example; he is charged with sex offences and housed in a social work institution at the time of the first interview. The interviewer asks him to explain how he came to be in the institution, and he responds as follows.

Example 4.10

1   KX: [. . .] Em, I was taken away from my real family at five months.
2   I: Mmm.
3   KX: Then went into care until I was eleven *(clears his throat)* in a foster family.
4   I: Mmm.
5   KX: (.) *(Groaning) Yeah, and I* sometimes *(laughing) did shit, right?* Y:eah, and when I was fourteen
6   (..) I crossed the line with girls.
7   I: Mmm.
8   KX: I've done a few courses of therapy already, not finished right, still doing therapy. (.) [*Name of a*
9   *psychosocial intervention*] in [*city in western Germany*].
10   I: Mmm.
11   KX: With Mr [incomprehensible name]. (.) E:m. But that's finishing soon too.
12   I: Mmm.
13   KX: Yeah, and (. . .) I'm- (.) well was in different group homes. (.) The last one was in [*city in western*
14   *Germany*], in [*name of a social work institution*]. It was like a special (.) specialised (.) group for
15   young (.) sex offenders.
16   I: Mmm.
17   KX: Em:, and (.) what's it called- yeah and then I, then there was like bother and that, and so I ran off
18   last year [*date*].
19   I: Mmm.
20   KX: So em then they told me "Yeah, you can't go home. Your parents will call the police". (. . .)
21   *(Groaning) Yeah,* I come from [*city*
22   *in western Germany/place of birth*]. (..) And em then I was in [*city in western Germany, place of birth*] over
     night, right, and then in the morning went to my guardian,
23   sorted everything out, then a night in a hotel. Took all day then to sort it all out with the youth welfare
24   services. (.) Yeah, and then I was here. (.) It's a pretty cool group, actually-
25   I: Mmm.
26   KX: Because I go through the youth welfare services, right, and have (.) like more opportunities than
27   the others.
28   I: Mmm.
29   KX: I've got a room upstairs, with another boy here. (.) Em (..) yeah, and now we've- eh, been
30   allowed a PlayStation. There's another one over there. We're maybe getting it (.) today, if we're
31   lucky, upstairs as well. That needs to be checked.
32   I: Mmm.
33   KX: Yeah because upstairs there's a four down here's a three. Yeah, (..) and what else, school, year
34   ten. Doing my school leaving certificate soon. Em have the chance to do gardening, landscaping
35   training.
36   I: Mmm.
37   KX: At [*name of firm*]. (..) Yeah:, looking forward to it already. In four weeks time (.) I've now got (.)
38   a three-week placement from school. [KX, Int. 1, lines 9–51]

KX starts his narrative by presenting himself as a small child of five months who is "taken away" from his "real family" (line 1); in other words, he is denied a 'normal' childhood. A child is removed from the place where it 'really' belongs and becomes a victim of outside circumstances. As no reason is specified, all that we have is the dramatic act of removal. This is followed by being taken into a "foster family" (line 3) that is not described in more detail, either. The story told in the passive continues the theme of KX being removed from his "real family"; he now categorises himself as a 'foster child' (line 3). Criminality is mentioned in the subsequent narrative in which KX describes his stay in social work institutions, but for that criminality, too, no further reasons or justifications are given. He tells the interviewer that he "crossed the line with girls" (line 6), in other words committed sex offences. The German original ("übergriffig Mädchen gegenüber") does not express active commission of the offences. Instead – unlike the "did shit" (line 5) that indicates agency, but also more or less trivial incidents – the narrator also uses the passive voice. This and subsequent developments appear as a series of points in his life journey through which he passes without any personal involvement. One exception is his running away, which is narrated in the active voice (line 17–18); he links this to the experience that he cannot go to his parents (line 20). He thus became active by trying to get away from bother, by trying to return to his place of birth and to his parents, but he is frustrated in the attempt – by an unspecified "they" (line 20) and the parental wishes relayed by this "they". Until this point, he categorises himself primarily as a child or young person who does not receive a normal upbringing, who experiences problems or bother and whose actions are not successful.

This narrative changes with the place category "here" (line 24), the description of the social work institution in which he is staying at the time of the interview. This new place is the first to be associated with positive experiences, as KX recounts positive emotions in terms of his social integration ("cool group", line 24). He has a comparatively large range of play options ("PlayStation", line 30), will soon be able to "do my secondary school leaving certificate" (line 34; German original "*Hauptschulabschluss*", a lower secondary education qualification) and is to start training (line 34–35) and a "placement" (line 38). The category 'foster child with almost no agency', i.e. the child to whom things happen and who has, in the course of his non-normal development, committed sex offences apparently incidentally, has thus become transformed. He is now a young man who is able to engage in activities and experience things that young people should, and who will seemingly be able successfully to integrate into the labour market. As he details in the second interview, he is "a perfectly normal young person again" (KX, Int. 2, 417). He associates this with a "youth welfare service status" (KX, Int. 2, 417, see also line 26); in other words, he is in this positive place primarily not because of his illegal acts but for social work reasons. They do not interfere with his normality as he associates this status with 'normal' activities and experiences: they transform him from a member of the category passive 'foster child' or 'criminal' to 'a normal young person' (with even "more opportunities" than others, line 26).

The excerpt printed in example 4.10 may therefore be somewhat lacking in possible details, but it does show a success story which relocates KX morally by his self-categorisation (Jayyusi 1991). He underpins his 'normality' with the activity that he has worked for the privileges that he now enjoys himself (KX, Int. 1, 522), and with the quality that he has an acute "sense of guilt" (KX, Int. 1, 640) towards the victims of his offences. Both in terms of his activity status and in terms of his moral focus, he is thus categorising himself – as a narrator – as a 'normal', rehabilitated young person. He is active and regrets his past wrongful behaviour, despite the highly stigmatised offence with which he has been charged.

With this deliverance from a sad story, KX positions himself in rehabilitation-friendly penal welfarism: according to this narrative, it is possible to put an end to criminality and a troubled past. Even difficult circumstances and serious offences are transformable into a positive present and future. Maruna (2001) writes that with a view to long-term desistance, it can be useful for delinquents to free themselves from a negative past – a past that appears to retain a relatively strong influence on the present for the first two versions of the sad story presented here. Holding on to negative events in the past and experiences of one's own failures can, according to Maruna, prevent someone from actively rising to life's current and future challenges and can thus hinder successful desistance. The data used here does not allow an empirical analysis of this hypothesis (for a discussion, see for example Andrews et al. 2011; Farrall 2002; Farrall et al. 2014; Ward/Maruna 2007). However, the *deliverance from the sad story* version at least interactively gives the impression of a (possible) positive development. An improvement seems already to have taken place as KX has left or is leaving his negative past behind. In the context of criminal proceedings and the threat of punishment, this narrative fulfils key functions for self-presentation as a reformed *former* delinquent.[11]

4.3 Calls for punitivity

It may appear surprising that the young defendants did not simply present penal welfarism narratives, for those are the narratives from which they would apparently benefit the most.[12] Although they did, of course, primarily emphasise lenient responses or legal diversion instead of imprisonment for themselves, narratives of severity nonetheless played a significant part. The defendants in fact repeatedly exacted tough approaches to crime. In the political discourse, demands for 'tough action' increasingly came to play an important role as necessary atonement or as a deterrent (see Chapter 2.2). Even in social work, this tendency became more and more influential in the context of mounting calls for 'confrontational' interventions (see Chapter 3.2). In the case of the young defendants, this tough approach appears in two ways: firstly, as a claim that, had a defendant received more restrictive punishment earlier in his life, this would have prevented him from entering the downward spiral of a criminal career; and secondly, in comparisons with other offences and offenders.

Severity as a biographical demand

Quite frequently, the interviewees presented themselves as delinquents who were previously not treated restrictively enough to give their lives a turn for the better. Although there are also opposing narratives, as example 4.9 shows, the complaint that the justice system was too lax in its response to their own criminality had an important role in the defendants' moral self-categorisation. IU – placed in a juvenile prison at the time of the interviews – provides one example. Before the passage cited, he has told the interviewer about community service that he had previously been given.

Example 4.11

```
1    I: And what's your position on other things like that? I mean long-term detention, that's a different
2    experience from being remanded in custody or a young offenders' institution. /Em-\
3    IU: /I- I'm\ if I'm honest
4    long-term detention, community service and (.) young offenders that's KINDERgarten.
5    I: This here is kinder/garten?\
6    IU: /Yes.\ What- I've- I've already said that to the staff here too, I- what we-
7    honestly: what we buggers need when we get up to shit is a boot camp.
8    I: /Okay.\
9    IU: /I reckon\ it doesn't work otherwise.
10   I: Mmm.
11   IU: Because this is like proper luxury. You can shop here, you've got television, you can write letters,
12   you can call people.
13   I: Mmm.
14   IU: It's not- it's no punishment.
15   I: Mmm.
16   IU: It's just (.) chilling out and killing time, (.) wasting time. You can work here.
17   I: Yes.
18   IU: (Quietly) Yes.
19   I: So what do you think would have WORKED with you in inverted commas?
20   IU: A real boot camp, right? Where you really get sorted out.
21   I: Yes?
22   IU: Up at four in the morning, off you go.
23   I: Mmm.
24   IU: I mean with real rules (.) it might- would have- could've worked. [IU, Int. 1, lines 536–561]
```

At the start of the passage, the interviewer qualifies various different sanctions: long-term detention *(Dauerarrest)* as different from being remanded in custody or imprisoned (lines 1–2). According to the interviewer, there is a logic of escalation as the measures are not equally strict. IU contradicts: with "if I'm honest" (line 3), he disagrees by terming all types of sanctions listed as "KINDERgarten" (line 4), in other words as far too soft. He demands tough measures, but not for him directly as an individual; he categorises himself as a member of difficult or criminal young people ("we buggers", line 7). As he identifies himself as a respective member of that category and that category needs tough punishment, the call for punishment is transferred to him. If ending careers in crime is to "work" (line 9), stricter measures are needed, i.e. not what he sees as the "luxury" (line 11) of detention but rather some kind of "boot camp" (lines 7, 20).

Examples 4.3 and 4.4 presented narratives from IU in which he reduced his personal responsibility for 'his' offences by recounting a difficult life story. This is in principle compatible with penal welfarism positions: if people have experienced problems in their life and those problems cause them to become criminal, addressing or solving the problems would appear the logical step to avoiding further offences. In Germany, this is the predominant rationale in the legal approach to delinquency. Even the primary justification given for imprisonment is addressing the so-called harmful inclinations (section 17 par. 2 JGG) of a young offender (Ostendorf 2013, 171): prison is to have a rehabilitative effect. It is worth highlighting this stance here, as IU puts forward the opposite view. He does not advocate leniency or rehabilitative intervention. What he explicitly calls for is punishment equivalent to the tough measures of a boot camp. A difficult life story from this perspective demands severity: strict rules can turn the young person around.

This rejection of rehabilitative (or educational) demands is no exception. Other interviewees also firmly denied that they were in need of or would respond to rehabilitative measures (Dollinger et al. 2017a, b). They called for relatively lenient, non-custodial measures and endorsed practical help (e.g. when dealing with formalities or seeking a job), whereas they were often critical of interventions in their 'core identity'. Yet not even calls for this practical version of penal welfarism were beyond dispute, as IU illustrates. His demand for tough sanctions communicates a continuing rejection of personal responsibility for delinquency. In the light of the problems he has experienced, he appears to bear almost no responsibility for his delinquency; and lenient measures by the criminal justice system are part of his problem-fraught past. Not he but the state or criminal justice system appears to give rise to delinquency through its leniency. He is a 'problem criminal' who has been incorrectly treated.

Another example reinforces this moral externalisation of responsibility. It comes from RV, who had already been imprisoned multiple times prior to his upcoming trial.

Example 4.12

1 RV: Right and (.) yeah (.) eh youth court judges (..) okay they really are rubbish. They. They're- I
2   mean (..) they give too h-h- too low a sentence. I mean if I were to say, if really (.) they should be
3   more on top of things (.) dole out more tougher sentences (.) because those people, right? I I reckon if
4   in my- if my first trial, if I'd got four, five years then, see?
5 I: Mmm.
6 RV: Let's just say, I'd not have coped with that emotionally, right? Right and eh I'd not have forgot it.
7   I reckon I'd never have done another crime, see? [RV, Int. 1, lines 683–690]

RV also firmly advocates tougher sanctions. His own life story serves as justification for his call for greater severity by youth court judges (lines 3–4). Despite the emotionally overwhelming challenge of several years' youth custody (line 6), he is demanding just that, as it would have prevented him from engaging in further delinquency (line 7). He says this despite telling the interviewer in the interview following the trial that he was satisfied with the relatively lenient sentence he had received (RV, Int. 2, 977). Clearly, he had not hoped for tough sanctions for himself in the present. However, in the interview situation he describes himself as someone who did previously need and should have received such a tough sentence. He is thus recounting himself as able to look beyond his own short-term well-being and indeed accepting an emotional challenge in order to avoid long-term criminality. At the same time, he is transferring responsibility for his repeated reoffending after earlier sentences to the youth court judges: had they acted differently, he would not have become delinquent again. The blame appears to rest with them, while he himself would even have accepted emotional problems caused by a justifiably harsh sentence. He categorises himself as a 'problem criminal' whose difficulties have been and still are caused by others, while putting himself in the moral position of wanting to change this situation or at least of knowing how a change could be achieved – by others.

A social comparison of severity

Other narratives demanding severity refer to other offences and to other offenders, with whom the narrator compared himself. Such comparisons are very common. The interviewees often presented themselves in relation to others whom they knew personally or about whom they had heard in order to demonstrate a form of moral superiority (Copes 2016; Dickinson/Wright 2017; Sandberg 2010, 459). These comparisons are relevant here insofar as the defendants demanded relatively lenient sentences for themselves or condemned what they saw as too tough a sentence on the grounds that others who had committed comparable or more serious offences, or who were 'more deserving' of punishment, had received more lenient sanctions than they had. The opposite case did occur as well. For example, one young man was surprised that he had been able to commit many more offences before his first prison sentence than "Moroccans" imprisoned with him; they "were locked up for nicking FOUR times and me not until [. . .]. I don't know how many times" (KM, Int. 2, 891–894). However, narratives criticising that others were apparently treated more softly are much more common. One example comes from the second interview with KL, who was very dissatisfied with the sentence that had been imposed on him.

Example 4.13

1   KL: So (.) *(angry) you should*, well I always say it's best for me not to compare myself with
2   other people that have done offences.
3   I: Uh-huh.

4   KL: I just get angry about it, you know (..). It's like with that Tuğçe case back then, maybe
5   *(mumbling) you know about it.*
6   [. . .]
7   KL: So I think to myself, woah (.) well (.) I dunno. With me, nobody died. Maybe they've got
8   psychological harm. But, as well, they didn't – but although they were WITH me (.) well
9   they're (.) also BECAUSE of me, but not (. . .) what can I say, well, after all I'm not THE ONE,
10 *(angry) still, the one who went in.* [KL, Int. 2, lines 347–372]

The example references a widely known case, "Tuğçe" (line 4), which had occurred in Germany in November 2014 and been widely discussed in the media.[13] KL uses this case to make his own position clear (Dollinger 2017). He categorises himself as an offender who is less deserving of punishment than the Tuğçe offender. Beginning with a disclaimer (lines 1–2), KL rejects any suggestion that he would make loose comparisons, and in so doing prepares the interviewer for just such a comparison.

KL uses two references in his comparison. The first is that offenders whose offences have serious consequences, like the death of Tuğçe in the case mentioned, are particularly deserving of punishment. No one has died as a result of KL's offences, on the other hand (line 7); a comparison on the basis of the consequences ought therefore to mean KL receiving a lesser sentence. The interactive impression is that KL wrongly received a restrictive sentence. KL then changes his narrative by admitting that his actions also had serious consequences ("psychological harm", line 8). He had previously established the category 'offender particularly deserving of punishment' and associated this with death in the Tuğçe case, and distanced himself from this category. However, by stressing that his actions also caused serious harm to the victims, he reduces the gap between himself and this category. In both interviews, KL recounted at length how much he regretted his actions, and repeatedly referred to the significant impact on the victims of his offences. The "psychological harm" is therefore a very serious (and delicate) matter in his narratives. In this context, KL introduces a second comparative reference to define the category of 'offender particularly deserving of punishment' and to differentiate himself from that category: responsibility for an offence. He sees his responsibility in his case as reduced because he – as he also details at other points in the interviews – was only one of a number of offenders and not the principle perpetrator of the offences for which he was being prosecuted. This becomes evident in the excerpt when he tells the interviewer that he was "not THE ONE, *(angry) still, the one who went in*" (lines 9–10). According to KL's narrative, the principle perpetrator entered the place in question in a robbery but KL did not. KL did therefore not take an active part in the robbery and bears little responsibility for it. Following this line of argument, relatively tough punishment is deserved not by someone who is simply present at a crime, but by the person who is primarily responsible for that crime. Now it is responsibility – and no longer the consequences of a crime – that is being linked to punishment. This modifies the category of 'offender particularly deserving of punishment', to which KL once again does not belong.

KL is not explicitly saying that other offenders should be punished severely. Nonetheless, his self-categorisation as an 'offender less deserving of punishment' implies that there are other offenders – those who cause particularly serious harm to their victims or who are the principle perpetrators of a crime – for whom repressive sanctions are legitimate. KL's relational self-positioning only makes sense following this line of argument. He cannot demand that these other offenders also be treated leniently, because this would undermine his stated objection to his sentence. Others, so the narrative runs, could be punished restrictively; only in his case is a tough sentence unfair.

Conclusion

This chapter presented narratives of young defendants who had to fear imprisonment in the context of their trials. The analysis focused on categories that they used to describe themselves, i.e. particularly as offenders little deserving of punishment. It should be stressed that this is only one snapshot of the many narratives of people who, for whatever reason, emerge as (alleged) offenders. It is quite possible, for example, that persons charged with minor offences, female defendants or persons of other ages would provide different narratives.[14] Nonetheless, the people studied here are particularly relevant for it is they – often categorised as 'persistent offenders' – who have been at the centre of the political, public and academic debate on crime over recent decades.

As we are dealing with young people with long histories of crime and sanctions, it is hardly surprising that sad story narratives are of central importance. Yet these narratives are not uniform; they cover different forms of self-categorisation, in some cases involving elements of agency and a degree of responsibility (and repentance) for delinquency. Narratives that present the narrator's upbringing or childhood as particularly difficult are nonetheless a central aspect of the interviewees' stories, and such narratives fulfil the interactive function of making punishment appear more or less obsolete. In keeping with basic principles of penal welfarism, the narrators often categorise themselves as 'problem criminals' who can hardly be blamed for the many difficulties in their lives.

In this context, it may seem surprising that punishment is not in principle rejected, and that narrators in fact even express demands for severity. We need to look at each individual story to reconstruct what contextual function the corresponding narrative serves. For example, criticism of the criminal justice system for failing to take earlier and tougher action against the narrator's own delinquency can pass on responsibility for criminality to that system. Political and public narratives in which the courts are 'too soft' in their sentences (see Chapter 2) are thus used and modified by the young defendants to enable a form of self-categorisation that renders them deserving of little punitive intervention.

The defendants largely accept that delinquency brings a negative institutional response. None of those we interviewed fundamentally disputed the fact that punishment *must* follow crime. Delinquency and punishment appear almost 'naturally' linked. What was a matter for dispute, however, was the specific form and extent of punishment for which the interviewees were hoping for themselves. They categorised themselves as 'problem offenders', i.e. as burdened with a troublesome past, thus rendering a relatively light sentence plausible. The measure of what constituted a fair sentence for them was often taken from comparisons with other offenders and offences.

Notes

1 Offenders are the core of the membership categorisation "device 'parties to the offense'" (Stetson 1999, 82). Without offenders, there is no crime, which at least in exceptional cases may be conceivable without other parties. Apart from offenders, victims would appear the other most necessary group. However, there are so-called victimless crimes (Schur/Bedau 1974) in which the offender and victim are identical (for example drug-taking) or which involve only abstract categories of victim (for example environmental crime).
2 The time between the first interview and the trial varied from two days to five months, and the time between the trial and the second interview from one day to 83 days. Problems with access to the interviewees and the late announcement of some court dates meant it was not possible to standardise these periods.
3 The available studies on offender narratives describe a great diversity in offender portrayals both from interviewee to interviewee and in some cases in narratives from one and the same person (e.g. Andersson 2008; Brookman et al. 2011; Maruna 2001; O'Connor 2000; Presser 2008; Presser/Sandberg 2015b; Sandberg 2009; Sandberg et al. 2015; Spies 2010; Yardley et al. 2015).
4 In the following excerpts and citations, "Int. 1" refers to the first interview, "Int. 2" to the second. I use the following transcription symbols:

(.)	Pause (1 second)
(..)	Pause (2 seconds)
(...)	Pause (3 seconds)
[...]	Omission from the excerpt
[*text*]	Omission to protect anonymity and explanation of content
[incomprehensible]	incomprehensible word
[untranslatable fragment]	untranslatable fragment or expression
(number sec.)	measured pause
(*text*)	Comment on the speech quality or non-linguistic peculiarity; following cursive lettering shows the duration of the peculiarity
/text\	Overlapping of the speakers (start and end)
TEXT	Emphasis
–	Abruption
:	Lengthening

5 In German: "Wer einmal leckt, der weiß wie es schmeckt".
6 "Einrichtung für Verselbstständigung", a group home designed to teach self-reliance.
7 Maruna (2001, 73) talks in a similar context of a "condemnation script": a script demonstrating a linear negative development in which a more positive development in the future appears almost impossible. His reference to a "lack of efficacy" (Maruna 2001, 77) does, however, need to be detailed further for the type of sad story illustrated by LE's narrative, for LE does in fact recount possible agency – only in a way that does not lead to improvement but rather worsens his situation or perpetuates his problems. LE bears (some) responsibility for the fact that he was difficult, is difficult and will likely remain difficult.

8 The exact sentence has been omitted to ensure anonymity. It was a custodial sentence of several years.

9 Exact sentence has been omitted.

10 Exact sentence has been omitted.

11 It is worth mentioning that a high degree of remorse and self-blame can also go against young defendants. For example, BK – a 16-year-old facing charges including assault and property offences – clearly expressed his regret and remorse for his acts at his trial. During the hearing, he received the support of a number of institutional representatives in his desire to be placed in a social work facility instead of prison. The judge contacted youth welfare services during a break in proceedings; however, the latter refused to cover the costs of a social work facility place. The judge then issued BK with a prison sentence on the grounds that BK had demanded penance for his actions.

12 I am referring here to the programmatic, as it were, 'friendly side' of penal welfarism. It should be remembered, however, that it also has an 'unfriendly', restrictive side. The relatively wide scope of discretion for professionals can be used for severe measures: "Offenders identified as dangerous, recidivistic or incorrigible could be detained for lengthy periods" (Garland 2001a, 35). This restrictive side will be in the foreground in this section.

13 A 22-year-old woman named "Tuğçe" had been hit and died of the injuries suffered when she then fell.

14 The data used here were compared to the narratives of six young people charged with minor offences who have only received non-custodial sentences (such as training courses or community service). Their narratives of themselves were less shaped by criminality; however, aspects like social comparisons and a practical interest in getting along and being respected differed relatively little from that of the narratives presented here (Dollinger et al. 2017b).

5 Commonalities

How society got lost and was re-narrated

The previous chapters set out the main findings from three discourses of narrating youth crime. They are now to be related to each other in order to ascertain commonalities and actual historical changes of key narratives. In this process, I deliberately do not, as detailed in the preface of this book, assume influences that are external to the narratives. Abstract variables such as neoliberalism, the late modern period, globalisation, etc. may be relevant to theoretical explanations of changes in narratives. Analyses and debates in this area and on this basis are important: of course we cannot and should not ignore theory. Nonetheless, it is also important to *determine changes empirically on the basis of the material examined*. Below, I will therefore reconstruct changes within narratives without referring to possible external influences. The central question here is how narratives have changed over time in the discourses on youth crime, and how the changes relate to each other.

5.1 Preliminary remarks

The first two discourses in Chapters 2 and 3 provide information on a period ranging from 1970 to 2009 (or 2012). The findings presented in Chapter 4, on the other hand, all come from case studies with 15 young defendants. The type of data differs: the longitudinal results are predicated on parliamentary debates (Chapter 2) and on magazines that published articles by police officers or social workers (Chapter 3). The data from the case studies in Chapter 4 stems from interviews, in which young defendants talked about themselves, 'their' crimes and life stories and about other people.

Despite these differences, the data and findings do have much in common. In formal terms, one basic commonality is the narrative quality of the material. It comprises of stories on crime which are directed at a specific audience: the parliamentary debates at the public to gain approval for a specific political stance; the journal articles at a professional readership in the police and social work sectors to mark out the positions and competencies of the given profession; the interview data at an interviewer in the context of a trial in which the defendant's case and delinquency are being presented to legal professionals. Despite these different audiences, one thing is true for all material: the way in which each narrator talks about youth crime is designed to convince a specific group of listeners or readers of a specific 'nature' of crime. In light of the "lack of any intrinsic quality of an act which defines an event as crime" (Hillyard/ Tombs 2008, 7), youth crime is a project of narrative convincing. It is that of which people can be convinced. Since convincing is essential to establish particular understandings of youth crime, the three discourses do not exist in parallel. Narratives in the three discourses do not represent discrete systems, but combine and form coalitions. For example, professionals who work with delinquents operate within political and legal structures, i.e. they must be able to follow respective requirements. Similarly, if they want to achieve a favourable judgment, young defendants must work with legal positions and the expectations of prosecutors and judges. Politicians, too, do not speak in a narrative vacuum; they are, at least in democracies, reliant on approval among the population and bound by legal options.

It must therefore be possible to identify points at which the discourses coincide. The narrative construction of a specific meaning of crime represents – to borrow a term from Presser's (2008, 122) analysis of "heroic" struggles of violent men – a "battlefront", in that only narratives that are shared or approved of by various audiences are viable in the long term. As the respective narrative coalitions are flexible, predominant narratives of crime can change and adapt to new challenges (Kiesling 2006, 262). Hegemonic discourses are "contradictory and shifting", even if for a certain time they appear "as stable monolithic forces" (Chase 2011, 422; see also Pfohl 1994, 502–503).

Based on the analyses in the previous three chapters, a comparison makes it possible to reconstruct hegemonies as well as temporal changes. Commonalities of narratives represent a form of malleable, culturally established (or 'hegemonic') knowledge about youth crime that can be used and reproduced in particular discourses. That shared knowledge is 'functional' in diverse contexts.

How do we get there? How can something as abstract as a flexible narrative 'hegemony' be ascertained? The answer given here is: by disclosing empirically recurring "patterns" as "general tendencies in the way issues are viewed and dealt with by the communities to which individuals belong" (De Fina 2013, 45). Patterns are commonalities of narrating youth crime, which become visible through "the comparison of data from different participants" (De Fina 2013, 46).[1]

A stable pattern indicates a culturally predominant (or hegemonic) way to narrate crime. A brief recourse to Laclau's (or Laclau's and Mouffe's) theory of hegemony is helpful to address this point.[2] This theory renounces an extra-discursive reality; just like here it is assumed that there is no extra-narrative 'nature' of youth crime. There exists "no beyond the play of differences, no ground which would a priori privilege some elements of the whole over the others" (Laclau 2005, 69). Nevertheless, hegemonic manners of construing crime do exist (Melossi 2000). As I stated before, crime is in itself a multifaceted and heterogeneous phenomenon, yet concomitantly also represents consensus and unity, "a shared consensual normative order" (Reiner 2016, 67). Criminal law in particular testifies to hegemonic narratives as it assumes a general binding character within the framework of a nation state. Even if disputes and disagreement endure with regard to individual criminal law norms (e.g. relating to abortion, drug use, sexual and other laws), criminal law claims relative uniformity in its reference to "substantive rules of conduct addressed to citizens" (Lacey/Zedner 2012, 160).

Laclau (2004, 280) refers to this uniformity as a "logic of equivalence", meaning a type of coalition of different discursive positions. The basis for such a coalition in the context of youth crime is a shared understanding of it, a unifying narrative. Crime implies the notion that an accord on something unwanted can be achieved (Dollinger et al. 2014b).[3] It represents a kind of negative reference with respect to which (apparently) all agree that it should be prohibited and sanctioned. As the definition of crime generalises (or establishes as hegemonic) partial proscriptions and "rules of conduct", criminal law aspires to structure how people should and should not behave.[4] It thus appears to integrate diverse options to define social relationships and standards.[5] At least temporarily, differences seem to be suspended in the collective project of condemning and, inversely, prescribing the abovementioned "substantive rules of conduct". This "process of one demand assuming the representation of many others" is, according to Laclau (2004, 281), what can be called "hegemony". It becomes visible when joint narratives can be empirically identified. The foundation for a coalition of different positions can therefore not be found in a putative objective quality of crime, nor in a specific form of society. Instead, this foundation lies in joint narratives. If there is a coalition of different discourses with particular key narratives, then a hegemonic narrative becomes evident. A culturally predominant understanding of youth crime is thus accessible as a shared narrative.[6]

To the extent that differences as heterogeneous discursive positions continue to exist, however, a "logic of difference" also persists (Laclau 2004, 280). Differences cannot and do not have to be fundamentally eliminated if a hegemonic narrative is established. Certain narratives on crime are culturally predominant at given times, without alternative or subversive narratives being completely abandoned.[7] For instance, social work does not become identical with police even if they align their narratives on crime. Based on joint narratives, social work and police can cooperate and form a coalition, even though they are independent institutions. Hegemonic narratives on crime integrate divergent positions, which in themselves do not disappear despite the establishment of a hegemony.

These assumptions were discussed widely and controversially (e.g. Butler et al. 2000; Critchley/Marchart 2004). I mention them here briefly in order to illustrate that narratives of crime are contingent but don't vary arbitrarily. They exhibit manifold differences and are still structured and marked by specific (or hegemonic) ways of telling crime.

5.2 Narrative convergences: the long-term success of police narratives

The previous empirical chapters highlighted that one category is crucial in narratives on youth crime: the *offender*. I will use this category as a starting point for the search for narrative patterns and respective coalitions.

5.2.1 *Offender categorisations*

With regard to categorisations of offenders, there are three distinct versions that play a part in all three discourses.

a) **Offenders as victims:** Offenders do not necessarily bear the responsibility for 'their' offences. In fact, the opposite can be argued when the focus is on people who have violated norms, but whose breach is considered (more or less) irrelevant in terms of criminal responsibility. The criminal law category of a responsible offender is suspended when a criminal act is a symptom and indication of external factors or problems of the person. The category-bound feature of needing help replaces demands for punishment. Characteristic of this approach is defining offences as "indicators" in example 2.3 (Chapter 2.2). As the political speaker in 1979 argued, offences can point to problems affecting an offender; the speaker in this case was focusing in particular on serious issues in offenders' environment. An offender is thus replaced with a victim of circumstances beyond his or her control; his or her need for support is the central issue. The focus is then not on the problems caused by a person when they harm others, but on problems that person is facing. As a victim of circumstances, the offender is placed in criminogenic social structures that affect his or her personal history. It is this environment that causes criminality; the young persons in question cannot defend themselves from these external factors on their own or appear unable to make their own decisions.

   Interventions with individual youths could be justified in this context; people like "Pimo" (example 3.2) were supposed to benefit from social support despite all criminogenic effects of their environment. Yet in the more radical form of this narrative, the personality of the offender disappeared completely: measures were to be directed exclusively at the offender's social environment. In keeping with principles of a critical, politically oriented criminology, which primarily focuses on criminalisation through bodies of social control and social power relations, but much less on individual behaviour (e.g. Lilly et al. 2011, 166–198), this approach looks at 'unjust' social structural conditions. Society produces crime, while the punishment of individuals only increases social injustices. Criminality is thus, in this radical approach, not simply a sign of a criminogenic environment, but "an indicator, a sign, of a much broader crisis" (Melossi 2008, 183–184), in other words a genuinely political and/or structural issue.

   Despite these disparities between individual positions that differ in the significance they lend to the personalities of offenders, their common feature is that offenders are not to be held accountable for offences. Offenders are victims of social issues. It would therefore be unjust to punish them.

b) **Offenders as hybrid offenders/victims:** An offender considered 'purely' as a victim is more or less out of the question for criminal law discourses. If a social environment causes delinquency and not a person himself or herself through individual actions, this renders criminal law sanctions obsolete. The category of hybrid offender/victim is less extreme. It presents an offender as someone who has violated criminal law norms and to whom corresponding – possibly supportive – measures are to be applied; the purpose of these measures is to prevent crime (and not to foster the offender's well-being in itself). Where the criminal justice system and criminal policy are fundamentally criticised in the 'offenders as victims' narrative, this criticism is not voiced here, or it is at most directed against the excessive severity of some individualised measures. The offender/victim is affected by social problems and thus requires support. Despite his or her reduced agency, he or she is however *also* a criminal whose actions are not to be accepted. On this point, it is worth looking at a description of European youth criminal law by Dünkel et al. (2010b, 1813). Despite the heterogeneous nature of the national systems that they reconstruct in detail, they find the following common point of reference: "the common and principle aim of juvenile justice is to act in the best interests of the juvenile and to provide education, support and integration into society". Numerous political and professional narratives reconstructed in Chapters 2 and 3 agree with this assessment. They portray offenders as delinquents in need of help who face criminogenic social difficulties. Unlike in the personalised, moderate form of the offender-as-a-victim category, there is no fundamental criticism of society. The focus is instead on helping the individual to be integrated into the *existing* social order so as to prevent reoffending. Changes to the social structure and order tend to be irrelevant, as crime is addressed through personalised help such as advice, organising vocational training, training courses, etc. Where force is necessary, it is to this end legitimate. The authoritative police concept of (re-)education (Chapter 3.2) typifies this mixture of support and restriction in an amalgam of well-meaning coercive power.

c) **Offenders as offenders:** Over the course of the narratives presented in Chapters 2 and 3, the focus gradually shifted to the 'pure' criminal law category of young offenders. An offender simply became a person who had violated what were in themselves legitimate criminal laws and was to be held to account accordingly. This category of offender had already appeared on a few occasions in early speeches and texts from the 1970s. Police and conservative politicians were never entirely convinced that offenders were sheer victims of social circumstance and that the focus had to be on help as a countermeasure. Initially, in exceptional cases at least, then increasingly widely, confronting offenders by taking tangible and repressive action was considered necessary in the service of society. Various social institutions – not just social work and the police but also schools, parents and ultimately all bodies working with young people – were called on to take preventive action to stop the development of criminal careers. Prevention and measures by the criminal justice system could have welfarist side-effects, but their pivotal role was to prevent threats to safety and public order. The respective categorisation of offenders proliferated in the political and professional narratives analysed here since the mid-1990s. Yet, as Ashworth and Zedner (2014, 37) note, this line of argument points back to the growing "establishment of laws, institutions, and regulatory measures designed to anticipate threats to safety, welfare, and social order" in the nineteenth century. The point of reference for these measures is the effective prevention of risks. If deemed necessary, this can be achieved restrictively and with a disregard for the welfare of those persons who are, by their actions, causing risks for others. In the political and professional discourses examined here – but not in those of the defendants, who used this category differently with a more 'welfarist' focus – this personalisation of order and security risks is crystallised in the category of the *persistent offender*, which became popular in the 1990s. For politicians, police and social work professionals, the 'persistent offender' implied a need and justification for taking firm action against youth crime as he or she caused relevant harm to society. 'Persistent offenders' were associated with the commission of many and serious crimes, in particular violent and sexual offences. They needed to be dealt with preventively and repressively, and in all cases cooperatively.

There are shades and nuances to the categorisations of individual offenders. However, these three categories were at the centre of the membership device "parties to the offense" (Stetson 1999, 82), whose members differed depending on the invoked offender category: victims of crimes, society, social workers, parents etc. were optional parties or parties with widely differing features and roles depending on the specific categorisation of offenders. This is now to be explored in more detail, focusing also on the narrators themselves as they always had a central role in the narrations they undertook.

5.2.2 Marginal and hegemonic narratives

Based on the reconstruction of offender categorisations, the next step of the analysis is to broaden the perspective by disclosing marginal and hegemonic narratives. I will particularly focus on coalitions of narrators in order to determine the respective status of the narratives they employed.

a)   *The first, minor coalition* becomes visible in the critical self-positioning of social workers and the Green Party. The central narrative here is that of *a structural criticism of society*. It is 'critical' insofar as society is branded an offender and the criminal justice system and the police are presented as the adversaries of the young people. A symptomatic feature here is the talk of violence (see examples 2.1 and 3.1). Youth crime is currently strongly linked to the commission of violence as a threat to society (Muncie 2015, 8–11; Zimring 2014). Yet social work in the 1970s and 1980s and the early Green Party after its formation in the 1980s discussed violence in a very different way, namely as the illegitimate exercise of the state monopoly on the use of violence: the state worked with its institutions and organisations to preserve the social order. This appeared to be at the expense of young people. State or institutional oppression (as in example 3.4) isolated and predestined them for long-term criminality: social structures were the causes of crime and the real culprits, and the co-offenders were the criminal justice system and the police. Youth crime as individual acts committed by young people was hardly discussed; the focus was on a battle of the institutions. In this battle, social work and the Green Party had only marginal roles in the confrontations between professions and parties respectively. They clearly had no discursive predominance. For a long time, the Green Party had only minimal success in quantitative terms, for example obtaining just 1.5% of the vote in the national parliamentary elections in 1980 (Probst 2013, 171). Social work discussed at length its marginal, suppressed relevance in the context of work with young people, and in the specified period saw itself as facing the constant of dominance by the police and criminal justice system (Dollinger et al. 2015b, c). In their discussions of youth crime, social work and the Green Party expressed this marginality and their solidarity with young people, whom they also saw as victims of society; they appeared to be on the same (socially excluded) level. By putting themselves on the side of the delinquents and taking issue with the latter's oppression by the state, they themselves in turn became victims of the state. They could make their repression known and criticise it in their speeches and texts, but they did not have the resources to alter the situation fundamentally. The battle against youth crime was, for them, primarily a question of changing social structures in which they themselves had a relatively marginal and powerless position. Only in some cases did they recognise that help for individuals could in fact be useful. In social work, there were some calls to support individual young people (see example 3.2). However, these juvenile delinquents were the victims of society and the criminal justice system, and their support had to be explicitly justified by social work as that help was provided in the knowledge that it merely treated the symptoms of a deeper social issue. It thus potentially replicated the state rationality of exclusion and control.

Help for individual delinquents was in fact exactly what the major parties (CDU/CSU and SPD) were demanding of social work (see example 2.3). Social work was addressed by dominant positions in the youth crime discourse and called upon to act as an important player. Interestingly, however, this was a demand rejected by social work itself (or only admitted in exceptional cases). Social work was called upon, but without those making that call taking an interest in social works' self-categorisation as a determined critic of society. The only political body that agreed with the strong social and institutional criticism of social work was the Green Party, which also criticised personalising measures to fight youth crime. The two bodies formed their narrative coalition by declaring offenders 'social victims', leaving out the category 'victims of crime', and declaring society and the state to be the 'actual' perpetrators of youth crime. However, this coalition started to disintegrate in the early 1990s. Both of its members adapted to the hegemony of penal welfarism in which the individual offender was to be 'improved'.

b) *A second, much broader coalition* lies in the responses to the question of how "*atonement* can be combined with *preparation for a new life*" (see Seesing's 1989 speech in example 2.4). The core narrative of this coalition is a call for *restrictive integration*, which represents a hegemonic consensus that dominated for most of the period covered in the investigation of political and professional discourses in Chapters 2 and 3. That consensus also includes central narratives used in the self-categorisation of the defendants in Chapter 4. This hegemonic consensus illustrates a discursive pattern that Garland (2001a, 27) identified as "penal welfarism", in other words an effort to combine proportional punishment, limited by law, with benevolent rehabilitation. Seesing, in this regard, communicated a retributive criminal policy objective combined with a focus on the social integration of the offender. This offender has two personae: in terms of the criminal law, he or she is a violator of statutory regulations who is to be held to account. At the same time, he or she is deemed a socially excluded and strained person who is in need of help. The respective narratives demonstrate the elasticity of the term 'education' in German youth criminal law: it refers both to punishment and to options for social support (whereas it never did and still does not aim at a complete replacement of punishment with support measures; Cornel 2018; Gerken/Schumann 1988). The greater emphasis could be on either aspect. The focus on 'education' (or synonymously 'rehabilitation') allows both.

What is key is the overriding categorisation of an offender as an offender with individual problems. He or she is affected by structural factors or the immediate social environment, but the (imputed) fact remains that he or she has breached criminal law and is therefore *rightly* brought before the youth courts judge (or at least necessarily at the centre of a criminal investigation). In light of the fact of his or her illegal action, the institutions of the criminal justice system act legitimately. They do not oppress the offender and do not replicate society's injustices, as claimed by the small resistive coalition of social work and the Green Party. Instead, the institutions act in the interests of the offender, for although they (forcibly) intervene, "all interventions should be directed to meeting the needs of young people" (Muncie 2015, 275) so that they promote their individual rehabilitation.

A wide range of interests can feed into this hegemonic narrative. Social work and the Green Party arrived relatively late; only in the course of the 1990s did they withdraw their highly socially critical demands to join this grand coalition. The coalition's most important representative is the *police*, who insisted on the education of offenders throughout the entire period studied but were also always ready to take tough action against specific groups of offenders (a kind of action that was also termed a form of 'education'; Dollinger et al. 2012a). Confident in the belief that they could educate or rehabilitate offenders, the police were able to claim forms of youth work as their domain and thus enter social work territory (see example 3.9). They could, however, also demonstrate severity by interpreting education as confrontation and setting strict boundaries – a demand with which social work partly agreed from the mid-1990s on. Conservative parties did not need to be persuaded of the merits of joining this coalition; where their demands had previously been peripheral, they now became more explicit and were covered with principles of – if necessary: insistent and rigorous – education.

Society played an important role here – a double role aligned with the category of offenders as hybrid offenders/victims. In this grand coalition, society was not a structural, abstract cause of criminalisation. Instead, it was on the one hand a social environment that contributed to a criminogenic life story and socialisation. On the other hand, society was the point at which the social integration of offenders was aimed. Victims and victim protection were not yet as important as in the third coalition described below, in which a rhetoric of victim suffering was used to argue against help for offenders. What was more important here was a reference that Casparis had already raised back in 1978 with a demand for the assimilation of the "children of foreign workers" (example 3.3). Such a demand does not criticise society, at least not fundamentally. As discussed in the analysis of that example, while this position does work on the assumption of a social background to careers in crime, the existing society is the reference into which people who exhibit delinquency are to be fitted. It is only a small step from this stance to victims' suffering, but what is more important here is the authoritarian concept of education (or rehabilitation) that is to turn offenders into integrated fellow citizens. To legitimise help, it is assumed that offenders are not inherently 'evil' or 'brutal', for society shares some responsibility for their delinquency. At the same time and by integrating offenders, however, society has to be protected. Like the respective offenders, society is a hybrid offender/victim; it exerts criminogenic influence but has the right to see offenders punished and duly integrated.

The focus of conservative parties on teaching values (see example 2.5) and, more strongly advocated by the SPD, demands for integration opportunities in education and training (Lampe 2016) build on this position. Both approaches present social causes of youth crime while promoting rehabilitation through which youth crime should be addressed.

The police, and a social work sector that departed significantly from its fundamental social criticism from the 1990s on, were able to support this view without any significant issues. They could accept that youth crime had social causes, was reflected in the life story of the individual offender and could therefore be addressed with personal, integrative measures. In their specifics, however, the positions of the various players did differ. A degree of moderate criticism remained in the social work sector (Dollinger et al. 2012a); conservative parties and the police urged tougher measures for certain offenders at least, and the SPD tended to call for less restrictive socially integrative measures. This pattern, which conceived of offenders and society in the manner described and associated youth crime with demands for education – more or less authoritative or supportive depending on the interests at stake – was, however, a point of narrative convergence that allowed these stakeholders to cooperate.

The narratives of the defendants largely correspond to this point of convergence. As reconstructed in Chapter 4, a central narrative for the interviewees is that of a 'sad story'. This narrative was composed in different ways, but it fundamentally involves a difficult life story or upbringing that reduced individual responsibility for delinquency. The defendants do not really want to be educated, i.e. they do not want their personality to be changed (either through penal sanctions or through help from social work; Dollinger et al. 2016). However, in many cases they advocated integrative measures instead of restrictive sanctions for themselves. Sad stories demand social or socially integrative responses to youth crime. By creating this connection of a 'sad' biography and integrative measures, the interviewees drew on and replicated the hegemonic narrative pattern described here.

This replication even included demands for punishment. The interviewees sometimes criticised individual sentences for being too tough, but the principle that delinquency leads to punishment appeared almost 'naturalised' (see Chapter 4.2.a) – not unlike the relatively unquestioned role that society now played in politics and professional journals: criticised in part, but not fundamentally called into question in its current form.

In the light of this wide range of parties and players, we can legitimately talk of a grand coalition based on a hegemonic, widely shared narrative of youth crime. At the heart of that narrative are the offenders with their dual personae of being an offender and victim. It is clear that this narrative was not in itself entirely homogeneous, but this is ultimately a characteristic of hegemonies, as we can see from both hegemony theory following Laclau and Mouffe (1985) and narrative theory (Bamberg 2004; see also Kiesling 2006). The very possibility of integrating differences and representing commonalities is what defines a hegemony. In light of the issues and positions presented here, we can say that the golden age of this hegemonic narrative was in the 1990s, and it is still powerful today. The narrative was discernible already in the 1970s and 1980s, but it was not until it was also adopted by social work, a stakeholder with a key contribution to its practical implementation, that its hegemonic status unfolded. At this point, however, an opposing concept was already developing that will now be explored.

c) *A third coalition* advocates *tough measures and confrontation*. This narrative also already existed in the 1970s, but it was marginal at the time. One indication of that relatively lasting marginality is the considerable justification required in example 2.4 to legitimise tough action. Tough measures in that context were still part of the restrictive integration postulate. In opposition to this postulate, the third coalition demands a hard line against (certain) offenders. Their integration into society is optional only, and they are no longer dual personae but offenders who engage in delinquency and cause harm. Offenders act criminally more or less of their own free will and produce innocent victims, and must therefore be held accountable. Penance is an element here, but what is key is guaranteeing security: protection from risks emanating from the offenders. Melossi (2008, 6) refers to an "attitude of distance or antipathy toward the criminal", who is no longer a part of society but appears to stand in opposition to it because of the ill for which he or she is responsible.

The moral category of responsibility is a key point in this context. From the perspective of attribution theory, people appear sympathetic and in need of help when they are not themselves responsible for difficulties and are part of 'our own' social configuration, i.e. when they belong to an 'us' (Oorschot 2000). In the first two coalitions described, the small and the grand coalition, this impression stems from the talk of social causes of youth crime. If there are social causes of crime, offenders are at least not wholly responsible and are part of a social community. The case is different when there are no social causes and offenders appear simply 'evil'; when they are termed hedonistic, greedy or lazy, or labelled with other stigmatising personality traits. A good illustration here is the "Moroccan child gangs that peddle heroin", allegedly with a full understanding of right and wrong (see example 2.7). In this case, issues of foreignness come along with intentional harm to others. The speaker does not want to mobilise support; he tends to justify tough measures against persons whom he is portraying as "dangerous outsiders" (Loseke 2003, 85). A child in these gangs is supposedly "not one of us" (Loseke 2003, 85) and endangers a community of the threatened and the integrated that is presented narratively. In this narrative, delinquents are no longer part of a social community but a risk to it. This means that protection of the public is being demanded as a political maxim (Garland 2001a, 12), and in the face of this demand, the well-being of the delinquents is not of particular importance. Rehabilitation can still play a part, but it is strictly subordinate to the security imperative (Robinson 2008, 2016). This imperative makes it plausible to ignore rehabilitation in certain cases and pursue punishment or exclusion if an offender appears unable or unwilling to be rehabilitated.

Voices presenting this narrative of an evil offender were isolated and muted in the 1970s and 1980s; they became stronger from the mid-1990s on. Through the category of the 'persistent offender', this narrative became a fixture in the police and political field and – possibly surprisingly, considering its consistent earlier social criticism – even in social work. A symptomatic example is 3.11, in which two social workers set out the systematic humiliation of a violent offender as a legitimate social work measure. Offenders in this case do not deserve sympathy and there are no reasons that could excuse them or justify their actions. They are, instead, evil and can or indeed should be mistreated just as they have mistreated their victims. The category 'innocent victim' legitimises the required confrontation of offenders, which can even involve suggestions of violence ("gestured slaps in the face"; example 3.11). Social work had previously criticised the fact that offenders were not treated humanely by the police and the criminal justice system (see example 3.5), and in return for cooperation with the police, had demanded that offenders be respected as human beings. Later, however, in the context of the narrative of severity and confrontation, it was possible in social work to demand the inhumane treatment of offenders to bring home to them their inhumanity.

This position was not by any means accepted by the entire social work sector, as in political contexts too, such demands did *not* become hegemonic. However, postulates of severity and confrontation have proved to be references on which various professionals in the police, politics and social work have drawn since the mid-1990s without this having to be concealed or glossed over.

Insofar as education can hardly be presented as a legitimising argument here, this model threatens the continuing hegemony of restrictive integration but has yet to contribute to its fundamental revision. In Germany at least, strict confrontation and tough action in the case of youth crime remain limited to certain groups of offenders and offences, primarily in the field of violent and sexual offences (Dollinger 2011; Dünkel 2011, 2012). While Chapter 2 found that the political discourse on youth crime has overall become more restrictive, education (or rehabilitation) is and remains a key narrative in that discourse – even if there is a noticeable and growing tendency to infuse political crime narratives with strongly repressive demands.

Given the enduring relevance of educational goals of criminal justice, defendants who authentically recount 'sad' biographical stories can still reckon with judicial clemency for themselves. But even their narratives mirror calls for harsh treatment. The defendants hardly demand severity and intransigence against delinquents in general; this would run counter to their own interest in light sanctions. Nonetheless, Chapter 4 showed that a desire for tougher action emerged on the one hand in comparisons with other offenders and offences, and on the other from a biographical perspective as criticism of too 'lax' a justice system that should have punished the narrator's own previous crimes harder (see Chapter 4.3). These demands imply a reduction of personal responsibility. Despite the 'tough' appearance of these demands, they make a *lenient* sentence for the interviewees plausible. If their criticism is correct, then their criminal history is to blame more on the 'lax' and unjust criminal justice system than on themselves. However, with these postulates the defendants drew on the political and professional narratives of a too clement justice system.

This coalition is thus by no means small, as alongside the institutions mentioned it can even find supporters from among the offenders themselves. The defendants also provide a reason for tough measures, namely that crime is "fuckin' great" (example 4.1), in other words that it is fun and thus requires confrontation if offenders are to stop engaging in crime. This draws on the political and professional category of 'persistent offender', who quite simply enjoys harming others and therefore requires tough institutional action. But example 4.6 illustrates that the category 'persistent offender' was also used by defendants to argue the opposite: it was integrated into a sad story to achieve leniency and a light sentence. Categories used politically and professionally to legitimise tough measures can therefore be expropriated and adapted, yet at the cost of reproducing the respective category. In a punitive context, this is particularly ambivalent. When youths categorise themselves as 'persistent offenders', then they directly connect their personal identity to punitive public discourses on crime. As illustrated in detail by Matza (1969), subjects place themselves within a crime discourse by acknowledging and accounting for their own misconduct. This crime discourse has recently become stricter. While the defendants often still cite a troublesome social and biographical past to account for their actions, these arguments tend to disappear from politics and the professional public. They are gradually replaced with the suffering of victims, which now requires intransigence. Offenders in this coalition have become more or less identical with their offences.

It is worth noting that the establishment of hegemonic narratives has far-reaching consequences for defendants. It is particularly significant in the case of *youth* crime that the social and biographical background to offences has become less and less relevant in recent years. Defendants still recount at some length their earlier "sad stories" that turned them into offenders. Following the logic of penal welfarism, they often categorise themselves as 'problem offenders' who deserve a lenient verdict. Yet their stories must also reflect a current common sense that makes their actions plausible and explains them. Defendants must *adapt to the cultural hegemony of stories of crime*. In court, the challenge is twofold: they must introduce themselves as people and explain (or deny) their (possibly illegal) actions. In the highly formalised process of prosecution and judgment, the defendants are assessed in terms of their life story, moral qualities and actions. It is crucial for them to appear credible and authentic. As Komter has reconstructed, defendants often master this complex challenge by adapting to the (assumed) expectations of the court: "Suspects manage their dilemmas by appearing to give judges what they want: truth, cooperation, clarification, and moral confirmation" (Komter 1998, 132). Judges often doubt the authenticity of defendants' narratives, as defendants clearly have an interest in receiving a lenient sentence. Nevertheless, it is obvious that defendants attach importance to appearing in such a way that they portray themselves authentically. If they speak (or give the impression of speaking) in a credible and open manner without clearly revealing their interest in a light sentence, they can expect to be judged leniently. This must mean that they are guided by what they regard as plausible and authentic from the point of view of judges and other parties in the proceedings. Defendants must provide narratives and communicate self-categorisations that convincingly characterise them personally as people while at the same time adapting to the expectations of their audience.[8] The narratives of defendants are thus, in this respect, embedded in other narratives on youth crime. The narratives reconstructed in the interviews with the defendants reflect what the analysis of political and professional discourses revealed:

explanations of crime based on a fundamental critique of society are no longer relevant; principles of penal welfarism and demands for severity in responses to youth crime are much more important. It is no coincidence that both are to be found in the narratives of the defendants.

5.3 Youth crime in a political and institutional culture of consensus

To conclude, I contextualise the findings politically in order to outline how they may be specific to Germany. One significant result of the comparative narrative analysis undertaken here is the restricted punitive turn implied in many narratives since the mid-1990s. In this punitive turn, the earlies basic criticism levelled at society as the cause of youth crime largely disappeared. Offenders no longer embody structural disadvantages, discrimination and injustice. They cause harm and thus they have to be controlled and sanctioned. But this change has (until now) been restricted, as demands for sheer, *unmasked* intransigence against young offenders do not surface as a consensus of all relevant actors in the field. These demands exist, and they come up time and again, particularly connected to ascriptions like 'foreignness' and to sexual and violent offences. However, calls to 'tighten up' sanctions against offenders are often tellingly sugar-coated and veiled in a rhetoric of education. Young offenders, so the readjusted narrative goes, do need education – but this education can or should be restrictive and retributive.

Analysts of the German system of juvenile justice sometimes criticise this broad and inconsistent notion of education (e.g. Albrecht 2002; Cornel 2018; Dollinger/Schabdach 2013; Gerken/Schumann 1988). Why would it make sense to speak of a need to 'educate' offenders if this term covers measures as diverse as legal diversion, restorative justice, probation, fines, imprisonment or community work?[9] The answer to this question locates the German system of juvenile justice in a broader context. Cavadino and Dignan (2006, 101) term the German penal and (socio-)political system "archetypical corporatism". They highlight its composition of diverse entities with comparatively wide discretion, and a corresponding focus on stability and mutual consent. In their words:

> The political culture (in Germany; B.D.) prizes consensus and stability, with a 'social market' or 'stakeholder economy' based on consensus between workers, unions, employers, shareholders and politicians. The freedom of the free market is in practice significantly abridged by the duties of firms to act as good corporate citizens and take into account the interests and views of all sections of the community.
>
> (Cavadino/Dignan 2006, 102)

In a similar vein, Germany's culture of youth crime control is characterised by a drive to maintain a consensus of cooperating actors such as politicians, jurists, social workers, psychologists etc. A basic distinction in German youth law is

between a *Youth Courts Law* and a *Youth Welfare Law*, which makes the reten-
tion of a consensus particularly demanding. The former is to deal with young
offenders based on the main principles of the rule of law and meeting individual educational needs (Albrecht 2004; Cavadino/Dignan 2006; Dollinger/
Schabdach 2013); the latter is meant to ensure and regulate care for and protection of children, teenagers and their families (Jordan et al. 2012; Rätz et al.
2014). This legal double-track system was implemented in the 1920s (Hasenclever 1978), after decades of controversies. In the context of the criminal law,
conflicting legal doctrines and a passivity of the Germany parliaments contributed to what Oberwittler (2000, 134) calls an "extremely slow reform process"
leading to the implementation of the Youth Courts Law (*Jugendgerichtsgesetz*)
in 1923. In the field of civil (or social) law, much hope was initially placed in the
reform process, but financial restrictions and ideological disputes – including
between a strong confessional tradition and governmental institutions in the
welfare sector – brought about delays and moderations of what had originally
been hoped for. The result was an important but not sweeping reform with
the passage of the Youth Welfare Law (*Reichsjugendwohlfahrtsgesetz*) in 1922
and its delayed implementation in 1924 (Peukert 1986). Hasenclever (1978, 62)
appositely terms the Youth Welfare Law a "compromise of conflicting forces".
The double-track youth law – and with it the separation of young offenders
and young persons in need – remains in place to date, and also to date it proves
extremely challenging to reform either law. Despite their almost simultane-
ous implementation, the two laws were arranged largely independently, and
yet they brought about the necessity of close cooperation. For instance, social
work institutions are mandated in both laws and youth courts regularly impose
sanctions which have to be organised and overseen by social workers (whose
main reference is the Youth Welfare Law). A joint reference of different actors
is therefore indispensable. The umbrella term which characterises either law
is 'education'. Its exact meaning differs in the two laws,[10] but the rhetoric of
education still makes it possible to base all institutional efforts directed at young
people on their – at least programmatic – well-being. Education is the compromise formula which was instituted in the 1920s and which still functions
today as the least common denominator to which professionals and institutions
dealing with youth crime are obliged.

In the period analysed here, the minor coalition of social workers and the
Green Party dared to deviate from this compromise. Their strict criticism of
society's state of things resulted in calls for structural reforms and basic transformations of an unjust society, not for the education of individual offenders.
But even during this period, 'established' politicians and police relied on education. Politicians actually ignored that they were being assailed by these very
institutions when they commissioned "public and independent youth welfare
organisations" to educate young offenders, as Wolters did as a representative of
the federal government in 1979 in the German Bundestag (see example 2.3).

The hegemonic consensus on education persisted, and the left-wing crit-
ics eventually joined the major coalition in its effort to combine support and

punishment. The narrative according to which young offenders are in need of education proved insurmountable, even when it was later attacked by punitive-populist, right-wing campaigns. Until now, they had hardly been successful (Dollinger et al. 2017c).[11] The focus on education remains in place, even though it was recently extensively stretched as punitive reforms still relied on an educational rhetoric. For instance, the so-called *Warnschussarrest* was dubbed "*another educational measure in youth criminal law*", despite its actual expansion of options to take young offenders in stationary custody (see example 2.9). In spite of punitively turned and stricter professional and political conceptions of youth offending, demands for mere harshness do not represent a new hegemonic narrative. The consensus on education remains. But the meaning of education has been transformed from benevolent support to a postulate of restrictive integration. Harsh treatment and confrontation are no longer exceptions that have to be legitimised extensively, but they represent a new normality in the way young offenders are dealt with.

A detailed exploration of narratives on youth crime can detect these alterations. Given that the judiciary in Germany is relatively insulated from influences by the media and politics (Savelsberg 2000), the respective punitive transformation can remain more or less undiscovered under the radar of e.g. statistical analyses of rates of imprisonment. Sudden or radical changes of politics in Germany's current political system seem to be unlikely compared to e.g. the USA or England/Wales. Germany's political system and political elite favour stability and consensus. Changes in the German political landscape are therefore likely to take the form of readjustments of what has been established before, not a resolute abandonment of a compromise that was carved out arduously and that rendered possible the cooperation and coalitions which are (deemed) essential to political and institutional practice. A punitive trend has indeed taken place in Germany, but it is marked by particularities of Germany's culturally and politically established, consensus-based narratives of youth crime. They imply that young offenders need to be 'educated'. In this regard, the narrative of education is astonishingly durable and resilient, even if it has become more restrictive recently.

Conclusion

The comparison undertaken in this chapter revealed three coalitions. Firstly, a small coalition, highly critical of society, which remained marginal overall and had largely disappeared by the mid-1990s. It was formed primarily of social work and of the Green Party. Secondly, a hegemonic coalition that was (and is) most clearly epitomised by police narratives and that was gradually also joined by social work and the Green Party; it is characterised by a restrictive integration postulate. A key aspect of this coalition is its demand for offender education, education that can be repressive or benevolent to varying degrees. The categorisation of offenders as both responsible criminals and young people with a difficult background in need of help is a central feature of this coalition.

Thirdly, a coalition that has recently become stronger but not (yet) hegemonic. It consists of narratives of severity and intransigence. In these narratives, offenders may have a criminal history, but they hardly have a social biography and in particular cannot present excuses or justifications. They are 'bad' and act 'badly' by harming others, and thus threaten the security of society.

The three coalitions demonstrate a change over time in how youth crime is narrated and evaluated. On the one hand, crime is by definition negative and indicates a particularly serious situation (Hillyard/Tombs 2008, 8). On the other hand, the concept of crime became progressively more pejorative and threatening as illustrated in Chapters 2 and 3. In the socially critical positions of the 1970s and 1980, offences themselves were to be largely disregarded; criticism was directed primarily at society, the state and the criminal justice system and not at individual offenders or their offences. Over time, the opposite became predominant. Society was to an extent discursively excused: as offences and offenders were increasingly blamed to cause harm, society became increasingly blameless and the criminal justice system more legitimate, for it was acting against the now almost unquestioned evil of the crime. At the same time, we saw the rise of the innocent, 'pure' victim as an object to be protected by politics and the professions.

Youth crime thus demonstrates an amazing flexibility as regards evaluations and relevant categories. Offenders are by no means always offenders and victims are not automatically linked to specific offences. Offenders can be presented as victims of society; victims of crime can be ignored; society can be called to take (its share of) responsibility (or not); the police and criminal justice system can be criticised or invested with the authority of legitimate players. Nothing in the field of youth crime is thus a natural given, even though offenders themselves did not question the fact that they had to be punished (Chapter 4). They assumed an 'automatism' of repeat offending and sanctions, only calling for clemency for themselves. But this does not alter the overall picture that crime can be narrated in many different ways. Categories such as offender, victim, etc. make sense only within specific narratives that place those categories in relation to each other and associate them with characteristics and activities that communicate value judgements to an audience. This can be done by e.g. linking offenders to the activity of causing harm to victims – who are thus defined as such – and in so doing acting 'maliciously'. This is currently the best-known crime narrative, as it seems self-evident that the main characteristic of offenders is to cause harm. But it is not the only narrative on youth crime, and there are narratives which appear to be more in line with criminological findings on desistance and reoffending. The basic aim of this book is to present analyses of empirical data in order to reveal temporal changes of narratives on youth crime. Its aim is not to provide a criticism of the respective narratives. However, I should note that in the case of *youth* crime in particular, it is surely surprising that offenders, as demonstrated in Chapters 2 and 3, tended to lose their personal story and position within society over time. In politics and professional journals, they gradually became virtually in-human beings without a genuine biography: they appeared to cause harm to victims for almost no reason. Even social work as an institution, which should primarily be responsible for their support, called for their humiliation. The demand for integrating all people and renouncing severity as far as possible tended to fade away. Restoring it – and thus also a reliance on criminological findings, as they demonstrate the wide uselessness of overly tough interventions (e.g. Cullen/Jonson 2011; Petrosino et al. 2012, 2013; Travis et al. 2014) – should be a key concern, not just of criminologists. This study shows that this endeavour is not primarily a matter of presenting 'evidence-based' findings. Such findings are important, but 'good', convincing stories are of greater relevance.

Notes

1 While De Fina refers to comparisons of discourse analyses with ethnographically acquired knowledge, the search for recurring patterns can also be predicated on comparisons of different discourses. Even though not all potentially relevant discourses on youth crime could be brought together and analysed here, a conscientious selection and comparison of relevant narratives can make patterns visible.

2 Chapter 1 sets out my understanding of narratives, and illustrates why I do not refer to the concepts of hegemony that are employed in critical criminology. Take for example the major study by Hall et al. (1978), "Policing the Crisis". The authors attribute moral panics on crime (specifically on "mugging") to particular cultural, political and economic circumstances. They do not argue on a purely economic basis, instead taking a neo-Marxist approach and assuming a complex connection between culture and other areas of society. Nevertheless, they still maintain that there is a socio-economic basis of the discussion of crime. In their view, a moral panic points to a "deep-seated historical crisis" (Hall et al. 1978, 221). Questions of (criminal) law are, they believe, ultimately a product of "the question of the capitalist state and the class struggle" (Hall et al. 1978, 195). My narrative approach is not based on "deep-seated" conditions. I assume that diagnoses of societal crises can be important, but ultimately produce narratives and can therefore be analysed as such. In this regard, there is a connection between the approach of Laclau and Mouffe (1985) and my understanding of narratives, as they also argue in terms of a consistent cultural theory. Drawing on Laclau and Mouffe, I purposefully do not – unlike Hall et al. (1978) and the critical criminology approach that they represent – attribute the hegemony or dominance of certain narratives to conditions external to the narratives, but instead attribute hegemonies to the formation of discursive or narrative coalitions (or in the words of Laclau and Mouffe: equivalences).

3 Developments in US criminal policy give one instructive example of the potency of discursive coalitions. Particularly since the late 1960s, both politically 'left' and politically 'right' criticised a relatively broad discretionary scope for criminal justice professionals as unjust (e.g. Tonry 2016; Western 2006, 62–63). Crime was to be fought more consistently, more fairly and more effectively by largely ignoring the previous history – except particularly previous convictions – and personality of individual offenders. At the same time, standardised procedures (such as 'three strikes and you're out', 'truth in sentencing', minimum mandatory sentences and risk assessments) became increasingly popular. Criticism of the established criminal justice system from the 'left' and the 'right' also helped make the fight against crime in the (rhetorical) service of the protection of society a prominent political issue. The subsequent escalation of this fight to an ever more punitive approach (e.g. Beckett/Sasson 2000; Garland 2001a, b) united different political positions (Pratt 2007; Roberts et al. 2003). For example, it involved both neoliberal demands for the responsibilisation of offenders and conservative calls for the protection

of traditional values. It remains to be seen whether trends towards a bipartisan policy of decriminalisation will be able to deliver the same impact.

4   The assumption of *partial* proscriptions and prescriptions rests on Laclau's reasoning that a "fullness of society" cannot be achieved; it is "an impossible object which successive contents try to impersonate through catachrestical displacements" (Laclau 2000, 79; on the role of antagonisms and the impossibility of fixing discourses, see Laclau/Mouffe 1985).

5   From the perspective of discourse and hegemony theory, crime functions as a negatively rated but nonetheless broadly used reference in the attempts to achieve a hegemonic representation of society. Crime narratives symbolise an order in which there are offenders, victims, criminal prosecution institutions, etc. Crime always communicates concepts of how society should 'correctly' be structured. The fact that prescriptions of 'proper' conduct can remain implicit in the discursive fight against crime is probably one reason why criminal policy is such a highly attractive topic for politicians to gain approval.

6   The political discourse is thereby not to be treated as a kind of macro-level that would be distinct from the professional discourse as a meso-level and the defendants' discourse as a micro-level. Instead, the three discourses are separate discourses that each discuss youth crime in a particular, context-specific way that exhibits commonalities among the three discourses. Those commonalities emerge in narrative patterns of youth crime. Such patterns indicate (at most) a coalition of political, professional and individual players.

7   On dominant and counter narratives, see also Bamberg/Andrews (2004); Page (2014).

8   The same applies to the judges and the other parties in the proceedings. In their assessment of narratives, they are guided by not only legal categories but also an implicit common sense that provides information on how people 'normally' behave (Arnauld/Martini 2015; Garfinkel 1967; Komter 1998; Scheppele 1994). This common sense attribution of normality is necessarily based on culturally hegemonic narratives of youth crime.

9   Formally, legal sanctions against youthful offenders in Germany can take the form of so-called educational measures (*Erziehungsmaßregeln*), disciplinary measures (*Zuchtmittel*) or youth imprisonment (*Jugendstrafe*). The umbrella term to cover all three is 'education', which is primarily meant to prevent reoffending by fostering the offender's social integration through education (according to section 2 subsection 1 of the German Youth Courts Law).

10   The meaning of education in the Youth Courts Law (section 2 subsection 1) is formally restricted to the prevention of reoffending, whereas in the Youth Welfare Law it aims at individual development and upbringing of a young person to a self-reliant, responsible and socially integrated personality (according to section 1 subsection 1 of the German Youth Welfare Law).

11   Two important populist campaigns during the period examined here were the Hamburg election of 2001 and the Hesse election of 2008, when conservative politicians demanded, among other things, a particular harsh treatment of young (repeat) offenders with a migrant background. The campaign in Hamburg of Ronald Schill was only temporarily successful; he was soon dismissed after he had become Hamburg's Senator of the Interior. The campaign in Hesse of Roland Koch also failed; his party, the ruling CDU, incurred substantial electoral losses. More successful, but also more balanced, was a campaign by the social democrat and future Chancellor Gerhard Schröder in 1997 and 1998.

References

Agnew, R., 2011: *Toward a unified criminology*. New York: NYU Press.

Albrecht, H.-J., 2002: *Ist das deutsche Jugendstrafrecht noch zeitgemäß?* Munich: C.H. Beck.

Albrecht, H.-J., 2004: Youth Justice in Germany. In: M. H. Tonry/A. N. Doob (eds.): *Youth crime and youth justice. Comparative and cross-national perspectives*. Chicago, IL: University of Chicago Press, pp. 443–493.

Albrecht, P.-A., 2010: *Kriminologie*, 4th ed. Munich: C.H. Beck.

Alexander, M., 2010: *The new Jim Crow. Mass incarceration in the age of colorblindness*. New York: New Press.

Andersson, K., 2008: Constructing Young Masculinity. In: *Discourse & Society* 19: 139–161.

Andrews, D. A./Bonta, J./Wormith, J. S., 2011: The Risk–Need–Responsivity (RNR) Model: Does Adding the Good Lives Model Contribute to Effective Crime Prevention? In: *Criminal Justice and Behavior* 38: 735–755.

Arnauld, A. V./Martini, S., 2015: Unreliable Narration in Law Courts. In: V. Nünning (ed.): *Unreliable narration and trustworthiness*. Berlin: De Gruyter, pp. 347–370.

Arrigo, B. A., 2003: Postmodern Justice and Critical Criminology: Positional, Relational, and Provisional Science. In: M. D. Schwartz/S. Hatty (eds.): *Controversies in critical criminology*. Cincinnati, OH: Routledge, pp. 43–55.

Arrigo, B. A./Milovanovic, D./Schehr, R. C., 2005: *The French connection in criminology*. Albany, NY: State University of New York Press.

Ashworth, A./Zedner, L., 2014: *Preventive justice*. Oxford: Oxford University Press.

Aspden, K./Hayward, K. J., 2015: Narrative Criminology and Cultural Criminology: Shared Biographies, Different Lives? In: L. Presser/S. Sandberg (eds.): *Narrative criminology*. New York: NYU Press, pp. 235–259.

Atkinson, J. M./Drew, P., 1979: *Order in court: The organisation of verbal interaction in judicial settings*. London: Palgrave Macmillan.

Atkinson, M. A., 1980: Some Practical Uses of 'A Natural Lifetime'. In: *Human Studies* 3: 33–46.

Atkinson, P./Delamont, S., 2006: Rescuing Narrative from Qualitative Research. In: *Narrative Inquiry* 16: 164–172.

Baldwin, C., 2013: *Narrative social work*. Bristol: Policy Press.

Bamberg, M., 2004: Considering Counter Narratives. In: M. G. W. Bamberg/M. Andrews (eds.): *Considering counter narratives*. Amsterdam: John Benjamins Publishing Company, pp. 351–371.

Bamberg, M., 2012: Narrative Practices and Identity Navigation. In: J. A. Holstein/J. F. Gubrium (eds.): *Varieties of narrative analysis*. Los Angeles: SAGE, pp. 99–124.

Bamberg, M./Andrews, M. (eds.), 2004: *Considering counter narratives*. Amsterdam: John Benjamins Publishing Company.

Bamberg, M./Georgakopoulou, A., 2008: Small Stories as a New Perspective in Narrative and Identity Analysis. In: *Text & Talk – An Interdisciplinary Journal of Language, Discourse Communication Studies* 28: 377–396.

Bannenberg, B./Coester, M./Marks, E. (eds.), 2005: *Kommunale Kriminalprävention*. Mönchengladbach: Forum-Verlag.

Barthes, R., 1972: *Mythologies*. New York: Jonathan Cape.

Baumann, E., 1973: Zusammenarbeit zwischen Polizei und Bewährungshilfe. In: *Bewährungshilfe* 20: 27–34.

Baumann, I., 2006: *Dem Verbrechen auf der Spur. Eine Geschichte der Kriminologie und Kriminalpolitik in Deutschland 1880 bis 1980*. Göttingen: Wallstein.

Becker, H. S., 1963: *Outsiders*. New York: The Free Press.

Becker, H. S., 2007: *Telling about society*. Chicago, IL: University of Chicago Press.

Becker, P., 2002: *Verderbnis und Entartung. Eine Geschichte der Kriminologie des 19. Jahrhunderts als Diskurs und Praxis*. Göttingen: Vandenhoeck & Ruprecht.

Beckett, K., 1997: *Making crime pay*. New York: Oxford University Press.

Beckett, K./Sasson, T., 2000: *The politics of injustice*. Thousand Oaks, CA: SAGE.

Bennett, J., 1981: *Oral history and delinquency*. Chicago, IL: University of Chicago Press.

Benwell, B./Stokoe, E., 2006: *Discourse and identity*. Edinburgh: Edinburgh University Press.

Bergmann, J. R., 2003: Ethnomethodologie. In: U. Flick/E. von Kardorff/I. Steinke (eds.): *Qualitative forschung*, 2nd ed. Reinbek b. Hamburg: Rowohlt, pp. 118–135.

Bernard, T. J./Kurlychek, M. C., 2010: *The cycle of juvenile justice*, 2nd ed. New York: Oxford University Press.

Berns, U., 2014: Performativity. In: P. Hühn/J. C. Meister/J. Pier/W. Schmid (eds.): *Handbook of narratology*, 2nd ed. Berlin: De Gruyter, pp. 677–691.

Best, J., 2008: *Social problems*. New York: W. W. Norton & Company.

Kögel, G./Karliczek, K.-M. (eds.), 2009: *Jugendliche Mehrfach- und 'Intensivtäter'*. Berlin: LIT.

Blumer, H., 1969: *Symbolic interactionism*. Englewood Cliffs, NJ: Prentice Hall.

Boje, D. M., 2008: *Storytelling organizations*. London, Thousand Oaks, CA: SAGE.

Bosworth, M./Hoyle, C., 2011: What Is Criminology? An Introduction. In: M. Bosworth/C. Hoyle (eds.): *What is criminology?* Oxford: Oxford University Press, pp. 1–12.

Bottoms, A. E., 1977: Reflections on the Renaissance of Dangerousness. In: *Howard Journal of Penology and Crime Prevention* 16: 70–96.

Bottoms, A. E., 2012: Developing Socio-Spatial Criminology. In: M. Maguire/R. Morgan/R. Reiner (eds.): *The Oxford handbook of criminology*, 5th ed. Oxford: Oxford University Press, pp. 450–489.

Bradt, L./Bouverne-De Bie, M., 2009: Social Work and the Shift from 'Welfare' to 'Justice'. In: *British Journal of Social Work* 39: 113–127.

Brookman, F., 2015: The Shifting Narratives of Violent Offenders. In: L. Presser/S. Sandberg (eds.): *Narrative criminology*. New York: NYU Press, pp. 207–234.

Brookman, F./Copes, H./Hochstetler, A., 2011: Street Codes as Formula Stories. How Inmates Recount Violence. In: *Journal of Contemporary Ethnography* 40: 397–424.

Brooks, P./Gewirtz, P. D. (eds.), 1996: *Law's stories*. New Haven: Yale University Press.

Brown, S. E./Esbensen, F.-A./Geis, G., 2010: *Criminology*, 7th ed. New Providence, NJ: Anderson.

Bruner, J., 1991: The Narrative Construction of Reality. In: *Critical Inquiry* 18: 1–21.

Bruner, J., 2003: *Making stories*. Cambridge, MA: Harvard University Press.

Buchna, J./Coelen, T./Dollinger, B./Rother, P., 2017: Abbau von Bildungsbenachteiligung als Mythos? Orientierungen pädagogischer Akteure in (Ganztags-)Grundschulen. In: *Zeitschrift für Pädagogik* 63: 416–436.

Burkhardt, A., 2003: *Das Parlament und seine Sprache*. Tübingen: De Gruyter.

Burkhardt, A./Pape, K. (eds.), 2000: *Sprache des deutschen Parlamentarismus*. Wiesbaden: Springer.

Burton, J./Broek, D. V. d., 2009: Accountable and Countable: Information Management Systems and the Bureaucratization of Social Work. In: *British Journal of Social Work* 39: 1326–1342.

Busch, H./Funk, A./Kauß, U./Narr W.-D./Werkentin, F., 1988: *Die Polizei in der Bundesrepublik*. Frankfurt a. M.: Campus.

Butler, F., 2011: Rush to Judgement: Prisoners' Views of Juvenile Justice. In: *Western Criminology Review* 12: 106–119.

Butler, J., 1997: *The psychic life of power*. Stanford: Stanford University Press.

Butler, J./Laclau, E./Žižek, S. (eds.), 2000: *Contingency, hegemony, universality*. London: Verso.

Case, S., 2007: Questioning the 'Evidence' of Risk that Underpins Evidence-Led Youth Justice Interventions. In: *Youth Justice* 7: 91–105.

Case, S./Haines, K., 2009: *Understanding youth offending. Risk factor research, policy and practice*. Cullompton: Routledge.

Casparis, J., 1978: Ein Fall von brutaler Jugendkriminalität. In: *Kriminalistik* 32: 123–126.

Cavadino, M./Dignan, J., 2006: *Penal systems*. London: SAGE.

Chase, S. E., 2011: Narrative Inquiry. In: N. K. Denzin/Y. S. Lincoln (eds.): *The Sage handbook of qualitative research*, 4th ed. Thousand Oaks, CA: SAGE, pp. 421–434.

Christie, N., 1982: *Limits to pain*. Oxford: M. Robertson.

Clear, T. R./Frost, N., 2015: *The punishment imperative*. New York: NYU Press.

Clifton, J./Van De Mieroop, D., 2016: *Master narratives, identities, and the stories of former slaves*. Amsterdam: John Benjamins Publishing Company.

Cohen, S., 1972/2002: *Folk devils and moral panics*, 3rd ed. London: Routledge.

Cohen, S., 1988: *Against criminology*. New Brunswick, NJ: Transaction Books.

Collins, R., 1990: Market Closure and the Conflict Theory of the Professions. In: R. Torstendahl/M. Burrage (eds.): *The formation of professions*. London: SAGE, pp. 24–43.

Coomber, R./Donnermeyer, J. F./McElrath, K./Scott, J., 2014: *Key concepts in crime and society*. Los Angeles, London, New Delhi: SAGE.

Copes, H., 2016: A Narrative Approach to Studying Symbolic Boundaries Among Drug Users. In: *Crime, Media, Culture* 12: 193–213.

Cornel, H., 2018: Der Erziehungsgedanke im Jugendstrafrecht: Historische Entwicklungen. In: B. Dollinger/H. Schmidt-Semisch (eds.): *Handbuch Jugendkriminalität*, 3rd ed. Wiesbaden: Springer, pp. 533–558.

Cornel, H./Kawamura-Reindl, G./Maelicke, B./Sonnen, B. R. (eds.), 2009: *Resozialisierung. Handbuch*, 3rd ed. Baden-Baden: Nomos.

Critchley, S. J./Marchart, O. (eds.), 2004: *Laclau. A critical reader*. London, New York: Routledge.

Cullen, F. T./Jonson, C. L., 2011: Rehabilitation and Treatment Programs. In: J. Q. Wilson/J. Petersilia (eds.): *Crime and public policy*. New York: Oxford University Press, pp. 292–344.

Cullen, F. T./Jonson, C. L./Nagin, D. S., 2011: Prisons Do Not Reduce Recidivism: The High Cost of Ignoring Science. In: *The Prison Journal* 91: 48S–65S.

Cunneen, C., 2011: Postcolonial Perspectives for Criminology. In: M. Bosworth/C. Hoyle (eds.): *What is Criminology?* Oxford: Oxford University Press, pp. 249–266.

De Fina, A., 2013: Positioning level 3. Connecting Local Identity Displays to Macro Social Processes. In: *Narrative Inquiry* 23: 40–61.

De Fina, A./Georgakopoulou, A., 2012: *Analyzing narrative*. Cambridge: Cambridge University Press.

Decker, F./Neu, V. (eds.), 2013: *Handbuch der deutschen Parteien*, 2nd ed. Wiesbaden: Springer.

DeKeseredy, W. S./Dragiewicz, M. (eds.), 2012: *Routledge handbook of critical criminology*. Abingdon, Oxon: Routledge.

Denzin, N. K., 1992: *Symbolic interactionism and cultural studies*. Oxford: Blackwell.

Denzin, N. K., 2003: Symbolischer Interaktionismus. In: U. Flick/E. von Kardorff/I. Steinke (eds.): *Qualitative forschung*, 2nd ed. Reinbek: Rowohlt, pp. 136–150.

Denzin, N. K., 2011: The Politics of Evidence. In: N. K. Denzin/Y. S. Lincoln (eds.): *The Sage handbook of qualitative research*, 4th ed. Thousand Oaks, CA: SAGE, pp. 645–657.

Deppermann, A., 2013: How to Get a Grip on Identities-in-Interaction: (What) Does 'Positioning' Offer More Than 'Membership Categorization'? Evidence from a Mock Story. In: *Narrative Inquiry* 23: 62–88.

Deppermann, A., 2015: Positioning. In: A. De Fina/A. Georgakopoulou (eds.): *The handbook of narrative analysis*. Chichester, West Sussex: Wiley Blackwell, pp. 369–387.

Dickinson, T./Wright, R., 2017: The Funny Side of Drug Dealing: Risk, Humor, and Narrative Identity. In: *Criminology* 55: 1–30 (online first; doi: 10.1111/1745-9125.12148).

Die Redaktion Sozialmagazin, 1979: Normalität oder die verdrängten Katastrophen. Über die pädagogische Beziehung als Marionettentheater. In: *Sozialmagazin* 4, H. 5: 31–33.

DiIulio, J., 1995: *The coming of the super-predators* (Weekly Standard, November 27). (www.weeklystandard.com/john-j-dilulio-jr/the-coming-of-the-super-predators; last accessed 29 August 2018).

Dinges, M./Sack, F. (eds.), 2000: *Unsichere Großstädte?* Konstanz: UVK.

Doering-Manteuffel, A./Raphael, L., 2012: *Nach dem Boom. Perspektiven auf die Zeitgeschichte seit 1970*, 3rd ed. Göttingen: Vandenhoeck & Ruprecht.

Dollinger, B., 2010: 'Konrad, sprach die Frau Mama ...' Keine Chance für die Pädagogik im Jugendstrafrecht? In: *Zeitschrift für Jugendkriminalrecht und Jugendhilfe* 21: 409–416.

Dollinger, B., 2011: 'Punitivität' in der Diskussion. Konzeptionelle, theoretische und empirische Referenzen. In: B. Dollinger/H. Schmidt-Semisch (eds.): *Gerechte Ausgrenzung? Wohlfahrtsproduktion und die neue Lust am Strafen*. Wiesbaden: Springer, pp. 25–73.

Dollinger, B., 2014a: 'Intensivtäter' zwischen kriminalpolitischem Interesse und empirischen Befunden. Kritische Anmerkungen. In: *Diskurs Kindheits- und Jugendforschung* 9: pp. 81–91.

Dollinger, B., 2014b: Soziale Arbeit in der Politik. Eine Diskursanalyse von Parlamentsdebatten am Beispiel Jugendkriminalität. In: *Neue Praxis* 44: 439–454.

Dollinger, B., 2017: Subjects in Criminality Discourse: On the Narrative Positioning of Young Defendants. In: *Punishment & Society* 19 (online first; doi: 10.1177/1462474517712977).

Dollinger, B./Fröschle, T., 2017: Me and My Custodial Sentence: A Case Study on Categorization Work of Young Defendants. In: *Narrative Inquiry* 27: 66–84.

Dollinger, B./Fröschle, T./Gilde, L./Vietig, J., 2016: Junge Menschen vor Gericht: Fallstudien zum subjektiven Erleben von Verhandlungen durch das Jugendgericht. In: *Monatsschrift für Kriminologie und Strafrechtsreform* 99: 325–341.

Dollinger, B./Fröschle, T./Gilde, L./Vietig, J., 2017a: Zwischen Ohnmacht und der Suche nach Selbstbestimmung: Verurteilung und Inhaftierung aus der Sicht junger Angeklagter. In: M. Schweder (ed.): *Jugendstrafvollzug – (k)ein Ort der Bildung!?* Weinheim: Beltz Juventa, pp. 141–157.

Dollinger, B./Gilde, L./Heppchen, S./Vietig, J., 2017b: Junge Angeklagte im Kampf mit dem Erziehungsanspruch des Jugend(straf)rechts. Empirische Erkundungen. In: H. Weinbach/

T. Coelen/B. Dollinger/C. Munsch/A. Rohrmann (eds.): *Folgen sozialer Hilfen*. Weinheim: Beltz Juventa, pp. 168–185.

Dollinger, B./Lampe, D./Rudolph, M./Schmidt-Semisch, H., 2017c: Maneuvering with Crime. An Empirical Reconstruction of 'Populist' Stances on Youth Crime in German Parliamentary Debates. In: *European Journal on Criminal Policy and Research* 23: 193–210.

Dollinger, B./Lampe, D./Rudolph, M./Schmidt-Semisch, H., 2015a: Ist die deutsche Kriminalpolitik populistisch? Eine konzeptionelle und empirische Annäherung. In: *Kriminologisches Journal* 47: 3–21.

Dollinger, B./Rudolph, M./Schmidt-Semisch, H./Urban, M., 2015b: Von Marionettentheatern und Teufelskreisen. Punitive Entwicklungen der Sozialen Arbeit und Polizei in den vergangenen vier Jahrzehnten. In: P. Bauer/B. Dollinger/C. Füssenhäuser/F. Kessl/S. Neumann (eds.): *Praktiken der Ein- und Ausschließung in der Sozialen Arbeit*. Weinheim: Beltz Juventa, pp. 92–106.

Dollinger, B./Rudolph, M./Schmidt-Semisch, H., Urban, M., 2015c: Von Spitzeln, Zeitbomben und der sozialen Feuerwehr: Die Analyse von Interdiskursen und Kollektivsymbolen am Beispiel von Jugendkriminalität in den 1970er und 1980er Jahren. In: S. Fegter/F. Kessl/A. Langer/M. Ott/D. Rothe/D. Wrana (eds.): *Erziehungswissenschaftliche Diskursforschung*. Wiesbaden: Springer, pp. 283–299.

Dollinger, B./Lampe, D./Schmidt-Semisch, H., 2018: Konturen einer 'Sicherheitsgesellschaft'. Diskursanalytische Hinweise am Beispiel Jugendkriminalität. In: J. Puschke/T. Singelnstein (eds.): *Der Staat in der Sicherheitsgesellschaft*. Wiesbaden: Springer, pp. 217–242.

Dollinger, B./Rudolph, M., 2016: Der 'Kampf' gegen Jugendkriminalität im historischen Wandel: Vom Schutz junger Menschen zur Aufwertung gesellschaftlicher Sicherheitserwartungen. In: *Zeitschrift für Diskursforschung* 4: 51–70.

Dollinger, B./Rudolph, M./Schmidt-Semisch, H./Urban, M., 2012a: *Zwischenbericht der Projektbearbeitung 'Jugendkriminalität im Interdiskurs'*. (www.bildung.uni-siegen.de/forschung/workingpapers/wopa/zwischenbericht_jugendkriminalitaet_im_interdiskurs.pdf; last accessed 26 May 2017).

Dollinger, B./Rudolph, M./Schmidt-Semisch, H./Urban, M., 2012b: Ein goldenes Zeitalter der Integration? Die Repräsentation von Jugendkriminalität in polizeilichen und sozialpädagogischen Zeitschriften der 1970er Jahre. In: *Kriminologisches Journal* 44: 279–297.

Dollinger, B./Rudolph, M./Schmidt-Semisch, H./Urban, M., 2013: Jugend und Kriminalität – Symbolisierungen von Devianz in Zeitschriften der Jugendhilfe und Polizei. In: A. Groenemeyer/D. Hoffmann (eds.): *Jugend als soziales problem – Probleme der Jugend?* Wiesbaden: Beltz Juventa, pp. 140–157.

Dollinger, B./Rudolph, M./Schmidt-Semisch, H./Urban, M., 2014a: Jugend und Kriminalität – Symbolisierungen von Devianz in Zeitschriften der Jugendhilfe und Polizei. In: A. Groenemeyer/D. Hoffmann (eds.): *Jugend als soziales problem – soziale Probleme der Jugend?* Weinheim: Beltz Juventa, pp. 140–157.

Dollinger, B./Rudolph, M./Schmidt-Semisch, H./Urban, M., 2014b: Konturen einer Allgemeinen Theorie der Kriminalität als kulturelle Praxis (ATKAP). In: *Kriminologisches Journal* 46: 67–88.

Dollinger, B./Schabdach, M., 2013: *Jugendkriminalität*. Wiesbaden: Springer.

Dollinger, B./Schmidt-Semisch, H. (eds.), 2018: *Handbuch Jugendkriminalität*, 3rd ed. Wiesbaden: Springer.

Dollinger, B./Urban, M., 2012: Die Analyse von Interdiskursen als Form qualitativer Sozialforschung. In: *Forum qualitative Sozialforschung 13/Forum: Qualitative social research* 13. (http://nbn-resolving.de/urn:nbn:de:0114-fqs1202258; last accessed 15 December 2018).

Dörner, A./Vogt, L. (eds.), 1995: *Sprache des Parlaments und Semiotik der Demokratie.* Berlin: De Gruyter.

Downes, D./Hansen, K., 2006: *Welfare and punishment. The relationship between welfare spending and imprisonment.* (www.crimeandjustice.org.uk/sites/crimeandjustice.org.uk/files/Welfare_and_Punishment_webversion.pdf; last accessed 27 April 2017).

Dreyfus, H. L./Rabinow, P., 1983: *Michel Foucault,* 2nd ed. Chicago, IL: University of Chicago Press.

Drinan, C. H., 2018: *The war on kids.* New York: Oxford University Press.

Dünkel, F., 2011: Werden Strafen immer härter? In: B. Bannenberg/J.-M. Jehle (eds.): *Gewaltdelinquenz, Lange Freiheitsentziehung, Delinquenzverläufe.* Mönchengladbach: Forum-Verlag, pp. 209–243.

Dünkel, F., 2012: Neue Punitivität im Jugendstrafrecht? Anmerkungen aus europäisch vergleichender Perspektive. In: E. Hilgendorf/R. Rengier (eds.): *Festschrift für Wolfgang Heinz.* Baden-Baden: Nomos, pp. 381–397.

Dünkel, F./Geng, B., 2013: Die Entwicklung von Gefangenenraten im nationalen und internationalen Vergleich – Indikator für Punitivität. In: *Soziale Probleme* 24: 42–65.

Dünkel, F./Grzywa, J./Horsfield, P./Pruin, I. (eds.), 2010a: *Juvenile justice systems in Europe* (4 Volumes). Mönchengladbach: Forum-Verlag.

Dünkel, F./Grzywa, J./Pruin, I./Šelih, A., 2010b: Juvenile Justice in Europe – Legal Aspects, Policy Trends and Perspectives in the Light of Human Rights Standards. In: F. Dünkel/J. Grzywa/P. Horsfield/I. Pruin (eds.): *Juvenile justice systems in Europe* (4 Volumes). Mönchengladbach: Forum-Verlag, pp. 1813–1870.

Durkheim, E., 1893/1964: *The division of labor in society.* New York: The Free Press.

Durkheim, E., 1895/1964: *The rules of sociological method.* New York: The Free Press.

Edelman, M., 1971: *Politics as symbolic action.* Chicago, IL: Academic Press.

Edwards, D., 1991: Categories Are for Talking. In: *Theory & Psychology* 1: 515–542.

Eglin, P./Francis, D., 2016: Editors' Introduction. In: S. Hester (ed.): *Descriptions of deviance.* University of Southern Denmark, pp. 6–9. (http://emca-legacy.info/files/Descriptions_of_Deviance.pdf; last accessed 02 July 2017).

Eglin, P./Hester, S., 1992: Category, Predicate and Task: The Pragmatics of Practical Action. In: *Semiotica* 88: 243–268.

Eglin, P./Hester, S., 1999: Moral Order and the Montreal Massacre: A Story of Membership Categorization Analysis. In: P. L. Jalbert (ed.): *Media studies: Ethomethodological approaches.* Lanham: University Press of America, pp. 195–230.

Eisenberg, U., 2012: *Jugendgerichtsgesetz,* 15th ed. München: Beck.

Emerson, R. M., 1969: *Judging delinquents.* Chicago, IL: Transaction Publishers.

Emig, O., 2010: Kooperation von Polizei, Schule, Jugendhilfe und Justiz – Gedanken zu Intensivtätern, neuen Kontrollstrategien und Kriminalisierungstendenzen. In: B. Dollinger/H. Schmidt-Semisch (eds.): *Handbuch Jugendkriminalität.* Wiesbaden: Springer, pp. 149–155.

Enli, G. S./Skogerbø, E., 2013: Personalized Campaigns in Party-Centred Politics. In: *Information, Communication & Society* 16: 757–774.

Ewick, P./Silbey, S., 2003: Narrating Social Structure: Stories of Resistance to Legal Authority. In: *American Journal of Sociology* 108: 1328–1372.

Ewick, P./Silbey, S. S., 1995: Subversive Stories and Hegemonic Tales: Toward a Sociology of Narrative. In: *Law & Society Review* 29: 197–226.

Farrall, S., 2002: *Rethinking what works with offenders.* Cullompton: Routledge.

Farrall, S./Hunter, B./Sharpe, G./Calverley, A., 2014: *Criminal careers in transition.* Oxford: Oxford University Press.

Feltes, T., 2010: Polizei und Soziale Arbeit – die polizeiwissenschaftlich-kriminologische Sicht. In: K. Möller (ed.): *Dasselbe in grün? Aktuelle Perspektiven auf das Verhältnis von Polizei und Sozialer Arbeit.* Weinheim: Juventa, pp. 28–36.

Ferrell, J./Hayward, K. J./Young, J., 2015: *Cultural criminology,* 2nd ed. London: SAGE.

Findlay, M., 2010: Stanley Cohen (1942–). In: K. J. Hayward/S. Maruna/J. Mooney (eds.): *Fifty key thinkers in criminology.* London: Routledge, pp. 242–249.

Fitzgerald, R., 2012: Membership Categorization Analysis: Wild and Promiscuous or Simply the Joy of Sacks? In: *Discourse Studies* 14: 305–311.

Fitzgerald, R./Housley, W. (eds.), 2015: *Advances in membership categorisation analysis.* London: SAGE.

Fleck, L., 1935/1980: *Entstehung und Entwicklung einer wissenschaftlichen Tatsache.* Frankfurt a.M.: Suhrkamp.

Fleck, L., 1935/1981: *Genesis and development of a scientific fact.* Chicago, IL: University of Chicago Press.

Foucault, M., 1972: *The archaeology of knowledge & the discourse on language.* New York: Tavistock Publications.

Foucault, M., 1975/1979: *Discipline and punish.* New York: Viking.

Francis, D./Hester, S., 2004: *An invitation to ethnomethodology.* London: SAGE.

Freeman, M., 2015: Narrative as a Mode of Understanding: Method, Theory, Praxis. In: A. De Fina/A. Georgakopoulou (eds.): *The handbook of narrative analysis.* Chichester, West Sussex: Wiley Blackwell, pp. 21–37.

Frehsee, D., 2010: Korrumpierung der Jugendarbeit durch Kriminalprävention? In: B. Dollinger/H. Schmidt-Semisch (eds.): *Handbuch Jugendkriminalität.* Wiesbaden: Springer, pp. 351–364.

Freidson, E., 2001: *Professionalism.* Cambridge: University of Chicago Press.

Gängler, H., 1998: Vom Zufall zur Notwendigkeit. Materialien zur Wissenschaftsgeschichte Sozialer Arbeit. In: A. Wöhrle (ed.): *Profession und Wissenschaft Sozialer Arbeit.* Pfaffenweiler: Centaurus.

Garfinkel, H., 1967: *Studies in ethnomethodology.* Cambridge: Polity Press.

Garfinkel, H./Sacks, H., 1970: On Formal Structures of Practical Action. In: J. C. McKinney/E. A. Tiryakian (eds.): *Theoretical sociology.* New York: Appleton-Century-Croft, pp. 337–366.

Garland, D., 1985/2018: *Punishment and welfare.* New Orleans: Quid Pro Books.

Garland, D., 1993: *Punishment and modern society.* Chicago, IL: University of Chicago Press.

Garland, D., 2001a: *The culture of control.* Chicago, IL: Oxford University Press.

Garland, D. (ed.), 2001b: *Mass imprisonment.* London: SAGE.

Garofalo, R., 1885/1968: *Criminology.* Montclair, NJ: Petterson Smith.

Gensing, A., 2010: Jurisdiction and Characteristics of Juvenile Criminal Procedure in Europe. In: F. Dünkel/J. Grzywa/P. Horsfield/I. Pruin (eds.): *Juvenile justice systems in Europe* (4 Volumes). Mönchengladbach: Forum-Verlag, pp. 1581–1622.

Gerken, J./Schumann, K. F. (eds.), 1988: *Ein trojanisches Pferd im Rechtsstaat. Der Erziehungsgedanke in der Jugendgerichtspraxis.* Pfaffenweiler: Centaurus.

Goffman, E., 1961/1991: *Asylums.* London: Penguin Books.

Goffman, E., 1963: *Stigma.* Englewood Cliffs, NJ: Penguin Books.

Goodwin, C., 2015: Narrative as Talk-in-Interaction. In: A. De Fina/A. Georgakopoulou (eds.): *The handbook of narrative analysis.* Chichester, West Sussex: Wiley Blackwell: pp. 197–218.

Graham, T./Jackson, D./Broersma, M., 2016: New Platform, Old Habits? Candidates' Use of Twitter During the 2010 British and Dutch General Election Campaigns. In: *New Media & Society* 18: 765–783.

Green, D. A., 2008: *When children kill children. Penal populism and political culture.* Oxford: Oxford University Press.

Gubrium, J. F./Holstein, J. A., 2009: *Analyzing narrative reality.* London: SAGE.

Hafemann, H., 1994: 'Gewaltprävention' – eine Gratwanderung. Pädagogische und politische Probleme mit Anti-Gewalt-Maßnahmen. In: *Sozial Extra* 18: 9–12.

Hall, C., 1997: *Social work as narrative.* Aldershot: Avebury.

Hall, C./Juhila, K./Matarese, M./van Nijnatten, C. (eds.), 2014: *Analysing social work communication.* New York: Routledge.

Hall, C./Matarese, M., 2014: Narrative. In: C. Hall/K. Juhila/M. Matarese/C. van Nijnatten (eds.): *Analysing social work communication.* New York: Routledge, pp. 79–97.

Hall, C./Slembrouck, S./Sarangi, S., 2006: *Language practices in social work.* London: Routledge.

Hall, S. M./Critcher, C./Jefferson, T./Clarke, J./Roberts, B., 1978: *Policing the crisis.* London: Palgrave Macmillan.

Hammerschmidt, P./Aner, K./Weber, S., 2017: *Zeitgenössische Theorien Sozialer Arbeit.* Weinheim, Basel: Beltz Juventa.

Hannah-Moffat, K., 2005: Criminogenic Needs and the Transformative Risk Subject. Hybridizations of Risk/Need in Penalty. In: *Punishment & Society* 7: 29–51.

Hardyns, W./Pauwels, L. J. R., 2018: The Chicago School and Criminology. In: R. A. Triplett (ed.): *The handbook of the history and philosophy of criminology.* Hoboken, NJ: Wiley Blackwell, pp. 123–139.

Harrington, J. F., 2013: *The faithful executioner.* New York: Picador.

Hasenclever, C., 1978: *Jugendhilfe und Jugendhilfegesetzgebung seit 1900.* Göttingen: Vandenhoeck & Ruprecht.

Hasenfeld, Y., 2010: Worker–Client Relations. In: Y. Hasenfeld (ed.): *Human services as complex organizations,* 2nd ed. Los Angeles: SAGE, pp. 405–425.

Have, P. ten, 2014: *Bibliography on Membership Categorization Analysis.* (http://www.paulten have.nl/MCA-bib.pdf; last accessed 14 April 2019).

Heinz, W., 1991: Das Erste Gesetz zur Änderung des Jugendgerichtsgesetzes (1.JGGÄndG). Rückblick, Zwischenbilanz und Ausblick auf ein 2.JGGÄndG. In: *Zeitschrift für Rechtspolitik* 24: 183–189.

Heinz, W., 2008: Bekämpfung der Jugendkriminalität durch Verschärfung des Jugendstrafrechts!? In: *Zeitschrift für Jugendkriminalrecht und Jugendhilfe* 19: 60–68.

Heinz, W., 2012: Aktuelle Entwicklungen in der Sanktionierungspraxis der Jugendkriminalrechtspflege. In: DVJJ (ed.): *Achtung (für) Jugend! Praxis und Perspektiven des Jugendkriminalrechts.* Mönchengladbach: Forum-Verlag, pp. 513–562.

Heinz, W., 2014: *Das strafrechtliche Sanktionensystem und die Sanktionierungspraxis in Deutschland 1882–2012 (Stand: Berichtsjahr 2012; Version: 1/2014).* (www.uni-konstanz.de/rtf/kis/ Sanktionierungspraxis-in-Deutschland-Stand-2012.pdf; last accessed 18 March 2017).

Heinz, W., 2016: *Kriminalität und Kriminalitätskontrolle in Deutschland (Stand: Berichtsjahr 2013; Version: 1/2016).* (www.uni-konstanz.de/rtf/kis/Kriminalitaet_und_Kriminalitaets kontrolle_in_Deutschland_Stand_2013.pdf; last accessed 27 January 2017).

Heritage, J., 1990/1991: Intention, Meaning and Strategy: Observations on Constraints on Interaction Analysis. In: *Research on Language and Social Interaction* 24: 311–332.

Hester, S., 2016: *Descriptions of deviance. A study in membership categorization analysis.* University of Southern Denmark. (http://emca-legacy.info/files/Descriptions_of_Deviance.pdf; last accessed 30 March 2017).

Hester, S./Eglin, P. (eds.), 1997a: *Culture in action.* Washington, DC: University Press of America.

Hester, S./Eglin, P., 1997b: Membership Categorization Analysis: An Introduction. In: S. Hester/P. Eglin (eds.): *Culture in action*. Washington, DC: University Press of America, pp. 1–23.

Hester, S./Eglin, P., 2017: *A sociology of crime*, 2nd ed. Abingdon, Oxon: Routledge.

Hilgartner, S./Bosk, C. S., 1988: The Rise and Fall of Social Problems: A Public Arenas Model. In: *American Journal of Sociology* 94: 53–78.

Hillyard, P./Tombs, S., 2008: Beyond criminology? In: D. Dorling/D. Gordon/P. Hillyard/ C. Pantazis/S. Pemberton/S. Tombs (eds.): *Criminal obsessions: Why harm matters more than crime*, 2nd ed. London: Centre for Crime and Justice Studies, pp. 6–23.

Hofinger, V., 2015: *Die Konstruktion des Rückfalltäters*. Weinheim: Beltz Juventa.

Holland, S./Scourfield, J., 2015: *Social work*. Oxford: Oxford University Press.

Holstein, J. A./Miller, G., 2003: Social Constructionism and Social Problems Work. In: J. A. Holstein/G. Miller (eds.): *Challenges and choices. Constructionist perspectives on social problems*. New York: Aldine Transaction, pp. 70–91.

Housley, W./Fitzgerald, R., 2015: Introduction to Membership Categorisation Analysis. In: R. Fitzgerald/W. Housley (eds.): *Advances in membership categorisation analysis*. London: SAGE, pp. 1–22.

Howell, J. C./Lipsey, M. W./Wilson, J. J., 2014: *A handbook for evidence-based juvenile justice systems*. Lanham, MD: Lexington Books.

Höynck, T./Ernst, S., 2014: Jugendstrafrecht: Ein Vierteljahrhundert schlechte Zeiten für rationale Kriminalpolitik. In: *Kritische Justiz* 47: 249–260.

Hugman, R., 2008: An Ethical Perspective on Social Work. In: M. Davies (ed.): *The Blackwell companion to social work*, 3rd ed. Malden, MA: Wiley Blackwell, pp. 442–448.

Hutcheon, L., 1994: *Irony's edge: The theory and politics of irony*. London: Routledge.

Jayyusi, L., 1984: *Categorization and the moral order*. Boston: Routledge.

Jayyusi, L., 1991: Values and Moral Judgement: Communicative Praxis as Moral Order. In: G. Button (ed.): *Ethnomethodology and the human sciences*. Cambridge: Cambridge University Press, pp. 227–251.

Jonson, C. L., 2013: The Effects of Imprisonment. In: F. T. Cullen/P. Wilcox (eds.): *Criminological theory*. Oxford: Oxford University Press, pp. 672–690.

Jordan, E./Maykus, S./Stuckstätte, E. C., 2012: *Kinder- und Jugendhilfe*, 3rd ed. Weinheim: Beltz Juventa.

Kahl, G., 1979: Wer die Spielregeln einhält ist mein Feind. In: *Sozialmagazin* 4: 30–37.

Katz, J., 1988: *Seductions of crime*. New York: Basic Books.

Kawamura-Reindl, G., 2018: Bewährungshilfe für Jugendliche und Heranwachsende im Spannungsfeld von Resozialisierung und Kontrolle. In: B. Dollinger/H. Schmidt-Semisch (eds.): *Handbuch Jugendkriminalität*, 3rd ed. Wiesbaden: Springer, pp. 443–460.

Kawamura-Reindl, G./Schneider, S., 2015: *Lehrbuch Soziale Arbeit mit Straffälligen*. Weinheim: Beltz Juventa.

Kessl, F., 2011: Von der Omnipräsenz der Kooperationsforderung in der Sozialen Arbeit. Eine Problematisierung. In: *Zeitschrift für Sozialpädagogik* 9: 405–415.

Kiesling, S. F., 2006: Hegemonic Identity-Making in Narrative. In: A. De Fina/D. Schiffrin/ M. Bamberg (eds.): *Discourse and identity*. Cambridge: Cambridge University Press, pp. 261–287.

Kipke, R., 1995: Der Zwischenruf – ein Instrument politisch-parlamentarischer Kommunikation? In: A. Dörner/L. Vogt (eds.): *Sprache des Parlaments und Semiotik der Demokratie*. Berlin: De Gruyter, pp. 107–112.

Kipp, A., 1994: Wer braucht eigentlich Hilfe? Paradigmenwechsel in der Straffälligenhilfe. In: *Sozialmagazin* 22: 46–51.

Klug, W., 2003: 'Risk Management'? Anfragen an Selbstverständnis und Methodik Sozialer Arbeit in der Straffälligenhilfe. In: *Sozialmagazin* 28: 28–37.

Komter, M., 1998: *Dilemmas in the courtroom*. London: L. Erlbaum Associates.

Komter, M., 2014: Conversation Analysis in the Courtroom. In: J. Sidnell/T. Stivers (eds.): *The handbook of conversation analysis*. Chichester, West Sussex: Wiley Blackwell, pp. 612–629.

Krämer, W., 2006: *So lügt man mit Statistik*, 8th ed. Munich: Piper.

Kreiswirth, M., 2000: Merely Telling Stories? Narrative and Knowledge in the Human Sciences. In: *Poetics Today* 21: 293–318.

Kreuzer, A., 2008: Ursprünge, Gegenwart und Entwicklungen des deutschen Jugendstrafrechts. In: *Zeitschrift für Jugendkriminalrecht und Jugendhilfe* 19: 122–131.

Labov, W., 1997: Some Further Steps in Narrative Analysis. In: *Journal of Narrative and Life History* 7: 395–415.

Labov, W., 2011: Narratives of Personal Experience. In: P. C. Hogan (ed.): *The Cambridge encyclopedia of the language sciences*. Cambridge: Cambridge University Press, pp. 546–548.

Labov, W./Waletzky, J., 1967: Narrative Analysis. In: J. Helm (ed.): *Essays on the verbal and visual arts*. Seattle: University of Washington Press, pp. 12–44.

Lacey, N., 2008: *The prisoners' dilemma*. Cambridge: Cambridge University Press.

Lacey, N., 2012: Punishment in the Perspective of Comparative Political Economy. In: *Kriminologisches Journal* 44: 9–31.

Lacey, N./Zedner, L., 2012: Legal Constructions of Crime. In: M. Maguire/R. Morgan/R. Reiner (eds.): *The Oxford handbook of criminology*, 5th ed. Oxford: Oxford University Press, pp. 159–181.

Lacey, N./Zedner, L., 2017: Criminalization: Historical, Legal, and Criminological Perspectives. In: A. Liebling/S. Maruna/L. McAra (eds.): *The Oxford handbook of criminology*, 6th ed. Oxford: Oxford University Press, pp. 57–76.

Laclau, E., 2000: Identity and Hegemony: The Role of Universality in the Constitution of Political Logics. In: J. Butler/E. Laclau/S. Žižek (eds.): *Contingency, hegemony, universality*. London: Verso, pp. 44–89.

Laclau, E., 2004: Glimpsing the Future. In: S. J. Critchley/O. Marchart (eds.): *Laclau. A critical reader*. London, New York: Routledge, pp. 279–328.

Laclau, E., 2005: *On populist reason*. London: Verso.

Laclau, E./Mouffe, C., 1985: *Hegemony and socialist strategy*. London: Verso.

Lagasnerie, G. D., 2016: *Juger*. Paris: Fayard.

Lampe, D., 2016: Ein goldenes Zeitalter des Jugendstrafrechts? In: *Soziale Probleme* 27: 95–118.

Lampe, D., 2017: Von Rockerhäuptlingen, Punks, Crash-Kids und Intensivtätern. Vier Jahrzehnte Konstruktion gefährlicher Jugend in der Hamburger Bürgerschaft. In: *Kriminologisches Journal* 49: 19–41.

Lampe, D./Rudolph, M., 2016: Jugendkriminalität als Ergebnis politischer Konstruktionsprozesse. In: J. Luedtke/C. Wiezorek (eds.): *Jugendpolitiken: Wie geht Gesellschaft mit 'ihrer' Jugend um?* Weinheim: Beltz Juventa, pp. 91–117.

Lappi-Seppälä, T., 2010: Vertrauen, Wohlfahrt und politikwissenschaftliche Aspekte – International vergleichende Perspektiven zur Punitivität. In: F. Dünkel/T. Lappi-Seppälä/C. Morgenstern/D. v. Zyl Smit (eds.): *Kriminalität, Kriminalpolitik, strafrechtliche Sanktionspraxis und Gefangenenraten im europäischen Vergleich* (2 Volumes). Mönchengladbach: Forum-Verlag, pp. 937–996.

Lappi-Seppälä, T., 2014: Imprisonment and Penal Demands. In: S. Body-Gendrot/M. Hough/K. Kereszi/R. Lévy/S. Snacken (eds.): *The Routledge handbook of European criminology*. London: Routledge, pp. 295–336.

Laubenthal, K./Baier, H./Nestler, N., 2015: *Jugendstrafrecht*. Berlin: Springer.

Lazai, H.-J., 1985: Das Problem Jugendkriminalität ... die Schule bietet eine Chance. In: *Der Kriminalist* 40: 231.

Lee, J., 1984: Innocent Victims and Evil-Doers. In: *Women's Studies International Forum* 7: 69–73.

Lehn, D. V., 2014: *Harold Garfinkel*. Walnut Creek: Left Coast Press.

Leidner, R., 2010: Work Cultures. In: J. R. Hall/L. Grindstaff/M.-C. Lo (eds.): *Handbook of cultural sociology*. London: Routledge, pp. 419–427.

Lemert, E. M., 1951/1981: Primary and Secondary Deviation. In: E. Rubington/M. S. Weinberg (eds.): *Deviance. The interactionist perspective*, 4th ed. New York: Palgrave Mac-Millan, pp. 407–409.

Lepper, G., 2000: *Categories in text and talk*. London: SAGE.

Leven, C., 1997: Crash-Kids. Zugleich ein Bericht über die Schwierigkeit der Zusammenarbeit im Jugendbereich. In: *Kriminalistik* 51: 52–55.

Licoppe, C., 2015: Categorization Work in the Courtroom. In: R. Fitzgerald/W. Housley (eds.): *Advances in membership categorisation analysis*. London: SAGE, pp. 71–98.

Liebling, A./Maruna, S./McAra, L., 2017: Introductions: The New Vision. In: A. Liebling/ S. Maruna/L. McAra (eds.): *The Oxford handbook of criminology*, 6th ed. Oxford: Oxford University Press, pp. 1–17.

Lilly, J. R./Cullen, F. T./Ball, R. A., 2011: *Criminological theory*, 5th ed. Thousand Oaks, CA: SAGE.

Lipsey, M. W., 2009: The Primary Factors that Characterize Effective Interventions with Juvenile Offenders: A Meta-Analytic Overview. In: *Victims & Offenders* 4: 124–147.

Lipsky, M., 2010: *Street-level bureaucracy*. New York: Russel Sage Foundation.

Loseke, D. R., 2003: *Thinking about social problems*, 2nd ed. New York: De Gruyter.

Loseke, D. R., 2018: Narrative and the Politics of Meaning in a 'Post-Fact' World. In: *Social Problems* 65: 1–10.

Lösel, F., 2012: Offender Treatment and Rehabilitation: What Works? In: M. Maguire/ R. Morgan/R. Reiner (eds.): *The Oxford handbook of criminology*, 5th ed. Oxford: Oxford University Press, pp. 986–1016.

Lutz, T., 2010: *Soziale Arbeit im Kontrolldiskurs*. Wiesbaden: VS.

Lynch, M., 1993: *Scientific practice and ordinary action*. Cambridge: Cambridge University Press.

Lynch, M. J., 2018: Conflict and Crime: Marx, Engels, Marxist/Radical Criminology and the Explanation of Crime. In: R. A. Triplett (ed.): *The handbook of the history and philosophy of criminology*. Hoboken, NJ: Wiley Blackwell, pp. 84–101.

Lyng, S., 2004: Crime, Edgework and Corporeal Transaction. In: *Theoretical Criminology* 8: 359–375.

Mäkitalo, Å., 2014: Categorisation. In: C. Hall/K. Juhila/M. Matarese/C. van Nijnatten (eds.): *Analysing social work communication*. New York: Routledge, pp. 25–43.

Mäkitalo, Å./Säljö, R., 2002: Invisible People: Institutional Reasoning and Reflexivity in the Production of Services and 'Social Facts' in Public Employment Agencies. In: *Mind, Culture, and Activity* 9: 160–178.

Mandelbaum, J., 2014: Storytelling in Conversation. In: J. Sidnell/T. Stivers (eds.): *The handbook of conversation analysis*. Chichester, West Sussex: Wiley Blackwell, pp. 492–507.

Mannheim, K., 1980: *Strukturen des Denkens*. Frankfurt a.M.: Suhrkamp.

Maruna, S., 2001: *Making good. How ex-convicts reform and rebuild their lives*. Washington, DC: American Psychological Association.

Matthews, R., 2005: The Myth of Punitiveness. In: *Theoretical Criminology* 9: 175–201.

Matza, D., 1969: *Becoming deviant*. Englewood Cliffs, NJ: Prentice Hall.

Maynard-Moody, S./Musheno, M., 2003: *Cops, teachers, counselors.* Ann Arbor: University of Michigan Press.

McAra, L., 2017: Youth Justice. In: A. Liebling/S. Maruna/L. McAra (eds.): *The Oxford handbook of criminology,* 6th ed. Oxford: Oxford University Press, pp. 938–966.

McRobbie, A./Thornton, S. L., 1995: Rethinking 'Moral Panic' for Multi-Mediated Social Worlds. In: *The British Journal of Sociology* 46: 559–574.

Melossi, D., 2000: Changing Representations of the Criminal. In: *British Journal of Criminology* 40: 296–320.

Melossi, D., 2008: *Controlling crime, controlling society.* Cambridge: Polity Press.

Melossi, D., 2015: *Crime, punishment and migration.* Thousand Oaks, CA: SAGE.

Meuter, N., 2014: Narration in Various Disciplines. In: P. Hühn/J. C. Meister/J. Pier/ W. Schmid (eds.): *Handbook of narratology,* 2nd ed. Berlin: De Gruyter, pp. 447–467.

Meyer, S., 2016: Still Blaming the Victim of Intimate Partner Violence? Women's Narratives of Victim Desistance and Redemption When Seeking Support. In: *Theoretical Criminology* 20: 75–90.

Miller, G./Holstein, J. A. (eds.), 1997: *Social problems in everyday life. Studies of social problems work.* Greenwich/London: JAI Press.

Mills, C. W., 1940: Situated Actions and Vocabularies of Motive. In: *American Sociological Review* 5: 904–913.

Miner-Romanoff, K., 2014: Juvenile Offenders Tried as Adults: What They Know and Implications for Practitioners. In: *Northern Kentucky Law Review* 41: 205–224.

Möller, K. (ed.), 2010: *Dasselbe in grün? Aktuelle Perspektiven auf das Verhältnis von Polizei und Sozialer Arbeit.* Weinheim: Beltz Juventa.

Moore, D./Hirai, H., 2014: Outcasts, Performers and True Believers: Responsibilized Subjects of Criminal Justice. In: *Theoretical Criminology* 18: 5–19.

Morath, R./Reck, W., 2002: Intensivtraining für Gewalttäter in Kooperation zwischen Kommune und Justiz. In: *Bewährungshilfe* 49: 313–327.

Muncie, J., 2008: The 'Punitive Turn' in Juvenile Justice: Cultures of Control and Rights Compliance in Western Europe and the USA. In: *Youth Justice* 8: 107–121.

Muncie, J., 2015: *Youth & crime,* 4th ed. London: SAGE.

Muncie, J./Goldson, B. (eds.), 2009: *Comparative youth justice.* London: SAGE.

Nagin, D. S./Cullen, F. T./Jonson, C. L., 2009: Imprisonment and Reoffending. In: *Crime and Justice* 38: 115–200.

Newburn, T., 2013: *Criminology,* 2nd ed. Abingdon: Routledge.

O'Connor, P. E., 2000: *Narratives of prisoners.* Lincoln: University of Nebraska Press.

O'Connor, P. E., 2015: Telling Moments: Narrative Hot Spots in Accounts of Criminal Acts. In: L. Presser/S. Sandberg (eds.): *Narrative criminology.* New York: NYU Press, pp. 174–203.

Oberwittler, D., 2000: *Von der Strafe zur Erziehung? Jugendkriminalpolitik in England und Deutschland (1850–1920).* Frankfurt a.M.: Campus.

Ogrodowski, J., 2008: (Geschlossene) Unterbringung von Kindern und Jugendlichen. In: *Kriminalistik* 62: 583–589.

Olschewski, A., 2000: Die Verschriftlichung von Parlamentsdebatten durch die stenographischen Dienste in Geschichte und Gegenwart. In: A. Burkhardt/K. Pape (eds.): *Sprache des deutschen Parlamentarismus.* Wiesbaden: Westdeutscher Verlag, pp. 336–353.

Olson, G., 2014: Narration and Narrative in Legal Discourse. In: P. Hühn/J. C. Meister/ J. Pier/W. Schmid (eds.): *Handbook of narratology,* 2nd ed. Berlin: De Gruyter, pp. 371–383.

O'Malley, P., 2010: *Crime and risk.* Los Angeles: SAGE.

Oorschot, W. V., 2000: Who Should Get What, and Why? On Deservingness Criteria and the Conditionality of Solidarity Among the Public. In: *Policy & Politics* 28: 33–48.

Ostendorf, H., 2013: *Jugendgerichtsgesetz*, 9th ed. Baden-Baden: Nomos.

Otto, H.-U./Polutta, A./Ziegler, H. (eds.), 2009: *Evidence-based practice. Modernising the knowledge base of social work?* Opladen: Budrich.

Page, R., 2014: Counter Narratives and Controversial Crimes. In: *Language and Literature* 23: 61–76.

Patzelt, W. J., 2005: Der Bundestag. In: O. W. Gabriel/E. Holtmann (eds.): *Handbuch Politisches System der Bundesrepublik Deutschland*, 3rd ed. Munich, pp. 159–231.

Payne, M., 2014: *Modern social work theory*, 4th ed. Basingstoke: Lyceum Books.

Pearson, G., 1983: *Hooligan*. Houndmills: Palgrave Macmillan.

Peters, H., 2017: Über das Selbstverständliche. Invarianzen der Devianzthematisierungen. In: *Kriminologisches Journal* 49: 255–274.

Petrosino, A./Turpin-Petrosino, C./Guckenburg, S., 2013: *Formal system processing of juveniles: Effects on delinquency* (No. 9 of Crime Prevention Research Review. Washington, DC: U.S. Department of Justice). (http://ric-zai-inc.com/Publications/cops-w0692-pub.pdf; last accessed 23 July 2014).

Petrosino, A./Turpin-Petrosino, C./Hollis-Peel, M. E./Lavenberg, J. G., 2012: *Scared straight and other juvenile awareness programs for preventing juvenile delinquency: A systematic review* (Campbell Systematic Reviews). (www.campbellcollaboration.org/media/k2/attachments/Petrosino_Scared_Straight_Update.pdf; last accessed 18 December 2016).

Peukert, D. J. K., 1986: *Grenzen der Sozialdisziplinierung. Aufstieg und Krise der deutschen Jugendfürsorge 1878 bis 1932*. Cologne: Bund-Verlag.

Pfohl, S., 1994: *Images of deviance and social control*, 2nd ed. New York: McGraw-Hill.

Phoenix, J./Kelly, L., 2013: 'You Have to do it for Yourself': Responsibilization in Youth Justice and Young People's Situated Knowledge of Youth Justice Practice. In: *British Journal of Criminology* 53: 419–437.

Polletta, F./Chen, P. C. B./Gardner, B./Motes, A., 2011: The Sociology of Storytelling. In: *Annual Review of Sociology* 37: 109–130.

Pollner, M., 1978: Constitutive and Mundane Versions of Labeling Theory. In: *Human Studies* 1: 269–288.

Potting, C., 1979: Kein Umschluß für Heiner und Charly. In: *päd.extra/sozialarbeit* 3: 21.

Pratt, J., 1997: *Governing the dangerous*. Sydney: Federation Press.

Pratt, J., 2007: *Penal populism*. London: Routledge.

Pratt, J./Brown, D./Brown, M./Hallsworth, S./Morrison, W. (eds.), 2005: *The new punitiveness*. Cullompton: Routledge.

Presser, L., 2008: *Been a heavy life. Stories of violent men*. Urbana: University of Illinois Press.

Presser, L., 2009: The Narratives of Offenders. In: *Theoretical Criminology* 13: 177–200.

Presser, L., 2010: Collecting and Analyzing the Stories of Offenders. In: *Journal of Criminal Justice Education* 21: 431–446.

Presser, L., 2016: Criminology and the Narrative Turn. In: *Crime, Media, Culture* 12: 137–151.

Presser, L./Sandberg, S., 2015a: Introduction. What Is the Story? In: L. Presser/S. Sandberg (eds.): *Narrative criminology*. New York: NYU Press, pp. 1–20.

Presser, L./Sandberg, S. (eds.), 2015b: *Narrative criminology*. New York: NYU Press.

Probst, L., 2013: Bündnis 90/Die Grünen (Grüne). In: F. Decker/V. Neu (eds.): *Handbuch der deutschen Parteien*, 2nd ed. Wiesbaden: Springer, pp. 166–179.

Rajack-Talley, T./Talley, C. R./Tewskbury, R., 2005: The Knowledge of Detained Juveniles About the Juvenile Justice System. In: *Juvenile and Family Court Journal* 56: 29–39.

Rajah, V./Kramer, R./Sung, H.-E., 2014: Changing Narrative Accounts: How Young Men Tell Different Stories When Arrested, Enduring Jail Time and Navigating Community Reentry. In: *Punishment & Society* 16: 285–304.

Rap, S./Weijers, I., 2014: *The effective youth court.* The Hague, Netherlands: Eleven International Publishing.

Rapley, T., 2012: Order, Order: A 'modest' Response to Stokoe. In: *Discourse Studies* 14: 321–328.

Rätz, R./Schröer, W./Wolff, M., 2014: *Lehrbuch Kinder- und Jugendhilfe,* 2nd ed. Weinheim: Beltz Juventa.

Redding, R. E./Fuller, E. J., 2004: What Do Juvenile Offenders Know About Being Tried as Adults? Implications for Deterrence. In: *Juvenile and Family Court Journal* 55: 35–44.

Reiner, R., 2007: *Law and order.* Oxford: Polity Press.

Reiner, R., 2016: *Crime.* Malden, MA: Polity Press.

Reinke, H./Schierz, S., 2010: Konjunkturen der Gefährlichkeit? Das wissenschaftliche und praxisbezogene Sprechen über kriminelle Jugendliche in den 1970er Jahren in der Bundesrepublik. In: L. Böllinger/M. Jasch/S. Krasmann/A. Pilgram/C. Prittwitz/H. Reinke/D. Rzepka (eds.): *Gefährliche Menschenbilder.* Baden-Baden: Nomos, pp. 356–373.

Riessman, C. K./Quinney, L., 2005: Narrative in Social Work. In: *Qualitative Social Work* 4: 391–412.

Roberts, J. V./Stalans, L. J./Indermaur, D./Hough, M., 2003: *Penal populism and public opinion.* Oxford, New York: Oxford University Press.

Robinson, G., 2008: Late-Modern Rehabilitation: The Evolution of a Penal Strategy. In: *Punishment & Society* 10: 429–445.

Robinson, G., 2016: The Rise of the Risk Paradigm in Criminal Justice. In: C. Trotter/G. McIvor/F. McNeill (eds.): *Beyond the risk paradigm in criminal justice.* Basingstoke, Hampshire: Palgrave Macmillan, pp. 9–23.

Robinson, G./Crow, I., 2009: *Offender rehabilitation.* Los Angeles: SAGE.

Rock, P., 2017: The Foundations of Sociological Theories of Crime. In: A. Liebling/S. Maruna/L. McAra (eds.): *The Oxford handbook of criminology,* 6th ed. Oxford: Oxford University Press, pp. 21–56.

Rogowski, S., 2010: *Social work. The rise and fall of a profession?* Bristol: Policy Press.

Roper v. Simmons 543 U.S. 551 (2005) (https://supreme.justia.com/cases/federal/us/543/551/; last accessed 30 August 2018).

Sack, F., 2013: Social Structure and Crime Policy: The German Case. In: *Punishment & Society* 15: 367–381.

Sack, F./Schlepper, C., 2011: Das Sexualstrafrecht als Motor der Kriminalpolitik. In: *Kriminologisches Journal* 43: 247–268.

Sacks, H., 1979: Hotrodder: A Revolutionary Category. In: G. Psathas (ed.): *Everyday language.* New York: Irvington, pp. 7–14.

Sacks, H., 1984: On Doing 'being ordinary'. In: J. M. Atkinson/J. Heritage (eds.): *Structures of social action.* Cambridge: Cambridge University Press, pp. 413–429.

Sacks, H., 1995: *Lectures on conversation* (2 Volumes). Oxford: Blackwell.

Sacks, H./Schegloff, E. A./Jefferson, G., 1974: A Simplest Systematics for the Organization of Turn Taking for Conversation. In: *Language* 50: 696–735.

Sandberg, S., 2009: Gangster, Victim or Both? The Interdiscursive Construction of Sameness and Difference in Self-Presentations. In: *The British Journal of Sociology* 60: 523–542.

Sandberg, S., 2010: What Can 'Lies' Tell Us About Life? Notes Toward a Framework of Narrative Criminology. In: *Journal of Criminal Justice Education* 21: 447–465.

Sandberg, S., 2016: The Importance of Stories Untold. In: *Crime, Media, Culture* 12: 153–171.

Sandberg, S./Tutenges, S./Copes, H., 2015: Stories of Violence. In: *British Journal of Criminology* 55: 1168–1186.

Sarcinelli, U., 2011: *Politische Kommunikation in Deutschland*, 3rd ed. Wiesbaden: Springer.

Sasson, T., 1995: *Crime talk. How citizens construct a social problem.* New York: Aldine Transaction.

Savelsberg, J. J., 1987: The Making of Criminal Law Norms in Welfare States: Economic Crime in West Germany. In: *Law and Society Review* 21: 529–561.

Savelsberg, J. J., 2000: Kulturen staatlichen Strafens: USA und Deutschland. In: J. Gerhards (ed.): *Die Vermessung kultureller Unterschiede.* Wiesbaden: Westdeutscher Verlag, pp. 189–209.

Schegloff, E. A., 2007: A Tutorial on Membership Categorization. In: *Journal of Pragmatics* 39: 462–482.

Scheppele, K. L., 1994: Practices of Truth-Finding in a Court of Law: The Case of Revised Stories. In: T. R. Sarbin/J. I. Kitsuse (eds.): *Constructing the Social.* London: SAGE, pp. 84–100.

Schlepper, C., 2014: *Strafgesetzgebung in der Spätmoderne.* Wiesbaden: Springer.

Schmidt, M. G., 2011: *Das politische System Deutschlands*, 2nd ed. Bonn: C.H. Beck.

Schur, E. M./Bedau, H. A., 1974: *Victimless crimes.* Englewood Cliffs/NJ: Prentice Hall.

Schütz, A./Luckmann, T., 2003: *Strukturen der Lebenswelt.* Konstanz: UTB.

Scott, M. B./Lyman, S. M., 1968: Accounts. In: *American Sociological Review* 33: 46–62.

Shuman, A., 2015: Story Ownership and Entitlement. In: A. De Fina/A. Georgakopoulou (eds.): *The handbook of narrative analysis.* Chichester, West Sussex: Wiley Blackwell, pp. 38–56.

Silverman, D., 1998: *Harvey sacks. Social science and conversation analysis.* Cambridge: Polity Press.

Simon, J., 2007: *Governing through crime.* Oxford: Oxford University Press.

Smith, D., 2015: What Evidence for Youth Justice? In: B. Goldson/J. Muncie (eds.): *Youth crime & justice*, 2nd ed. London: SAGE, pp. 83–99.

Spies, T., 2010: *Migration und Männlichkeit. Biographien junger Straffälliger im Diskurs.* Bielefeld: Transcript.

Spitczok von Brisinski, U., 1981: Und plötzlich war Pimo weg . . . In: *Sozialmagazin* 6: 6–8.

Steinacker, S., 2007: *Der Staat als Erzieher.* Stuttgart: Ibidem.

Steinert, H., 2003: The Indispensable Metaphor of War: On Populist Politics and the Contradictions of the State's Monopoly of Force. In: *Theoretical Criminology* 7: 265–291.

Stetson, J., 1999: Victim, Offender and Witness in the Emplotment of News Stories. In: P. L. Jalbert (ed.): *Media studies: Ethnomethodological approaches.* Lanham, MD: University Press of America, pp. 77–110.

Stevenson, B., 2014: *Just mercy.* New York: Spiegel & Grau.

Stokoe, E., 2009: 'I've got a girlfriend': Police Officers Doing 'self-disclosure' in Their Interrogations of Suspects. In: *Narrative Inquiry* 19: 154–182.

Stokoe, E., 2012: Moving Forward with Membership Categorization Analysis: Methods for Systematic Analysis. In: *Discourse Studies* 14: 277–303.

Stokoe, E./Attenborough, F., 2015: Prospective and Retrospective Categorization. In: R. Fitzgerald/W. Housley (eds.): *Advances in membership categorisation analysis.* London: SAGE, pp. 51–70.

Stuart, K., 2006: *Defiled trades and social outcasts.* Cambridge: Cambridge University Press.

Stump, B., 2003: *'Adult time for adult crime' – Jugendliche zwischen Jugend- und Erwachsenenstrafrecht.* Mönchengladbach: Forum-Verlag.

Stümper, A., 1971: Zur Jugendkriminalität. In: *Kriminalistik* 25: 393–397.

Sutton, J. R., 2004: The Political Economy of Imprisonment in Affluent Western Democracies, 1960–1990. In: *American Sociological Review* 69: 170–189.

Sykes, G. M./Matza, D., 1957: Techniques of Neutralization: A Theory of Delinquency. In: *American Sociological Review* 22: 664–670.

Tabbert, U., 2015: *Crime and corpus*. Amsterdam: Benjamins.

Thole, W., 2010: Die Soziale Arbeit – Praxis, Theorie, Forschung und Ausbildung. Versuch einer Standortbestimmung. In: W. Thole (ed.): *Grundriss Soziale Arbeit*, 3rd ed. Wiesbaden: Springer, pp. 19–70.

Timmermans, S./Oh, H. O., 2010: The Continued Social Transformation of the Medical Profession. In: *Journal of Health and Social Behavior* 51: S94–S106.

Toch, H., 1993: Good Violence and Bad Violence: Self-Presentations of Aggressors Through Accounts and War Stories. In: R. B. Felson/J. T. Tedeschi (eds.): *Aggression and violence*. Washington, DC: American Psychological Association, pp. 193–204.

Tonry, M., 2007: Determinants of Penal Policy. In: *Crime and Justice* 36: 1–48.

Tonry, M., 2013: Evidence, Ideology, and Politics in the Making of American Criminal Justice Policy. In: *Crime and Justice* 42: 1–18.

Tonry, M., 2016: *Sentencing fragments*. Oxford: Oxford University Press.

Tonry, M. H./Doob, A. N. (eds.), 2004: *Youth crime and youth justice. Comparative and cross-national perspectives*. Chicago, IL: University of Chicago Press.

Travis, J./Western, B./Redburn, F. S., 2014: *The growth of incarceration in the United States*. Washington, DC: National Academies Press.

Trenczek, T., 2009: § 42 Inobhutnahme von Kindern und Jugendlichen. In: J. Münder/ T. Meysen/T. Trenczek (eds.): *Frankfurter Kommentar zum SGB VIII: Kinder- und Jugendhilfe*, 6th ed. Baden-Baden: Nomos, pp. 390–403.

Trenczek, T., 2018: Mitwirkung der Jugendhilfe im Strafverfahren – Jugend(gerichts)hilfe. In: B. Dollinger/H. Schmidt-Semisch (eds.): *Handbuch Jugendkriminalität*, 3rd ed. Wiesbaden: Springer, pp. 411–426.

Trenczek, T./Goldberg, B., 2016: *Jugendkriminalität, Jugendhilfe und Strafjustiz*. Stuttgart: Boorberg.

Urban, M., 2014: *Von Ratten, Schmeißfliegen und Heuschrecken. Judenfeindliche Tiersymbolisierungen und die postfaschistischen Grenzen des Sagbaren*. Konstanz: UVK.

Victor, J./Waldram, J. B., 2015: Moral Habilitation and the New Normal: Sexual Offender Narratives of Posttreatment Community Integration. In: L. Presser/S. Sandberg (eds.): *Narrative criminology*. New York: NYU Press, pp. 96–121.

Voruz, V., 2010: Michel Foucault (1926–1984). In: K. J. Hayward/S. Maruna/J. Mooney (eds.): *Fifty key thinkers in criminology*. London: Routledge, pp. 152–158.

Wacquant, L., 2010: Crafting the Neoliberal State: Workfare, Prisonfare, and Social Insecurity. In: *Sociological Forum* 25: 197–220.

Wacquant, L. J. D., 2009: *Punishing the poor*. Durham, NC: Duke University Press.

Walsh, M., 2014: Der Umgang mit jungen Intensivtätern im Deutschen Justizsystem. In: *Recht der Jugend und des Bildungswesens* 62: 346–362.

Walter, M., 2003: Jugendkriminalität in zeitbedingter Wahrnehmung: Der Intensivtäter – empirische Kategorie oder kriminalpolitischer Kampfbegriff? In: *Recht der Jugend und des Bildungswesens* 51: 272–281.

Ward, G./Kupchik, A., 2009: Accountable to What? Professional Orientations Towards Accountability-Based Juvenile Justice. In: *Punishment & Society* 11: 85–109.

Ward, T./Maruna, S., 2007: *Rehabilitation*. London: Taylor & Francis.

Watson, D. R., 1976: Some Conceptual Issues in the Social Identification of Victims and Offenders. In: E. C. Viano (ed.): *Victims and society*. Washington, DC: Visage Press, pp. 60–71.

Watson, D. R., 1978: Categorization, Authorization and Blame – Negotiation in Conversation. In: *Sociology* 12: 105–113.

Watson, D. R., 1997: The Presentation of Victim and Motive in Discourse: The Case of Police Interrogations and Interviews. In: M. Travers/J. F. Manzo (eds.): *Law in action*. Aldershot: Ashgate, pp. 77–97.

Watts, R./Bessant, J./Hil, R., 2008: *International criminology*. London: Routledge.

Wehler, H., 2008: *Deutsche Gesellschaftsgeschichte 1949–1990* (Volume 5). Munich: C.H. Beck.

Weidner, J./Kilb, R. (eds.), 2010: *Konfrontative Pädagogik*, 4th ed. Wiesbaden: VS.

Welsh, B./Farrington, D. P. (eds.), 2012: *The Oxford handbook of crime prevention*. New York: Oxford University Press.

Weinhauer, K., 2000: 'Staatsbürger mit Sehnsucht nach Harmonie': Gesellschaftsbild und Staatsverständnis in der westdeutschen Polizei. In: A. Schildt/D. Siegfried (eds.): *Dynamische Zeiten: die 60er Jahre in den beiden deutschen Gesellschaften*. Hamburg: Christians, pp. 444–470.

Weinhauer, K., 2003: 'Staatsbürger mit Sehnsucht nach Harmonie' – Gesellschaftsbild und Staatsverständnis in der westdeutschen Polizei. In: A. Schildt/D. Siegfried/K. C. Lammers (eds.): *Dynamische Zeiten*, 2nd ed. Hamburg: Christians, pp. 444–470.

Weinhauer, K., 2008: Polizeikultur und Polizeipraxis in den 1960er und 1970er Jahren: Ein (bundes)deutsch-englischer Vergleich. In: C. Benninghaus/S. O. Müller/J. Requate/ C. Tacke (eds.): *Unterwegs in Europa. Beiträge zu einer vergleichenden Sozial- und Kulturgeschichte*. Frankfurt: Campus, pp. 201–218.

Western, B., 2006: *Punishment and inequality in America*. New York: Russel Sage Foundation.

White, S./Featherstone, B., 2005: Communicating Misunderstandings: Multi-Agency Work as Social Practice. In: *Child and Family Social Work* 10: 207–216.

White, S./Hall, C./Peckover, S., 2009: The Descriptive Tyranny of the Common Assessment Framework: Technologies of Categorization and Professional Practice in Child Welfare. In: *British Journal of Social Work* 39: 1197–1217.

Yardley, E./Wilson, D./Kemp, D./Brookes, M., 2015: Narrative Beyond Prison gates. In: *International Journal of Offender Therapy and Comparative Criminology* 59: 159–179.

Youngs, D./Canter, D. V., 2012: Narrative Roles in Criminal Action. In: *Legal and Criminological Psychology* 17: 233–249.

Zeh, W., 1989: Theorie und Praxis der Parlamentsdebatte. In: H.-P. Schneider/W. Zeh (eds.): *Parlamentsrecht und Parlamentspraxis in der Bundesrepublik Deutschland*. Berlin: De Gruyter, pp. 917–937.

Zehetmair, H. (ed.), 2004: *Das deutsche Parteiensystem*. Wiesbaden: Springer.

Ziegler, H., 2005: Soziale Arbeit als Garant für 'das Soziale' in der Kontrolle? In: *Kriminologisches Journal* 37: 163–182.

Zimring, F. E., 2014: American Youth Violence: A Cautionary Tale. In: F. E. Zimring/D. S. Tanenhaus (eds.): *Choosing the future for American juvenile justice*. New York: NYU Press, pp. 7–36.

Index